ISRAEL

idea and reality

ISRAEL
idea and reality

Emil Lehman

UNITED SYNAGOGUE COMMISSION ON JEWISH EDUCATION

NEW YORK

To

Ezra Millgram
Pathfinder in Jewish education who
sparked the idea of this volume

Petty
My wife, taking part in this work with
never-failing helpfulness and never-
ending concern

Carol Rena
My daughter to whom, like to others of
her age, this book may open gates to
understanding and sharing Jewish destiny

Israel is in the news almost every day, and the young Jewish State just having passed its Bar Mitzvah age, has achieved matter of fact standing in Jewish affairs and in the affairs of the world. So much so, that American Jewish youth takes the existence of the Jewish State for granted, while the older generations are beginning already to forget, that in their own lifetime there had been long stretches of years that knew nothing of Jewish sovereignty and only of a long protracted and bitter struggle to end Jewish homelessness. A state of normalcy has set in, that may be only for the good, but that strikingly demonstrates that it takes little to separate a miracle from the routines of reality.

There is another aspect to consider in this context of circumstances. Our young people today, as well as many of their elders, have come to look upon the establishment of the State of Israel as an outgrowth of political predicaments, as the crowning development of an heroic pioneering effort, and last but not least as the telling and glowing result of a gigantic exercise in Jewish philanthropy. Little thought and less recognition is progressively given to the impact of that profound revolution in Jewish life that history has marked as Zionism, as that political and cultural movement that has changed the face of the Jewish experience in the past hundred years. Moreover, there is even lesser grasp of the commonplace factuality and insight that Zionism as a political movement is but the transfer into modernity of a spiritual force that has motivated the continuation of the Jewish people ever since the prophets of old envisioned its physical rehabilitation and the restoration of its spirit to the soil of the ancient homeland. Zionism is therefore no "ism" like any other sociological or ideological trend, fraught with the frailties of fashionable and perishable transition, and tainted with the splashes of political partisanships. If Zionism is to be given its proper status in the line-up of "isms" in history, it will find its rightful place in those categories of thought that connote the perennial power of sublime values, inherent, for instance, in Judaism. It is, indeed, the interlocking combination of Judaism and Zionism, that opens the secrets of Jewish destiny.

It is to these constellations of historic continuity that this book addresses itself. Its scope therefore encompasses the wide span of Jewish history, serving as one massive background for "Israel—Idea and Reality." And its aim is to provide, through the presentation of historic continuity, the prerequisites of perception, of that unique phenomenon that is Israel of today, and to help create that sense of participation that is indispensable for every Jew everywhere in fulfilling himself by sharing, personally, or vicariously, in the building of the Israel of tomorrow.

Naturally, this is a matter of emotion. Nevertheless, the faithfulness to the spirit of history demands detachment and factuality. They have been given their place in this book to the best of the author's judgment and ability. Yet, if the facts by their very nature, strike a chord of responsiveness in the reader and spark his readiness for personal involvement, they are only living up to a famous poet's deep intuition: "It is the purpose of history to engender enthusiasm."

N.Y., June/1961

A textbook devoted specifically to the history of modern Israel and to its "pre-history," to the development, namely, in Jewish thought and life of the perennial attachment to Zion, has been long overdue. This book therefore should begin filling a need that has been widely felt in ever-growing measure.

Designed for use in Jewish schools in the first place, the present volume will be accompanied, it is hoped, in due course by a work book that may follow up in depth on the variety of materials, that necessarily had to be presented in a compactness dictated by both the abundance of subject matter and the limitations of space. I am conscious of a number of missing parts as well as of the process of slenderizing that had to be applied so that a proper framework of conciseness and continuity could be maintained. In this respect, I have guided myself by the maxim of a famous Jewish artist, the painter Max Liebermann: "To draw means to omit!"

If a series of questions following at the end of each chapter—a customary feature of textbooks—was left out, it was done so by intent. For it is hoped that this text may reach out beyond the delineation of classroom needs on the school level, and may also find its use for adult education purposes at large.

This is the time and place to acknowledge my indebtedness to all those whose active interest and participation have made the publication of this book possible. A first word of gratitude goes to Dr. Abraham Ezra Millgram, who initiated this project and who sustained it from its inception with his deep wisdom, with his loving kind care and with his minute attention to laborious detail. My most heartfelt thanks goes further to the Committee on Textbook Publication and its chairman, Mr. Henry R. Goldberg; to the official readers, Mr. Barnet Cohen, Dr. Samuel Dinin, Dr. Solomon Grayzel, Dr. Shlomo Noble, Mr. Levi Soshuk and Mr. Israel Soifer, for their constructive suggestions; to Mr. Eric Feldheim who also read the manuscript; and to Mr. David Boroff whose fine editorial judgment and assistance have been greatly appreciated.

Special acknowledgment is due to the Zionist Archives and Library that so generously supplied many illustrations accompanying the text. The Director of the Archives, Mrs. Sylvia Landress, and Miss Rebecca Zapinsky of the staff, have truly put me in their debt. In addition, I am much obliged to all the other members of the Library staff for their never-failing helpfulness. Miss Anna Kleban, Coordinator of Field Activities of the Library of the Jewish Theological Seminary of America, and Mr. Ezekiel Lifschutz, Archivist of the Yivo Institute for Jewish Research, have most graciously made additional photographs available. I am most thankful to them for all their courtesies.

This roster of expressions of gratitude would remain incomplete were it not to include the names of Miss Henrietta Cohen, secretary to Dr. Millgram, and of Mrs. Rose Festinger, my own secretary, who both gave so generously and willingly of their expertness and time in helping set this book on its course.

Contents

Preface v
Acknowledgments vii
Map of Israel x–xi

UNIT ONE *How Zion Lived in the Hearts of the Jewish People*

CHAPTER 1. Jerusalem the Holy 2
CHAPTER 2. The Mountain That Came to the People 7
CHAPTER 3. Waiting for the Messiah 16

UNIT TWO *How the Love of Zion Created Zionism* 32

CHAPTER 1. As Ghetto Walls Tumble 33
CHAPTER 2. Nine Years That Changed the Jewish World 50
CHAPTER 3. Steppingstones to Reality 63
CHAPTER 4. Herzl's Place in History 87

UNIT THREE *Zionism Strikes Roots* 89

CHAPTER 1. The Slow Decade 90
CHAPTER 2. The New World 105
CHAPTER 3. Engulfed by War 111
CHAPTER 4. Towards a New Dawn 123

UNIT FOUR *How the Jewish Homeland Developed* 136

CHAPTER 1. Advances and Setbacks 137
CHAPTER 2. Upheaval From Within and Without 145
CHAPTER 3. Shadows and Agonies 164
CHAPTER 4. Road Blocks to Fulfillment 172

UNIT FIVE *How the Jewish Homeland Became the State of Israel* 182

CHAPTER 1. A Nation Restored 183
CHAPTER 2. Building the New State 198
CHAPTER 3. Defending the Borders 204
CHAPTER 4. The Open Gates 214

Index 237

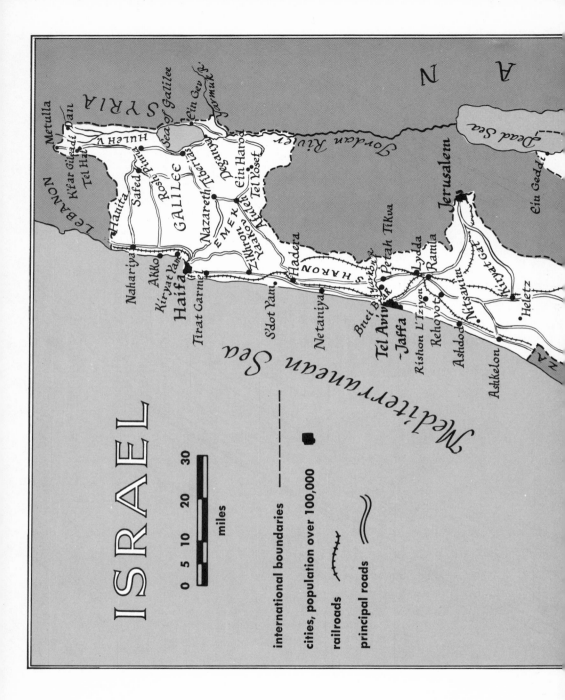

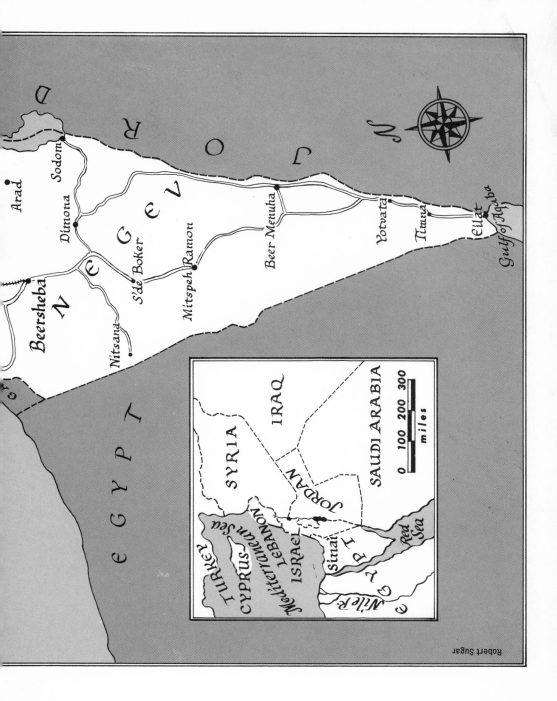

Map of Israel

Robert Sugar

UNIT ONE

*How Zion Lived in the Hearts
of the Jewish People*

THE *Seder* is drawing to its close. A long, beautiful evening has kept the family around the festive Passover table. There were the blessings and prayers, the singing, stories, the wine and *Matzot*, the dinner, the search for the *Afikomen*, and the opening of the door for the Prophet Elijah. There were moments of excitement, gladness, and even a bit of blessed tiredness as the celebration moved on. Then comes a moment of renewed vigor. Father, sitting at the head of the table, raises his voice in a solemn chant. "*Hasal Siddur Pesah*—the order of the Passover is now accomplished as prescribed." He intones the final sentences of the *Seder* ritual and exclaims, "*L'shanah Ha-Ba'ah B'rushalayim.*" Everyone joins in a chorus—"*L'shanah Ha-Ba'ah B'rushalayim*—next year in Jerusalem."

So it was last year in the Jewish home, here and all over the world. It was the same the year before, and for centuries, back through the ages. It is a shout that has made dull eyes sparkle, and that has sent joy into tired hearts. Eternal hope rings in that cry: "*L'shanah Ha-Ba'ah B'rushalayim*—next year in Jerusalem."

And when the year's holiest day, Yom Kippur, draws to a close, and the long-drawn sound of the *Shofar* signals the end of the great fast, again the cry of hope bursts out of many hearts in many lands: Next year in Jerusalem!

Why Jerusalem?

Why have the hopes and prayers of the Jewish people centered around Jerusalem throughout so many centuries?

Jerusalem has always been at the core of Jewish thinking and feeling. As the "Holy City" in which the Temple stood, it was the center of the

CHAPTER 1 *Jerusalem the Holy*

Jewish universe. Even after the Temple was destroyed, and the land of Israel made desolate, Jews looked to Jerusalem and recalled the days when the Jewish people had lived as a free, and proud, and independent nation.

Jerusalem has been laid low several times since the dawn of history. Six centuries before the common era (586 B.C.E.), the city and its Temple were destroyed by Nebuchadnezzar of Babylon; a second Temple went up in flames in the year 70 at the hands of the Roman legions; after Bar Kokhba's revolt in the year 132–135, the city was razed by the Roman Emperor Hadrian. But in Jewish hearts Jerusalem remained a city of glory. And legend built a city of dreams over its ruins. Thus one story tells of Jacob's ladder, reaching upward to the gates of heaven, from the exact site of the *Bet Hamikdash*, the Holy Temple. And according to another legend, its foundation stone was formed when the world was created.

No wonder that many people once thought Jerusalem to be the geographical center of the world. Of the ten measures of beauty that came

into this world, according to an ancient saying, nine were given to Jerusalem. And high above the earthly Jerusalem stood a heavenly Jerusalem.

The Biblical Oath

A solemn oath taken by Jewish captives of Babylonia after the first Temple was destroyed was pledged anew by Jews all over the world in every age. The psalm in which this oath is recorded reads:

> *By the rivers of Babylon, there we sat down,*
> *Yea, we wept, when we remembered Zion.*
> *Upon the willows in the midst thereof we hanged up our harps.*
> *For there they that led us captive asked of us words of song,*
> *And our tormentors asked of us mirth!*
> *"Sing us one of the songs of Zion."*
> *How shall we sing the Lord's song in a foreign land?*
> *If I forget thee, O Jerusalem,*
> *Let my right hand forget her cunning.*
> *Let my tongue cleave to the roof of my mouth,*
> *If I remember thee not;*
> *If I set not Jerusalem above my chiefest joy.*

"If I forget thee, O Jerusalem . . ." has become a people's oath, grave and haunting. Jews in every generation pledged not to forget Jerusalem and Eretz Yisrael. Indeed, they could not help but remember. The memory was renewed each time they opened their "book of books"—the Bible.

Recorded in the Bible

The Torah records repeatedly God's promise to Abraham, Isaac, Jacob, and their descendants of a land "flowing with milk and honey." Other books of the Bible recount Joshua's leadership as Israel conquered the

"By the Rivers of Babylon . . ."

At the Wailing Wall in Old City of Jerusalem

Land of Canaan and began to build its own national life under its judges, prophets, and kings. The Bible dwells on the pride and the love of the people for King David, whose royal descendants reigned for a stretch of about 500 years. A later tradition arose that a Messiah would emerge from the House of David to redeem his people from destruction and dispersion, and restore them to Eretz Yisrael. Throughout the Bible is expressed the vision of the Jewish people restored as a united, free, and independent nation.

Tishah B'Av

On Tishah B'Av, the ninth day of the Jewish month of Av, the synagogue is shrouded in darkness. There are only a few rows of flickering candles. Bare is the ark of any decorative curtain. Gloom hangs heavy. Some people squat on the bare floor, others sit on low stools. A sad mood grips the congregation as over their whispers rises a mournful melody, "*Ekhah yashvah vadad ha'ir* . . . —How has the city become deserted." It is a day of fasting and of mournful meditation, the darkest day of the Jewish calendar.

It seems as if the Ninth of Av has been singled out for the greatest calamities befalling the Jewish people, for on this day, in the year

> 586 B.C.E. the first Temple fell to the Babylonians;
> 70 C.E. the second Temple was destroyed by the Romans;
> 135 the Bar Kokhba revolt was crushed;
> 136 a plow was drawn over the Temple site in Jerusalem as a way of showing that the Temple, the city, and the land were completely destroyed;
> 1492 the Jews were expelled from Spain;
> 1914 the First World War broke out, bringing disaster to Europe and its many Jewish communities;
> 1929 an Arab revolt started in Palestine, causing destruction to some Jewish settlements, and opening a Moslem "Holy War" against the Jews.

Whatever one may think of such coincidence, a popular belief has labeled the Ninth of Av as a day that would change from a day of disaster to a day of great joy. One story tells that on the Ninth of Av the Messiah, the redeemer who will restore the Jewish people to their ancient homeland, will be born.

SOME three thousand years ago, in the days of King David, there stood on a hill of Jerusalem a mighty fortress called the "Stronghold of Zion." After King David captured Jerusalem from the Jebusites he gave the fortress a new name—the City of David. As the city grew, the name Zion came to stand for everything around the hill, including another

CHAPTER 2 *The Mountain That Came to the People*

mount, the one on which Solomon later built the Temple. Zion, Jerusalem, and the Holy Temple became one in the minds of the people. That single hill, Zion, later stood for the entire land of Israel. And the term *Bat Tzion* (Daughter of Zion) became a poetic expression for all the people of Israel.

When the Jews went into exile, the hope for the return to Zion never left them. The Mount of Zion was a towering symbol of their most fervent hopes for redemption.

In Daily Prayer

Could there be more striking proof of the living attachment of the Jewish people to Zion than that offered by the *Siddur*, the book of daily prayer? Each day, throughout the centuries, from the lips of Israel's faithful come prayers for redemption of Zion. Three times a day the pious Jew turns to God, while reciting the *Amidah* prayer, and pleads:

Sound the great *Shofar* for freedom; lift up the banner to gather our exiles; and gather us from the four corners of the earth.

Three times a day he prays:

And to Jerusalem, Thy City, return us in mercy, and dwell therein as Thou hast spoken, and rebuild it soon in our days as an everlasting structure.

And he adds:

And let our eyes behold Thy return to Zion in mercy! Blessed art Thou, O Lord, who restorest Thy divine presence unto Zion.

These prayers reflect the Jews' fervent hopes for an end to their exile, and a return to Zion—a new beginning.

On the Sabbath

When the Sabbath brings an end to the week's work, the observant Jew refreshes his spirit in the synagogue. His longings for the redemption of his people find expression in prayers at the Sabbath service. One prayer takes the form of a question:

Oh, *when* wilt Thou reign in Zion?

And then the congregation voices the hope:

Speedily in *our* days do Thou dwell there forever!

To this the chant of ages has added:

Mayest Thou be exalted and sanctified in Jerusalem, Thy City, throughout all generations and to all Eternity.

When the *Maftir* has completed the reading of the prophetic lesson, he concludes with special blessings, one of which pleads:

Be merciful unto Zion, for it is the fountain of our life, and mayest Thou soon in our own day deliver Zion that is grieved in spirit. Blessed art Thou, O Lord, who makest Zion rejoice with her children.

Joy and Zion are coupled again in the *Musaf* service when the congregation prays:

May it be Thy will, O Lord, our God, and God of our fathers, to lead us joyfully back to our land, and to establish us within its borders.

Remembrance Takes No Holiday

The holiday ritual is studded with reminders of "Jerusalem, Thy Holy City."

There are even special prayers for rain in Palestine. The *T'fillat Geshem*, a prayer recited on Sh'mini Atzeret, the eighth day of the Sukkot festival, shows how the Jew, no matter where he lived, continued

In Prayer at the Sukkot Service

to be concerned about the course of nature in the Holy Land. With much of Palestine a semi-desert, rainfall is of critical importance and could never be taken for granted.

Like rain, dew is especially important to the soil in Palestine and a prayer for dew, *T'fillat Tal,* is recited early in spring, on the first day of Passover.

Three Weeks of Mourning

The Jewish calendar has other reminders of the disaster that struck the first Temple. During the winter, the Fast of the Tenth of Tevet—Assarah B'Tevet—goes back to the beginning of Nebuchadnezzar's siege of Jerusalem. Another fast day comes in early summer, Shivah Asar B'Tammuz—the 17th of Tammuz—when the Babylonians broke through the walls of Jerusalem. The day also marks another catastrophic event, during the Jewish war with the Romans some 700 years later, when the tide of battle turned against the Jewish people. With this day begins the so-called "Three Weeks" of national religious mourning, climaxed by Tishah B'Av, symbol of the worst national disaster in Jewish history.

During the three joyless weeks between Shivah Asar B'Tammuz and Tishah B'Av, no weddings are permitted. Age-old custom has banned the cutting of the hair or the use of new clothes. During the final nine days, from the 1st to the 9th of Av, ancient custom decrees meatless meals except on Shabbat.

After Tishah B'Av, Jews turn from moods of despair to new hope for redemption. Prophetic readings on the seven Sabbaths leading to Rosh Hashanah express hope for Israel's return and restoration. "The Seven *Haftarot* of Comfort," as they are called, are all taken from the Book of Isaiah, Chapters 40 to 66. In them, the prophet predicts his people's liberation from Babylonian captivity, return to the Holy Land, and renewal as an independent nation. Thus Zion's saddest and happiest days are marked each year on the calendar of the synagogue.

Trees and Students

Two minor holidays of the Jewish calendar deal wholly with memories of the ancient land.

Tu Bishvat, the 15th day of Sh'vat, is observed in synagogue and

← *Roman Spoils from the Temple in Jerusalem*
Bas-Relief on the Arch of Titus, Rome

home as the New Year's day of the trees in Palestine. According to custom, a special fruit plate with different fruits, reminiscent of those grown in Palestine, is served.

Lag Ba-Omer, the thirty-third day during the counting of the *Omer*, was known as a "students' festival." Today Hebrew schools usually celebrate it by holding outings and other special events. Tradition has it that in the days of Rabbi Akiba, an epidemic among his pupils halted suddenly on that day. Again, Eretz Israel is the locale for the tradition that has made the *S'firah*, the period of counting the *Omer*, a time of mourning. Only on Lag Ba-Omer, Rosh Hodesh and Yom Atzmaut is the mourning interrupted, and only then are weddings permitted.

Turning Toward Jerusalem

The Bible describes how Daniel, an exile in Babylonia, stood in the upper chamber of his house at an open window facing Jerusalem when he prayed three times a day. This is the first known reference to the old Jewish tradition of turning toward Jerusalem while praying. In Western countries, the direction, of course, is eastward. That is why synagogues in the West are built so that the congregations face to the east. In many lands the eastern wall of a room in a Jewish home is adorned by a *Mizrah* (which means "east"), a drawing on parchment or in print to indicate the direction for prayer. The ornaments fancifully depict Jerusalem, or the Temple on Mount Moriah, or often a Menorah. The name of God, often in illuminated letters, appears in the center. For one who wishes to pray, say, in a field or forest, and does not know which direction is east, tradition holds that it is enough to think of Jerusalem.

Towards the end of a Jewish wedding ceremony, a blessing exultingly proclaims, "Blessed art Thou, O Lord, who makest the groom rejoice with the bride." Then comes a crunching sound, made by the bridegroom as

בְּקָרוֹב בִּמְהֵרָה בִּמְהֵרָה בְּיָמֵינוּ בְּקָרוֹב בְּנֵה בְנֵה בְּנֵה בֵּיתְךָ בְּקָרוֹב :
גָּדוֹל הוּא דָּגוּל הוּא יִבְנֶה בֵיתוֹ בְּקָרוֹב בִּמְהֵרָה בִּמְהֵרָה בְּיָמֵינוּ בְּקָרוֹב בְּנֵה
בְנֵה בְנֵה בֵּיתְךָ בְּקָרוֹב : הָדוּר הוּא וָתִיק הוּא זַכַּאי הוּא חָסִיד
הוּא יִבְנֶה בֵיתוֹ בְּקָרוֹב בִּמְהֵרָה בִּמְהֵרָה בְּיָמֵינוּ בְּקָרוֹב בְּנֵה בְנֵה בְנֵה בֵּיתְךָ
בְּקָרוֹב : טָהוֹר הוּא יָחִיד הוּא כַּבִּיר הוּא לָמוּד הוּא מֶלֶךְ הוּא נָאוֹר הוּא
סַגִּיב הוּא עִזּוּז הוּא פּוֹדֶה הוּא צַדִּיק הוּא יִבְנֶה בֵיתוֹ בְּקָרוֹב בִּמְהֵרָה
בִּמְהֵרָה בְּיָמֵינוּ בְּקָרוֹב בְּנֵה בְנֵה בְנֵה בֵּיתְךָ בְּקָרוֹב : קָדוֹשׁ הוּא רַחוּם הוּא
שַׁדַּי הוּא תַּקִּיף הוּא יִבְנֶה בֵיתוֹ בְּקָרוֹב בִּמְהֵרָה בִּמְהֵרָה בְּיָמֵינוּ בְּקָרוֹב
אֵל בְּנֵה אֵל בְּנֵה בְּנֵה בֵּיתְךָ בְּקָרוֹב :

"Oh may He who is mighty,
soon rebuild his house,
speedily, speedily, soon in
our days . . ."
  From an ancient
manuscript of the Passover
Haggadah: An artist's vision
of the Temple of the Future

he steps on a glass to shatter it. This is to introduce a brief sign of mourning at the height of his greatest joy. Even in the moment of greatest personal happiness, Jews have sworn to remember the loss of Zion.

The unending story of the love of the Jew for his homeland goes back to the Patriarch Jacob who willed that his remains be brought back from Egypt to the land of his fathers.

And his son, Joseph, left the same request. Two hundred years after Joseph's death, Moses and the children of Israel took his body with them into the Promised Land. For thousands of years to come, many more Jews had the same desire to be united in death with the Jewish land.

In the lands of the dispersion, many communities went out of their way to procure precious soil from the Holy Land to mingle with the soil of their local burial ground, thus giving the dead a last "touch of home."

At the End of Days

Countless generations have filled their lives with the fervent belief that a redeemer of the Jewish people, the Messiah, will appear at the "end of days." In the tradition, the Messiah would bring an end to all the misfortunes and miseries that had befallen Jews throughout the dispersion; he would gather the people from the four corners of the earth, bring them back to their ancient homeland, and restore them to greatness as a nation. Not only the Jewish nation would the Messiah glorify—he would establish the Kingdom of God on earth for all humanity.

The Messiah idea encompassed all the noble hopes of the people. The Prophets of the Bible, particularly Isaiah, Jeremiah, Ezekiel, Haggai, and Zechariah, told of magnificent things to come, when nations would not make war any more and the world would be filled with everlasting justice for all peoples. "The wolf shall dwell with the lamb and the leopard lie down with the kid." "They shall not hurt nor destroy in all my holy mountain; for the earth shall be full of the knowledge of the Lord." All mankind would be united in a brotherhood of man and the fatherhood of God. All would turn to God in reverence, or as the Scriptures say, "On that day God will be one and His name one."

This belief grew in intensity whenever the hardships of the Jewish people increased; it reached fresh heights of passion with each new agony.

In legend and fantasy, the Prophet Elijah became the "Guardian Angel of the Jewish people," its protector, comforter, and bearer of good tidings. The story is told that three days before the coming of the Messiah, the Prophet Elijah will announce the event on the hills and mountains of the Holy Land. The story has kept Jewish souls aglow throughout the ages. And every week, on *Motza'ei Shabbat*, the close of the Sabbath, the timeless hope rang out in heartlifting song:

May Elijah, the prophet, Elijah, the man from Gilead, soon come to us, together with the Anointed One, the son of David.

Galut—A State of Mind

The word *Galut* cannot actually be translated. Whether one renders it as "banishment," "exile," or "dispersion," the translation falls short of the full meaning of the Hebrew term. *Galut* means all these expressions and more. *Galut* is a state of mind. The soul of the Jew has been in a *Galut* throughout the course of time. For in all environments outside of the land of Israel, even were they the loveliest spots on earth, the Jewish people never forgot its homeland of old.

"And the wolf shall dwell with the lamb;
And the leopard shall lie down with the kid;
And the calf and the young lion and the fatling
together;
And a little child shall lead them . . ."

← *Isaiah 11:6*

FOR centuries a passionate longing for the arrival of the Messiah kept the Jewish people in a state of ceaseless expectation and tension. More than anything else, the misery of endless persecutions prompted them to dwell prayerfully on thoughts of a redeemer who would end all their suffering.

The grimmer their lot was, the greater was their longing, and the surer they became that the time for the Messiah was near. It was inevitable that from time to time—in one land or another—there would be some to announce that the promised Messiah had already arrived.

Mystical movements permeated by the promise of the Messiah marched across the pages of Jewish history. Often these ended in disillusion and despair. Still, no matter what their origin or outcome, they give eloquent testimony to the undying trust of the Jewish people in its rebirth as a nation in the holy Land of Israel.

CHAPTER 3 *Waiting for the Messiah*

The Roman oppression, when Judea was trampled by the empire's victorious legions, sparked the first real flame of messianic hopes. Some saw a
redeemer in an inspiring Jewish preacher from Galilee, Jesus of Nazareth.
His tragic death at the hands of the Romans sealed the fate of that
messianic movement and opened a new chapter in the history of man—
the beginning of Christianity. While the new faith spread and gained
many adherents in the pagan world, it failed, however, to convince most
of the people from whom Jesus sprang. To them it was clear that the
messianic kingdom on earth had not yet come. The promises of peace
and the redemption of the Jewish people from its oppressors had not been
fulfilled.

Years passed, but the terrible Roman occupation of Palestine continued and despondency grew. Then Bar Kokhba appeared on the horizon
of Jewish history, and in 132 C.E. he led a revolt against the Romans. At
first it was so successful that many Jews believed him to be the actual
Messiah. His real name was probably Simon, but the people called him
"Son of the Star." Even the famous Rabbi Akiba saw in Bar Kokhba the
fulfillment of a vision of Balaam, the pagan seer of the days of Moses.
Balaam tried his best to curse Israel, but from his lips he issued a blessing,
pronouncing what "This people shall do . . . in the end of days." His
prophecy proclaimed:

> *There shall step forth a star out of Jacob,*
> *And a sceptre shall rise out of Israel,*
> *And shall smite through the corners of Moab,*
> *And break down all the sons of Seth,*
> *And Edom shall be a possession. . . .*

Moab, Seth, and Edom were taken to be symbols of pagan Rome. Her
yoke was to be broken by the "Son of the Star"—Bar Kokhba.

"This is the King Messiah," Rabbi Akiba is supposed to have fer-
vently declared. Bar Kokhba started his revolt against the Romans during
the rule of the Emperor Hadrian (117–138). The Jewish general set the
hearts of his people ablaze with rebellion. Soon there were stories that he
possessed superhuman power and could work miracles. From many lands

where Jews lived outside Palestine came young Jews to join Bar Kokhba's army. Its ranks reached almost half a million. Sweeping victories marked the beginning of Bar Kokhba's uprising and more than fifty towns were liberated in one year. For a time, it really seemed as if the Roman tyranny had ended. Bar Kokhba proclaimed himself king and had coins struck as symbols of Jewish sovereignty. Redemption seemed close at hand.

However, the fortunes of war changed when the near-vanquished Romans shifted one of their outstanding generals, Julius Severus, from Britain to Palestine. After a bitter struggle, he crushed the rebellion. The last Jewish fortress of Betar fell, and Bar Kokhba lost his life. With him died the messianic illusion he inspired. But other deluded or fraudulent "redeemers" kept arising to take his place. And always, many were eager to follow.

Island and Mainland Messiahs

In the first half of the 5th century, the Jewish community of the Mediterranean island of Crete was thrown into a turmoil. A certain Moses convinced many Jews that he was the Messiah. He claimed he would bring the Jews of Crete to the land of Israel and they would walk dry-shod across the sea. At his word, many persons plunged into the sea and drowned.

An 8th century tailor, Abu Isa, convinced thousands of his fellow Persian Jews that he was the Messiah who would lead them back to Palestine. Raising an army of some 10,000, he attacked Persia's then Arab masters. He met defeat, imprisonment, and execution. But false messiahs

Coins Tell the Story:

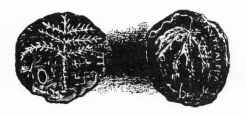

Bar Kokhba's Symbols of Independence in Bronze and Copper

continued to appear in Jewish communities across the Middle East and in Europe.

Messianic fever burst into flame during the times of the Crusades, when Christian armies sought to wrest their holy places in Palestine from Moslem rule. During this era of mass fanaticism and hysteria, many Jewish communities lying in the paths of onrushing forces were looted and burned. Thousands of Jews fell victim to either the crusading Christians or the defending Moslems. With each slaughter, messianic zeal burned brighter. Mass messianic delusions were recorded in places as widely scattered as France, Greece, Spain, Morocco, Persia, and Mesopotamia.

Maimonides Warns the Yemenites

At almost the same time in Yemen, at the southern end of the Arabian peninsula, Jews were suffering bitterly under pressure to convert to Islam. Then a man appeared who preached that all their hardships were only painful signs of redemption soon to come. Claiming to be a forerunner of the Messiah, he urged the Jews to prepare themselves by sharing their goods with the poor and also accepting his teachings, a hodgepodge of Jewish and Moslem beliefs.

The Yemenite Jews wrote for advice to the great Maimonides in Egypt. He replied with his famous letter, *"Iggeret Teman"*—"Letter to Yemen"—advising them to remain steadfast in their Jewish faith and to treat the pretender with calm and neglect. They did this, and eventually, the man was arrested by the Arab authorities. Believing he had super-

natural powers, he challenged them to behead him so he could prove the truth of his mission by returning to life. The challenge was accepted. His head was cut off and there was no "proof."

The Jews of Yemen remained ever grateful to Maimonides for his advice. And to this day, Yemenite Jews include the name of Maimonides in their *Kaddish* prayer to perpetuate his memory.

A Jewish Prince Visits the Pope

One day in the spring of 1524, all Italy was astir. A man called David Reubeni, who claimed to be a Jewish prince from a faraway country, was about to land at Rome. He had set sail from Venice in a magnificently decorated ship some months earlier, announcing at several Italian ports he touched that he had highly important political affairs to discuss with Pope Clement VII.

His appearance was dramatic and colorful. David Reubeni was swarthy, and of short stature. He was garbed in oriental costume. On a white steed, he rode to the papal palace, where he was received with royal honors.

Reubeni's story was that he came from Chaibar, a region of Arabia, where his brother, Solomon, was king of a sovereign Jewish state. He said the people were descendants of the tribes of Reuben, Gad, and half of Manasseh, which had settled on the eastern side of the Jordan, according to the biblical account.

Not only the Pope but, later, King João III of Portugal believed the story and showed the keenest interest in Reubeni's mission, which was to organize a Jewish army to fight the Turks. At the time, the Turks, who ruled the Middle East, were threatening Central Europe.

Reubeni was successful in his negotiations. He received the approval of the Pope, whose recommendations led the king of Portugal to promise cannons and other weapons for the proposed Jewish army.

Reubeni's appearance in Portugal made a deep impression on the Marranos, "secret Jews" who professed the Christian faith to avoid unspeakable persecution, but kept Jewish laws and traditions in secret. News of the Jewish ambassador revived messianic hopes and illusions. Marranos in Portugal and neighboring Spain were quick to believe that the Arabian Jewish prince could be no one else but a forerunner of the Messiah. Word of the Marranos' excitement soon reached the Inquisition, the Church court set up to punish heretics. The Inquisition accused Reubeni of promising Spanish Marranos that the Messiah would soon arrive to lead them to Palestine. Whether he actually made such claims is not known. Cautiously, Reubeni tried as best he could to avoid any contact with the Marranos. Nevertheless, the accusation eventually alienated King João and led to Reubeni's expulsion from Portugal.

Reubeni Acquires a Partner

A young Marrano, Diego Pires, who served as royal secretary to the Spanish High Court of Justice, became so fascinated by Reubeni that he decided to return openly to Judaism at the risk of his life. Reubeni, afraid for his own fortunes, advised Pires to flee. Calling himself Solomon Molkho, the young man went to Turkey and immersed himself in the study of the mysterious cabala. Soon Molkho told of having had weird visions, and claimed ability to interpret dreams. He gained fame as a fiery preacher, and wherever he went, people flocked to listen to him. Traveling through Palestine, he went to Safed, the center of cabalistic studies, and gained many followers. One day he startled them with a momentous announcement: The Messianic Kingdom will arrive in eleven years—in the year 1540.

Soon Molkho revised his prediction, and said the Messiah might come even earlier. Rome, capital of the Christian world, had been captured by the troops of the German Emperor, Charles V, and Molkho became convinced that this was a sure sign of the Messiah's coming.

According to an old folk fantasy, the Messiah would come from among the poor and the diseased in Rome. Molkho hurried to the city, clad himself in rags, blackened his face, and mingled with the crowd of beggars loitering near the papal palace. For thirty days, Molkho sat at one of the bridges of the Tiber River. Then, giving up the beggar's role, he appeared in Rome's largest synagogue and ascended the pulpit. With passionate singing and ringing words, he proclaimed that the arrival of the Messiah was at hand. His listeners were spellbound.

Also awe-struck were Pope Clement VII and other high church dignitaries whom Molkho later succeeded in meeting. Molkho warned them that Rome would be visited by a disastrous flood. Soon the Tiber's waters rose above its banks. He warned the Portuguese ambassador of earthquakes in his country, and in 1531, tremors almost destroyed the city of Lisbon.

These events—though undoubtedly coincidental—convinced Molkho that he had been chosen to do great things. As word spread, many people began to believe Molkho was the forerunner of the Messiah or even the Messiah himself.

But some Jews remained calm. They began to worry lest the rash promises by Molkho or his followers anger the Church and cost them their lives. Finally, one of them reported Molkho to the Inquisition as a former Christian who had deserted his faith. The Inquisition acted swiftly. Molkho was seized, tried, and condemned to be burned at the stake.

When the time for the execution arrived, Molkho was nowhere to be found. At the last moment, he escaped, chiefly through the assistance of the Pope himself. To his followers, this was Molkho's greatest miracle.

Molkho soon appeared in Mantua, where he met David Reubeni, and the two teamed up for new messianic adventures. They set out for Ratisbon, Germany, where Emperor Charles V was presiding at a diet, an important meeting of Germany's nobles. With a flair for showmanship, Reubeni and Molkho entered the city bearing a huge banner inscribed in bold Hebrew letters reading, "Maccabee." In solemn procession they made their way to the Emperor to whom they proposed a plan—like that submitted to the Pope—for organizing a Jewish army to make war against the Turks.

The Emperor listened, but he was not taken in by the theatrical pair. They were arrested, chained, and taken along as the Emperor moved on to Italy. In Mantua, the Emperor surrendered Molkho to the Inquisition as a former Christian who relapsed into Judaism. He was condemned to be burned to death. While bound to the stake, Molkho was offered reprieve and liberty if he would return to Christianity. He replied that he had always longed to die as a martyr, and he did, at the age of thirty-two.

The Inquisition—which dealt only with persons who were baptized, forcibly or otherwise—had no jurisdiction over Reubeni. Yet he remained a prisoner of the Emperor for the rest of his life. Wherever Charles went, Reubeni was taken along—in chains. His life ended in Spain. There are stories that he was poisoned in a Spanish prison. His was another dismal episode in a lengthy chain of Jewish disappointments growing out of an undying hope for messianic redemption, and return to nationhood.

The Amazing Story of Sabbatai Zevi

The messianic fever flared up frequently throughout the sixteenth and seventeenth centuries. Cabalistic calculations to determine the exact date of the Messiah's arrival became the chief activity for many Jews. Oddly enough, a messianic mood suddenly developed in Mexico, where Spanish Marrano settlers were sure the Messiah would appear there between 1642 and 1643. However, it was not in the Western Hemisphere nor in Europe but in the Near East where the messianic movement exploded into a real revolution, shaking the entire Jewish world to its very foundations.

A strangely beautiful young man, twenty-two-year-old Sabbatai Zevi, plunged into one of the biggest messianic adventures of all times by daring to do what had been forbidden by centuries of Jewish usage. He stood before a crowd in his native Smyrna, a town in Asiatic Turkey, and pronounced with great ceremony and in an amazingly melodious voice the four letters that form the Name of God. Only the High Priest, in the ancient Temple of Jerusalem, ever did so publicly, and then only at the climax of the Yom Kippur service. But young Sabbatai Zevi pronounced the Name deliberately as "proof" that he was the Messiah, who would abolish all earthly governments, institute the reign of God, make Jerusalem the center of the world, and redeem the Jewish people.

In cabalistic tradition, no one but the Messiah himself was privileged to pronounce the Name of God, and Sabbatai, steeped in cabalistic lore, knew this well. There was still another "sign": Sabbatai was born in 1626 on Tishah B'Av, the day marking the Jewish people's greatest calamity. And this was the day, according to legend, on which the Messiah would be born.

One of Sabbatai's growing band of followers came up with a most startling "discovery." He proclaimed that he had found an ancient manuscript, a book entitled *The Great Wisdom of Solomon*. On paper apparently withered with age, the book appeared to be written in archaic Hebrew characters. It began:

I, Abraham, was confined to a cave for forty years, and I wondered greatly that the time of miracles did not arrive. Then I heard a voice proclaiming: 'A son will be born in the year 5386 (1626 C.E.) to Mordecai Zevi; and he will be called Sabbatai. He will humble the great Dragon. . . . He, the true Messiah, will sit upon My throne.'

Repentance by Flagellation: Jews at Salonica at the time of Sabbatai Zevi upheaval

This was a fraud, but there were few cool heads to recognize it as such; and it appears that Sabbatai himself believed it as a revelation. Christians and Jews alike seemed to expect a major turning point in the destinies of the world and of the Jewish people. In the opinion of many Christians 1666 was the likely year for momentous happenings. Jews, generally citing an obscure passage in the *Zohar*, looked to 1648. That was the year which saw the end of the bitter Thirty Years' War in Europe, and it was the year Sabbatai Zevi "revealed" himself as the Messiah of his people.

Not all took to Sabbatai Zevi immediately. While he gained numerous followers in Smyrna, the rabbis turned against him because he had pronounced the Name of God, and he was driven out. In Salonika, Greece, he was expelled from the Jewish community for staging an outrageous, yet compelling, spectacle. Posing as the "Son of God," he arranged for a "marriage" to the Torah under the traditional wedding canopy. People were incensed and he had to leave. After wandering about in many places, he settled for a time in Cairo, Egypt, and there gained the patronage of a wealthy Syrian cabalist. Then Sabbatai moved on to Jerusalem. He arrived at a time when Turkish officials were threatening Jerusalem Jews

Sabbatai Zevi citing "proof" from the Bible

The "Messiah" ordaining a disciple

25

with doom unless they paid a high ransom. Sabbatai became a hero, winning Jewish acclamation as "the deliverer of the Holy City" when he returned to Cairo and procured the required funds from his rich friend.

While in Cairo, he heard stories about an orphaned Polish refugee girl, Sarah, who lived in Italy and claimed to have visions that she was chosen to be the bride of the Messiah. Sabbatai—asserting that the truth of her claims was revealed to him in a vision of his own—sent for Sarah. With the most lavish celebration ever witnessed by Cairo's Jews, they were married. With his bride, he returned to Jerusalem for a hero's welcome. Public acclaim truly intoxicated him and erased any doubts he may have entertained about his "messianic" mission.

A New Elijah

While passing through Gaza, in Palestine, Sabbatai met his most enthusiastic adherent, Nathan Gazati (that is, of Gaza), who opened a new phase in his messianic adventure. The man from Gaza soon became Sabbatai's chief propagandist and conspirator. Gazati announced in 1665 that the messianic era would commence next year and that he, Gazati, was the Prophet Elijah, reappearing now to usher in the Age of Redemption.

Extraordinary as it now seems, the mass of the people, in their misery and ignorance, believed what Gazati proclaimed—that he, the new Elijah, would conquer the earth in a sweeping, bloodless victory, to pave the way for the Messiah, who would be "riding on a lion with a seven-headed dragon in its jaws" to lead the return to Israel of the Lost Ten Tribes.

But the rabbis in Jerusalem opposed Gazati and Sabbatai as frauds and threatened to excommunicate them. So they turned towards Smyrna, the home town Sabbatai had fled some fifteen years earlier. Great throngs filled the streets to give Sabbatai a tremendous reception. The city's famous son had returned to begin another amazing episode.

King Messiah Has Come

On Rosh Hashanah in the year 1665, the main synagogue of Smyrna reverberated with the blaring of many *Shofarot*. From an enthralled congregation came hysterical cries. The crowd roared, "Long live our king, our Messiah." Sabbatai Zevi openly declared himself to be the Messiah!

A chain reaction rocketed across countries and continents. Jews in many lands, infected by the spirit of Smyrna, let their imaginations soar. The wildest and most fantastic tales about Sabbatai were believed.

Jewish communities began making serious preparations for an exodus to the Land of Israel. In Avignon, France, Jews gave up almost everything after hearing a rumor that a ship had appeared off Scotland with silken sails and ropes, manned by sailors who spoke Hebrew, and with a flag bearing the inscription, "The Twelve Tribes of Israel."

Not only Jews alone, but many Christians shared the excitement. An outstanding Christian scholar wrote to the Jewish philosopher Spinoza in Amsterdam that "all the world here is talking of a rumor of the return of the Israelites to their own country. Should the news be confirmed, it may bring about a revolution in all things." And many of the most intelligent rabbis began to believe in Sabbatai Zevi and his mission.

Sabbatai, decreeing the end of Jewish fast days, circulated a letter to Jewish communities. It read: "The first begotten son of God, Sabbatai Zevi, Messiah and redeemer of the people of Israel, to all sons of Israel, Peace! Since ye have been deemed worthy to behold the great day and the fulfillment of God's words by the Prophet, your lament and sorrow must be changed into joy, and your fasting into merriment, for ye shall weep no more. Rejoice with song and melody, and change the day formerly spent in sadness and sorrow into a day of jubilee, for I have appeared."

Sabbatai's propaganda chief, Nathan Gazati, predicted that Sabbatai would place the Turkish Sultan's crown on his own head. Sabbatai headed for Constantinople. When he landed, to his surprise he was met by a police officer. While a tumultuous crowd looked on, the officer slapped Sabbatai in the face and declared him under arrest. But Sabbatai displayed presence of mind. Calmly, he turned his other cheek. His followers were quick to explain this was in keeping with the role of a suffering Savior who must endure pain to redeem the world. Then Sabbatai managed to turn his arrest to advantage. Perhaps through bribery of government officials or fear of riots among the Jews, Sabbatai was removed from Constantinople to a castle on the Bosphorus, where he was held as prisoner, but with luxury befitting a king.

A Prison Palace

Nathan Gazati and his assistants began raising tremendous sums of money for Sabbatai. It poured in from followers all over the world. Stories about how Sabbatai was taken prisoner and then miraculously entered a life of royal splendor spread to a world-wide Jewish public that thrilled to every detail, no matter how false and fantastic. The prison fortress was called "*Migdal Oz*"—the Tower of Strength.

Followers came from all over to visit the prisoner, who held court like a glorious king. Their reports—exaggerated with each retelling—threw Jews in various parts of the world into a new turmoil of excitement and hectic expectancy. Sabbatai's initials were painted on many synagogue walls. Prayers of adoration for him were uttered in many congregations. His picture was printed in prayer books alongside that of King David.

Sabbatai reached dizzying heights of popularity. Then he made a fatal mistake. From some visitors he had heard that a "prophet" had arisen in Poland, heralding the coming of the Messiah. Sabbatai sent for him, and three months later, Nehemiah Ha-Kohen presented himself.

Sabbatai Discredited

Secret conversations between Sabbatai and Nehemiah left each convinced the other was a fraud. Each recognized the other as a rival in the business of deceiving the Jewish people. But Nehemiah acted first. He converted to Islam and then reported to Turkish authorities that Sabbatai was plotting against the Sultan. Transferred to a real prison in Adrianople, Sabbatai began to fear for his life. Before long, the would-be redeemer of the Jewish people decided to save himself. When brought before the Sultan, Sabbatai took off his Jewish headgear and placed a Turkish turban on his head to signify that he had converted to Islam. Pleased, the Sultan then appointed Sabbatai as doorkeeper of the palace. Sarah, his wife, also became a Moslem, and so did some of Sabbatai's followers. Later, Sabbatai tried to justify his disgrace by writing to the Jewish community in Smyrna, "God has made me an Ishmaelite. He commanded and it was done."

Holding Court in Prison:
Sabbatai Zevi receives delegation
of Constantinople Jews ➤➤

The news that Sabbatai had become a Moslem shocked countless masses of his followers. They suffered shame, disillusion, and disgrace.

Bitter disappointment swept across the Jewish communities of almost the whole world. For a time, Sabbatai played a double game. He told Jews he was secretly trying to win converts to Judaism from among the Moslems. He told the Turks the reverse. In the end, the Turks banished him to a small town in Albania where he died in complete isolation, cut off from a world that he truly had set on fire.

Pathetic Aftermath

But Sabbatai's lonely death did not bring to an end the movement he had started. A line of would-be successors followed. They claimed to be real or spiritual children of Sabbatai. Many deluded, miserable people steadfastly clung to their faith in Sabbatai for more than a hundred years after his death. Those who had followed Sabbatai into Islam formed a sect that came to be known as the Donmeh. Practicing a mixture of Moslem and Jewish customs, they kept alive the memory of this brilliant impostor. Some of their descendants remain in Turkey and Greece to this day.

Too many episodes of messianic frenzy, always ending in the bleakest despair, had assaulted the Jewish people. In a sense, the sickness and the cure came from identical sources. There was the hatred and persecution, and there was the unquenchable urge they forever felt to reestablish Jewish life in the Holy Land. Whoever hinted that he might fulfill this messianic dream was followed, whether saint or scoundrel. Yet the love of Zion and the messianic idea both proved to be among the most powerful forces for Jewish regeneration.

The True Messiah

After so many *false* messiahs have paraded across the pages of Jewish history, what is left to say about a *true* Messiah? Do Jews of today still cling to the belief that a flesh-and-blood descendant of King David will arise to redeem Israel and institute a world-wide reign of peace and justice? Many Jews hold this conviction as a precise, literal truth foreseen in prophesies that admit of no other interpretation. On the other hand, there are Jews who have given up the idea of a messianic *person*, one individual on whom the fate of Israel and the world will turn. Instead, they conceive of messianic possibilities residing in all of mankind—of a time when godly insight would so fill the world that all nations will renounce evil and promote universal good. This messianic age, they believe, must be a product of world-wide good will, understanding, and effort. Most Jews prefer still to employ in their prayers the traditional, vivid, graphic references to a personal Messiah, though they regard these only figuratively, holding them as symbols of a poetic truth, not a literal one.

Regardless of how interpretations may vary in modern Judaism, most of the *central* elements of the ancient Messiah *concept* continue to be cherished by the body of Jews the world over. Whether they "believe with perfect faith in the coming of the Messiah" as a man or an ideal, Jews still focus their goals on a brotherhood of mankind true to the

Fatherhood of God—a world-wide society founded on the messianic ideals of peace, justice, and love. As it always has done, the pulse of Israel continues to quicken at the prospect of Jews tilling the land of their fathers in a world free of hate and injustice.

How did the messianic hopes of the centuries help to create the modern State of Israel? The answer lies in the story of what happened in the nineteenth century, when the Jewish world was shaken again, but this time by a new movement—Zionism!

UNIT TWO

*How the Love of Zion
Created Zionism*

GHETTO walls, which had kept Europe's Jews penned up as despised aliens since the Middle Ages, were disappearing throughout Western and Central Europe towards the end of the eighteenth century. Jews began enjoying some of the rights and liberties they had lost centuries before. But many of the old problems remained.

Some Jews, weakened in their faith by the new enlightenment and humanism that gripped the intellectuals of Western Europe during the eighteenth century, took what seemed to be an easy way out. Like the German Jewish poet Heinrich Heine, they tried to get "the admission ticket to European culture" by converting to Christianity. But the great majority was not willing to pay the price of admission. They stood firm in their loyalty to Judaism and the Jewish people. They carried on with their Jewish tradition, though often they were deeply troubled. Where, they asked, would all this lead? Could the "Jewish problem" be solved? Where could Jews live a life of their own, free from all hatred, fear, and persecution? Again the old yearning gripped many—for a land the Jewish people could call its own—the ancient homeland in Palestine.

The Man Who Wanted to Forget

One of the first personalities to bring the new spirit into focus was Moritz Hess, a young German Jew who had once tried to forget completely his Jewishness. He came from a devoutly religious family, but he rebelled against his Jewish heritage. It seemed to him too narrow and too limited. He said he was interested in *all* people, *all* humanity, particularly the working people, living so often in poverty and in misery. He sought out the Socialist leaders of his day—Karl Marx, Frederick Engels, and Ferdinand Lassalle—and he saw Socialism as a great political and humanitarian movement.

He devoted all his energies to it. He wrote for it, spoke for it, fought for it. As a result, he was hounded by the German police, and finally he

CHAPTER 1 *As Ghetto Walls Tumble*

had to seek refuge in Switzerland and later in France. His return to Judaism had its beginnings in 1840, when he was twenty-eight and the city of Damascus in Syria became the center of world attention.

The Damascus Affair

1840

As Syrian Jews were preparing for Passover, a Catholic monk disappeared, and somehow the old falsehood that Jews needed Christian blood for their Passover ceremony was revived. Accused of murdering the monk for their ritual, thirteen Jews were arrested. That people could still believe such terrible lies jolted Jews the world over out of their sense of security, acquired in the wake of the French Revolution with its proclamation of equal rights for all. They felt that their rights everywhere were in danger. In France a defense organization, the Alliance Israelite Universelle, was founded. In England, the philanthropist Moses Montefiore emerged as the champion of Jewish rights. All over Europe, Jews fearfully watched what was happening in Damascus. Eventually the Jews were cleared of the absurd charge, but Moritz Hess remained deeply stirred. The Damascus Affair made him realize that he, too, was a Jew and that his fate was bound up with the destinies of all Jews. At a time when many Jews tried to hide their Jewishness by adopting fashionable names, Hess changed his first name to Moses. He wanted to make it clear that he was proud of his heritage. For years afterward, he devoted himself to writing about the Jewish situation. His most important work, *Rome and Jerusalem,* appeared in 1862. In it, he wrote that whatever Jews might try to do to the contrary, they never lose a sense of national

result

Can't hid "nationality".—

"*Every Jew, whether he likes it or not, is bound to his people in a bond of solidarity*"
Moses Hess in
"*Rome and Jerusalem*"

34

consciousness which is firmly rooted in the great national memories of the people. He said this was true even of his fellow Jews in Germany, where many felt strongly that the Jewish nation had ceased to exist and that they would be Germans forever.

But Hess argued that there *is* a Jewish people, however small its numbers, and it has much to give to humanity. Even the smallest people, he said, must have their voice in the concert of nations. They must have the same right to exist as the most powerful. The Jews, Hess reasoned, must have a homeland. The homeland of the Jewish people is Palestine. Therefore, the Jews must return to Palestine, and must colonize it. Bringing the Jewish people back to Palestine, Hess concludes, means creating for them a "center of activity" from which new men and new ideas will originate to connect mankind with its Creator.

The "First for Zion"

[handwritten annotation: Kalischer / orthodox — help speed coming of moshiach]

The first religious leader of the 19th century to endorse the idea of an actual return of the Jewish people to Palestine was Rabbi Zebi Hirsch Kalischer, who won the name, *Rishon L'Tzion*, the First for Zion.

A brilliant scholar, he served in Thorn, Prussia, as Rabbi and president of the Jewish court of law (*Bet Din*) and his reputation spread

Moses Montefiore and
Rabbi Zebi Hirsch Kalischer ➡

throughout Europe. Although many Jews believed that a return to Palestine must depend on the coming of the Messiah, Rabbi Kalischer held that under Jewish law and tradition, the process of redemption and return certainly could be speeded up. There is no reason to wait for the arrival of the Messiah, argued Kalischer. One could start rebuilding the Temple right now and even reinstitute the system of sacrifice in the Temple, as in the days of old. Whether or not such a venture would bring on the final salvation, a return could be started.

Much later, in 1864, Rabbi Kalischer formulated a program in a book, *Quest for Zion*. Declaring that Jews must help themselves if the Jewish nation is to be reconstituted on its own soil, he proposed a society to establish Jewish colonies in Palestine. They would buy land in Palestine and cultivate it. With the help of Jews all over, the society should purchase land to be worked by settlers returning out of their love for Zion. The book followed more than two decades of effort, during which Kalischer campaigned for a return through speeches, pamphlets, and letters. He turned for help to the famous English Jewish philanthropist, Moses Montefiore, who had visited the Holy Land a number of times. Montefiore promised to experiment with the idea of land purchase and colonization during his next trip to Palestine. In 1841, he kept his word and bought a piece of land near Jaffa. It marked the first Jewish orange grove in modern Palestine.

The "Love of Zion" Movement   *Hov'vei Tzion (From)*

A small committee that owed its formation to Kalischer's incessant endeavors was set up in Frankfurt in 1860 in the home of a physician. It became the nucleus of what later developed into an international organization that had a tremendous impact upon the return to Zion. The group and others like it became known as "Lovers of Zion," and the movement, which spread over Europe and to England and America, the *Hov'vei Tzion*, the Lovers of Zion Movement. It proved to be of great importance to later developments in the creation of the Jewish State.

Besides his deeply religious motives, Kalischer lived in an age of nationalism, when various peoples in Europe broke away from larger empires and formed their own independent nations. The Poles and Hun-

➠ *Expelled from St. Petersburg:*
Jews at the Railroad Station
in Czarist Russia's Capital

garians gained freedom as nations, and Kalischer asked why Jews should not do the same by systematic colonization of Palestine. Kalischer attracted many supporters, but it was only natural that he should also meet with bitter opposition. There were those who opposed the idea of a Jewish nation, believing in Judaism only as a religion, and those who, on religious grounds, insisted that only the Messiah could restore Zion.

But Kalischer's labors won at least some scattered results. The Alliance Israelite Universelle was finally persuaded to establish an agricultural school in Mikveh Israel in Palestine. This was a victory. Another came when the Society for the Colonization of Palestine purchased land in the area of Motza. Thus the large-scale colonization program of the Society was started just as it was conceived by Zebi Hirsch Kalischer, its first president.

The Pogroms   → *Pinsker*

The year 1881 was a year of untold horror for Jews in Russia. Pogroms —government-approved destruction of Jewish life and property— brought murder and loss of property to Jews throughout the large empire. Incited by government officials, gangs of peasants and soldiers rampaged, killing thousands of Jewish men, women, and children. In that year, Czar Alexander II was assassinated in the course of a revolt growing out of the misery and poverty of the oppressed Russian people. To

divert attention from the true causes of the political upheaval, the Russian government hastened to fasten the blame for the Czar's murder on the Jews and to unleash a reign of terror.

There was a mass flight of Jews from Russia. Tens of thousands escaped across the Russian borders with the active help of Jews in other lands. Most of them came to America; some went to Palestine.

The events in Russia shattered the illusions of many Russian Jews, who thought they could establish a peaceful life in the land of the Czar. Many gained a new awareness of Jewish realities and Jewish destiny. Five years earlier, one prominent Russian Jewish leader, Moshe Loeb Lilienblum, had strongly advocated that Palestine be bought for the Jews from the Sultan of Turkey. Lilienblum believed that this offered the only opportunity for solving "the Jewish problem." Another leader, Rabbi Samuel Mohilever, tried to persuade Jewish refugees bound for America to turn to Palestine instead, but only a few could be persuaded.

Leon Pinsker

For Leon Pinsker, one of the most prominent physicians of Odessa, the 1881 catastrophe destroyed his most fervent conviction—that the Jews should be "Russians first." Believing that Jews should embrace Russian culture fully he had joined the "Society for the Spreading of Culture Among the Russian Jews," and was one of its most influential leaders. He had taught the Russian language at a Jewish school, and proposed that the Bible and prayer book be translated into Russian. It was his conviction that rabbis should be trained in modern rabbinical seminaries and should be graduates of Russian universities. Only thus could Russian Jews be truly "enlightened" in the modern spirit, he believed.

When Pinsker witnessed the pogrom that had swept Odessa and

"Self-help: Now or Never!"
From "Auto-Emancipation" by Leon Pinsker

learned of the crimes perpetrated against Jews elsewhere in Russia, he understood that the Jews needed more than enlightenment. His horror was even greater because he recently had received a personal reward from the Czar for risking his life to bring a disastrous epidemic under control. And now Russians, some of the very same people he had cured, turned in blind fury against the Jews. Was it because Jews cannot be Russians and cannot be like Russians? His dream of Jewish "Russianization," of salvation through "enlightenment," collapsed.

What caused anti-Jewish attitudes throughout the world, it seemed to Pinsker, was a combination of strangeness and fear. This would change, Pinsker held, if Jews were represented by a *Jewish nation* that would live in freedom and dignity. As he wrote:

The proper, the only remedy would be the *creation* of a Jewish nationality, of a people living upon its own soil, the auto-emancipation of the Jews; their emancipation as a nation among nations by the acquisition of a home of their own.

"The international Jewish question must receive a national solution," he said, and Jews should not rely on others to achieve this goal. "We must take the first step towards national regeneration by organizing a 'congress of Jewish notables.' " The motto was:

"Help yourselves, and God will help you!"

He set forth this appeal for self-help in a book he called *Auto-Emancipation*, which was published anonymously in 1881 in Vienna. Only "A Russian Jew" was listed on the cover as the author, but it soon became known that Pinsker had written it. He approached leaders of various Jewish communities to enlist their support for a plan aimed at starting a movement for the colonization of Palestine.

Vienna, Berlin, Paris, and London were among his principal stops. Pinsker tried to persuade Jewish leaders through pleas and arguments. Some of their reactions were worse than disheartening.

"He is in a state of fever," was the comment of Dr. Adolf Jellinek, Chief Rabbi of Vienna. But Pinsker kept hammering. He insisted it was a case of "now or never" for the practical beginning of auto-emancipation. "Now or never" was the essence of all his personal discussions, of all his speech making and letter writing.

*Above: The "Biluim"—
Group Portrait at a
Reunion
Below: Heroine of the
Eighties—Many Years Later!*

His perseverance bore fruit. Three years after his small book had appeared, a conference in Kattowitz, Silesia, brought together delegates from societies that had sprung up in various parts for the purpose of colonizing Palestine. Now an over-all federation of the Lovers of Zion, the *Hov'vei Tzion*, was formally established. The movement spread rapidly from country to country and paved the way for setting up new Jewish settlements in Palestine. Pinsker, who had called the conference, became the president of the federation that fanned the "Love for Zion" into a glowing flame.

From America came a quick response from the poetess, Emma Lazarus, author of the famous sonnet, "The New Colossus," which pleaded on behalf of "those huddled masses yearning to breathe free." Speaking of Pinsker's book in her "Epistles to the Hebrews," she wrote:

With his fiery eloquence and his depth and fervor of conviction, this anonymous author could scarcely fail to rekindle the imagination of his Jewish readers, even if he stood alone.

"O House of Jacob, Come, Let Us Go"

By the time the Kattowitz conference was held, there already was a new fact in Jewish history. As Pinsker put it: "Russian Jews have already pioneered colonies by their own toil and sweat. They give us hope for the prosperous future of our brethren on the Hills of Zion."

It was not a well-organized action on a grand scale, but a first effort to do something concrete about the "Jewish question." Young Jewish students from Russian universities embarked for Palestine to start life anew as farmers. They lacked training, equipment, and money. Their only asset was courage.

For a name, they took a verse from the second chapter of the Book of Isaiah: "*Bet Ya'akov L'khu V'nelkha*—O House of Jacob, come, let us go." From the initials of the Hebrew words, they formed the word: *Bilu!* And proudly they called themselves "*Biluim.*"

The *Biluim* started as a band of about twenty students who set out from Charkov, Russia, determined to return to the ancient homeland. They traveled to Constantinople, the one-time capital of Turkey, and continued by sea to the Holy Land, landing at the harbor of Jaffa on

August 11, 1882. They were under oath to live up to an earlier declaration of principles.

The "Jaffa Compact" stipulated that each *Bilu* member must serve the Jewish people and the Jewish land for three years in agricultural settlements owned by the entire group; that each was to work not for his own interests but for a Jewish nation; after three years each member was to move to other settlements and help them organize; they pledged devotion to a new way of life, for "Israel on its land, the land of the prophets, will combine a new society with social justice, for that is the function of Israel in the land of Israel."

With the aid of Baron de Rothschild, the *Biluim* formed the settlement of Rishon L'Tzion (The First of Zion). Though it was founded by idealists who spoke of "social justice" and equality, Rishon L'Tzion was actually a settlement in which the labor was Arab and the administration Jewish. Here is how a young Zionist from Russia described his first visit to Rishon L'Tzion:

"We thought that to talk with the *Biluim* we would have to wait until sunset—we imagined a village like in Russia, hens pecking in the road and not a soul in sight while the sun is high and all the peasants are in the fields.

"But what was this? We were in a pretty street of neat brick houses with red tiled roofs, . . . the street full of people strolling up and down. We couldn't believe our eyes. We asked:

'Who are these?'

'*Biluim.*'

'And who does the work?'

'Arabs.'

'And what do the Jews do?'

'They are managers, supervisors.'

"It was a great shock to us. I said to myself: 'This isn't what I've come for,' and I could see that the others were disappointed as well."

It would be all too easy to condemn the *Biluim* for their supposed hypocrisy, but before one judges them too harshly, it is necessary to realize the great difficulties they had to face. Their first problem was economic survival and the most practical solution, at that time, was citrus-growing. With their long tradition of city living, it was hard for them to turn themselves into agricultural workers overnight. Added to this was the fact that they were unaccustomed to the climate and knew nothing about the soil. The Arabs, on the other hand, thought the work easy and were pleased with their earnings. The *Biluim* set the stage for the beginnings of the *Kibbutz* movement for they proved that the land could be settled and cultivated.

Except for these young pioneers, most of the Jews then in Palestine lived in the four "sacred cities" of Hebron, Jerusalem, Safed, and Tiberias. They were mainly pious Jews, dwelling in cabalistic dreams of the Jewish people's final redemption or waiting to die and be buried in "holy" soil. Wretchedly poor, they lived almost wholly on charity collected abroad by special emissaries. Jews in each *Kolel* (community) depended on the *Halukah* (distribution) of funds, and their settlements came to be known as *Halukah*. They were eyed with contempt by the new pioneering settlers, and they in return looked down upon the newcomers with equal contempt for impiety.

The *Biluim*, followed by other Lovers of Zion, constituted the first wave of Jewish immigrants in Palestine in modern times. Their arrival came to be known as the First *Aliyah*, and each succeeding wave of immigration was called another *Aliyah*.

The word *Aliyah* (ascent) usually refers to "going up" to the Torah during the services. It has also been used for centuries when referring to a return to Israel. The roots of this term are complex. The obvious geographical basis for "going up" to Jerusalem is that this city is set among the hills of Judea, one of the highest points of Israel. Berl Katznelson, one of the most influential leaders of the *Kibbutz* movement, epitomized the meanings of *Aliyah* in this way:

Going to any other land we call 'Immigration,' but returning to Zion, and to Zion alone, is *Aliyah*. *Aliyah* is a rise from the depths of the *Galut* (exile) to the homeland, to the land of liberty. We use *Aliyah* in both the material and the spiritual sense. There is an *Aliyah* of will and of hope. There is an *Aliyah* of the class and of the nation, and there is also an *Aliyah* of the individual. We have always looked upon ourselves as the pioneers of the people. Behind us, thousands await redemption. They shall come and, together with us, shall build this land.

Father of the Yishuv

Baron Edmund Rothschild, wealthy head of the Paris branch of the Rothschild family of financiers, took an increasing interest in the small, struggling colonies springing up in Palestine. Not less than twenty-seven settlements were supported by the Baron, who traveled to Palestine seven times to look after them personally. Tremendous vineyards and wine cellars were established at Rishon L'Tzion and Petaḥ Tikvah. Wide areas of barren land were purchased by him or with his financial assistance and were converted into model agricultural colonies. He appointed managers to run the settlements, which grew into a network of colonies.

For his efforts, the *Yishuv* (Palestine's Jewish community) spoke of the Baron as the Father of the *Yishuv*. But before long, it became clear that the process of reclaiming the homeland was going too slowly, and that too much reliance was being placed on the Baron's generosity. It seemed as if there was a whole desert waiting to be cultivated, and only a few small trees had been planted thus far. In fact, the whole colonization effort began to look like a failure.

"This Is Not the Way"

must be for the sake of the entire Jewish Nation

Why the *Hov'vei Tzion* movement achieved so little in Palestine began to concern Jews everywhere. Some blamed the system of "*Halukah.*" Others said it was the fault of Baron Rothschild. But deeper, more important reasons were advanced. These were set forth in a Hebrew daily newspaper published in Odessa, Russia. The newspaper article was called "This Is Not the Way." Its author was Asher Ginsberg, a writer

Aḥad Ha'am
One of the people

*Edmond de Rothschild—
"Father of the Yishuv"*

who became famous through the pen name of *Aḥad Ha'am* (One of the People).

Aḥad Ha'am said that the achievements were small because results were being sought too quickly. To want people to settle in Palestine is fine, he said, but the people who go there must be deeply convinced that the effort was worthwhile, not only for themselves, but for the entire Jewish people and for the sake of future Jewish life. Up to now, Aḥad Ha'am contended, the Lovers of Zion were mostly concerned with finding a better life in Palestine than they had in Europe. This is not enough, he said. What is needed are Jews who want to go to Palestine for the sake of the Jewish people, who would settle there for the future of the Jewish people. To create such attitudes takes time and understanding. With preparation and zeal to rebuild the Jewish nation on its own land, the will for practical action will come spontaneously. Then Jews will be ready for all the burdens of hard work, regardless of difficulties.

He did not advocate that colonization in Palestine be stopped; he said that work must go on, but in a different way. The effort must help create a national feeling among all the Jews by fostering a living Jewish culture of which Jews the world over will be proud. Then Palestine would become the spiritual center for all Jews.

Aḥad Ha'am said this should be attempted at first on a small scale only. What is needed is not a showing of many physical accomplishments, but quality in human material for truly Jewish achievement, he said.

Aḥad Ha'am, a master of Hebrew, modestly had claimed to be just "one of the people," but the article quickly established him as a leader

Aḥad Ha'am:
"This is not the Way . . . !"

of his people. A group devoted to his ideals formed into what was called the "*B'nei Moshe,*" the Sons of Moses. It admitted to membership only persons of the highest character who pledged themselves to fulfill the program enunciated by Aḥad Ha'am. All candidates had to know Hebrew.

For eight years the Sons of Moses tried to carry out this program. Then the organization broke up. The members simply could not live up to the high standards of personal conduct and idealism. There were also internal conflicts. Yet, what remained was of lasting impact. It was a concept of "spiritual Zionism," aiming at the establishment of a spiritual center in Palestine for the Jewish communities of the world. It was to be a center from which should flow creative ideas for Jewish living everywhere.

Haskalah

Aḥad Ha'am was only one of many who thought the Hebrew language essential to Jewish thinking. They looked at Hebrew as a vehicle for the creation of a new Jewish spirit, rooted in the Jewish past, but developing in consonance with modern ideas.

This was one of the avowed objectives of the so-called Haskalah movement, the movement of Jewish enlightenment that originated in Central and Eastern Europe, and aimed at the creation of a modern Jewish culture. It was sweeping the ranks of Jewish youth. The most powerful mouthpiece of the Haskalah movement was a periodical, "*Ha-Shaḥar*" —"The Dawn."

"*Ha-Shaḥar*" appeared in Vienna, the capital of the Austro-Hungarian monarchy, in 1868 and soon drew upon the outstanding Hebrew writers of the day. The editor was Russian-born Peretz Smolenskin, an outstanding Hebrew poet and novelist. In Russia, Poland, Galicia, and Rumania, Smolenskin found a tremendous following. With Jewish youth enmeshed in a struggle between advocates of complete assimilation and those who clung to the old tradition, Smolenskin became the champion of Jewish nationalism and called for fervent preservation of Jewish values. In Odessa, where a center for Jewish intellectuals had emerged, he came to the forefront of the *Hov'vei Tzion*—the Lovers of Zion—now a powerful organization.

What Smolenskin propounded in his book, *Am Olam* (The Eternal People) was this belief: that the Jews were a people eternally linked to Zion; its universal language, Hebrew, again must be its living expression; and that Jewish ideals demanded a return to Palestine. He said colonization must be the primary objective of all Jewish endeavors.

A Language Comes to Life

One certainly cannot say that Hebrew had become a "dead language." It lived every day in Jewish prayers and study. In every century, Jews throughout the world used and cherished the language they called holy. And Hebrew literature continued to be produced throughout the ages. Yet, since the disappearance of a Jewish nation, Hebrew had retreated into a holy language almost entirely reserved for ritual and study. It no longer existed as a tongue for ordinary, everyday use.

At the end of the 18th century and throughout the 19th century, Hebrew purists, and among them many Lovers of Zion, tried to revive the Hebrew for broader use. But still it was only the written word that came to life—in books and periodicals, in prose and poetry. To put the language of the Prophets back into the mouths of Jews was the avowed

Eliezer Ben Yehuda:
Prophet of Living Hebrew

purpose of Eliezer Ben Yehuda, a man of frail health but indomitable spirit. He saw in modern Hebrew a bond that could unify Jews all over and thought it an indispensable ingredient in the restoration of a Jewish homeland.

Born in Lithuania and educated in Paris, he was gripped there by a "magnificent obsession"—to live in Palestine and make Hebrew the living language of a people. Eliezer Perlman was the name he bore before he changed it to Ben Yehuda, the Son of Judea. He was literally a pioneer who opened up a new frontier for a language that had been held in bonds of holiness for so long. Now he gave it a new sanctification through his own life and through the daily lives of his people.

Living Hebrew begins at home, he realized, and it was in his own home where Hebrew was first spoken again as an everyday language. His wife, Deborah, promised she would speak only Hebrew. And thus Mrs. Ben Yehuda actually became—for ordinary household purposes— "the first Hebrew-speaking mother in nearly two thousand years."

With the zeal of a fanatic, Ben Yehuda fought many who opposed his passionate promotion of modern Hebrew. Foremost among his enemies were pious Jews who denounced him as a heretic for—in their view —he was desecrating the holy language by using it for non-religious purposes.

That fight went on for many years, and even landed Ben Yehuda in jail! Yet neither arrest nor condemnation could stop him. He continued to fight on for Hebrew. He spoke it wherever he could, and made his friends speak it. Slowly but steadily, Hebrew grew as a living language, finally bringing triumph to its great re-awakener. He had the satisfaction of seeing Hebrew gradually evolve as the common language of the Jews in the new settlements in Palestine, and take hold even in the lands of the dispersion.

In Israel today Hebrew is the language of home, street, and office. Most children use only Hebrew in schools; they play and sing in Hebrew; Hebrew newspapers, books, and magazines serve the country's needs; stage, screen, and radio resound to modern Hebrew's melodious cadences; the Hebrew University, the Technion in Haifa, and the Weizmann Institute in Rehovot conduct their classes in Hebrew. That all this could be possible, the whole range of the Hebrew vocabulary had to be tremendously expanded. Countless new words dealing with modern life had to be added or invented.

In biblical days, of course, there were no words for automobile, electricity, Socialism, cigarette, newspaper, and piano tuner. Many new terms were coined by Ben Yehuda by blending classic Hebrew with contemporary Arabic and other sources. He began compiling a dictionary of ancient and modern Hebrew. Though it was completed by others, it was a monument to his life and work.

Herzl

COMPARED to eighteen centuries of Jewish homelessness, nine years seem shorter than a single flicker of a tiny candle. But the time came when Jewish history took a leap—and in nine years accomplished what had been left untouched and undone for ages. These were the nine years from 1895 to 1904. For Theodor Herzl, they were crammed with inspiration, excitement, passion, struggle, hope, frustration, and heartbreak. But they were nine years that changed the Jewish world.

Early Years

There was nothing about Herzl's early life to mark him as one who was to become one of the greatest Jewish leaders of all times. He was born in Budapest, the capital of Hungary, in 1860. His well-to-do parents lived in a Jewish neighborhood that was renowned for its magnificent Reform Temple, one of the oldest in Europe. The Herzls attended services occasionally and Theodor had a private Hebrew tutor, as was customary among people of means. But apparently his Jewish studies made little impression on him. All that he seemed to remember vividly in later life was his Bar Mitzvah. Like many other Jewish boys with whom he grew up, he knew he was a Jew, although at first he cared little about it. But there were others who did care—the anti-Semites.

Anti-Semitism

Anti-Semitism was a new kind of Jew-hatred. It developed as Jews of the nineteenth century—leaving behind the ghettos that had kept them apart since the Middle Ages—sought to enjoy freedom and equality as citizens of the countries in which they lived. As Jews made their mark in business and the professions, and rose in society, they met intense resentment on the part of many non-Jews.

This was a time when class and social position mattered a great deal to many Europeans. And many could not bear the thought that the

CHAPTER 2 *Nine Years That Changed the Jewish World*

"lowly" Jew would dare, for example, to buy a fine house, attend a well-known school, hold an important position, and rub shoulders with "respectable" Christians. This also was an age of nationalism, and there were those who felt that Jews were aliens and could never possibly become "real Germans," "real Frenchmen," "real Austrians," or whatever.

In addition, there were new notions about the supposed importance of race and national origins. According to these beliefs—long since proven false—certain "races" were superior and others inferior. Usually, if the theory was put forward by a German, the Germans or the Nordic peoples were placed at the top of the list as the "master race"; if by an Englishman, then the English. In any case, the so-called Aryan, or Indo-European peoples, were proclaimed to possess far more desirable physical, mental, and moral qualities than Jews, who are a Semitic people. (Hence, the name anti-Semitism.) Nowadays, science holds the view that the terms Aryan and Semite apply mostly to *language* origins, rather than race. Scientists feel that there are almost no innate differences of intellect and character among various groups of people, and that the term "race" itself really has little meaning. And the Jews can hardly be considered a race, since they vary so greatly in physical appearance. Some are tall, some short; they are blue-eyed and brown-eyed; some are as blond and fair as a typical Swede; some are as dark-skinned as Negroes.

But in the nineteenth century, anti-Semitism, built on a false scientific basis, found many supporters.

In Eastern Europe, where Jews still lived in ghettos, they were still hated chiefly for their religion. In the West, hatred of the Jew for purely religious reasons had become less important, but traces of it still lingered.

And there were always the envious, who hated the Jew for his occasional successes; the opportunists, who tried to turn anti-Semitism to their own political or economic advantage; and the moral and physical bullies who assaulted the Jew because he still was relatively weak. All of

Market Day in the Ghetto

these—along with anti-Jewish nationalists, snobs, and "race scientists"—joined forces under the banner of anti-Semitism.

Anti-Semitism, of course, made its enemies, too—among great numbers of high-minded Christians who believed Jews should enjoy full civil and social equality and should be judged only as fellow human beings. But there were enough anti-Semites in Herzl's day to affect him deeply.

The First Blows

Herzl had his first taste of anti-Semitism early in his high school days. A history teacher, speaking of the word "pagan," said, "Well, there are various people who are pagans—among them are the idolators, the Mohammedans, and the Jews." Quite upset about this obvious falsehood, young Theodor told his parents, and they decided to take him out of the school. They transferred him to another one, where they hoped he would not be exposed to insults of an anti-Semitic teacher. True, the incident was not very important—yet, it was so significant to Herzl that he never forgot it.

Another episode he never forgot came when he was about eighteen years old. He read a newspaper story about a speech delivered by Fred-

erick Stoecker, leader of the German anti-Semites in Germany. Stoecker was a powerful politician, a member of the German Parliament, and a sworn enemy of the Jews. Reading of Stoecker's anti-Jewish outburst, Herzl suddenly had a thought and jotted it down in his notebook: "The Jews must look for a country of their own."

A few months later, Herzl entered the University of Vienna, in the city where his family had moved, and began the study of law.

Many professions were closed to the Jews in Austria. The laws of the land did not say so explicitly, but an unwritten practice made it impossible for a Jew to become a judge. This had been Theodor Herzl's great ambition, but upon graduation as doctor of law he realized that his efforts to embark upon a career in the judiciary were doomed to failure—unless he gave up his religion and converted to Christianity. True, Herzl knew very little about his Judaism, but he had too strong a sense of self-respect to give it up. So he looked for another career and finally decided to become a journalist.

"I was then a writer with little ambitions and little vanities," he said later in reviewing his literary beginnings. His experience and achievement were rather limited. He wanted to broaden his horizon and learn more about life. He therefore decided to travel.

One evening, as Herzl was leaving a crowded tavern in Mainz, Germany, somebody shouted, "Hep Hep," and the crowd roared with delight. Others joined in, and for a moment the tavern on the Rhine shook with the cry, "Hep Hep."

This slogan was said to have been the battle cry of the Crusaders when—during the Middle Ages—they stormed the city of Jerusalem. It

← Class in Ghetto School

Water Carriers in the Ghetto

stood for *"Hierosolyma est perdita"*—"Jerusalem must fall." Now it had become a battle cry of anti-Semites all over Germany. They shouted "Hep Hep" whenever they saw a Jew. The "Hep Hep" Herzl heard was another reminder for him that he was a Jew, that he was hated as a Jew, that all Jews were hated, and that he ought to do something about it!

The Dreyfus Affair

In October, 1894, while working as a reporter for the Vienna newspaper, *Neue Freie Presse*, Herzl was assigned to cover a trial that soon became one of the world's most famous courtroom cases. On trial in Paris on charges of treason was a Jewish officer, Captain Alfred Dreyfus, of the General Staff of the French Army. He was accused of selling secret plans of the French high command to agents of the German army. Though he protested his innocence, the cry went up that Dreyfus had betrayed his country because he was a Jew and not a real Frenchman; that a Jew could not be a loyal citizen of France, and that, therefore, it was obvious that Dreyfus had sold out to the Germans—the arch enemies of the French.

The charges aroused the passions of the French people. Many believed these accusations, in spite of the very flimsy evidence put forward against the captain. On the other hand, some of the most outstanding citizens of France—chief among them, the writer Emile Zola—rose in his defense. But to no avail! Dreyfus was found guilty by a Military Court; he was stripped of his military honor and of his rank and was sentenced to life imprisonment in the French penal colony on Devil's Island, off the coast of French Guiana.

Captain Dreyfus suffered the humiliation of a public degradation on the parade ground of the Ecole Militaire (Army School) in Paris. Thousands came to watch. They heard the sentence of guilt pronounced again and looked on as his epaulettes, the sign of his military rank, were torn from his uniform, and his saber was broken apart. The crowd was seized by an outburst of mass hysteria. "Down with Dreyfus," howled the mob; "Down with the Jew"; "Down with all Jews." The delirious shouting all but drowned out Dreyfus' pathetic plea before he was led away: "I am innocent! Long live France!"

It was in line of duty as a reporter that Theodor Herzl witnessed this scene of an agonizing personal tragedy. At first, Herzl was not sure whether Dreyfus was guilty or not. But the mob spectacle made it clear that there was more involved than the fate of Dreyfus. He had seen mob passions aroused against the Jews and he was afraid. Suppose Dreyfus was guilty, he reflected, why should hundreds of thousands of Jews suffer? Suppose *one* Jew was a traitor, why should blind rage lash out at *all* Jews? He had seen a thousand faces filled with blind hatred, and he asked: Why—why—why all this brutal hostility here, and all over?

Was this linked to the teacher in high school who called the Jews pagans? To Stoecker's wild tirade against the Jews? To the "Hep Hep" cry in a Mainz tavern? It's all one pattern, Herzl realized. And he knew that something radical had to be done.

His conviction did not change even when, years later, the innocence of Dreyfus was proved beyond a doubt, and he was brought back to France and restored to his military rank.

An Idea Takes Shape

Throughout the weeks and months that followed Captain Dreyfus' public humiliation, Herzl was obsessed with the broader problem that had presented itself. Like the prophets of old, he felt a call to serve his people, a call he could not deny. It took possession of all his thoughts, dominating every second of his waking hours. Ideas flowed so fast he hardly could keep up with them. As he wrote later, they utterly preoccupied him while walking, sitting, eating, riding the subway, hurrying to ap-

←* *Dreyfus on Trial*

Nine Years That Changed the Jewish World

pointments, attending meetings of the French Parliament, or covering other stories for his newspaper in Vienna. *– too fast*

Meeting With Baron de Hirsch *doesn't work – too brash*

One day Herzl, on the spur of the moment, wrote a letter to Baron Moritz de Hirsch, financier, in London, England. Baron de Hirsch was known to the Jewish world as the outstanding Jewish philanthropist of his age. The Baron had spent more than one hundred million dollars on a large scale project for resettling Jews as farmers, founded a Jewish Colonization Association (ICA), and established agricultural colonies in Argentina, the United States, and in Eastern Europe. In many ways he sought to alleviate the poverty of Jews in many parts of the world by training them as farmers and artisans. Everywhere, he had become a symbol of constructive Jewish charity.

In his letter, Herzl asked the Baron for "a talk with you on matters of Jewish politics." But the financier, who had never heard of Herzl before, was hesitant. It took a second letter, with Herzl writing, "Up to now you have been just a philanthropist . . . but I will show you that you can become more than that, and I will show you how," before Baron de Hirsch agreed to an interview on his next trip to Paris.

It was with a great deal of trepidation that Herzl prepared for the interview. As a newspaperman with only a limited reputation, Herzl felt at a disadvantage in facing the wealthy financier. So he struck a pose that almost smacked of arrogance. Brashly, Herzl asked at the beginning of the interview: "Do you have an hour for me? If it's not an hour, we'd better let it go!" Surprised, the Baron nodded approval. Herzl began to talk. He outlined a plan to establish a state for the Jews, a program that called for tremendous sums of money.

Herzl's proposals filled twenty-two pages of notes he had prepared. But when he had covered only six pages, the interview was suddenly terminated by the Baron. It was a failure.

Later, Herzl expressed his indignation in another letter to Baron de Hirsch. He wrote of Baron de Hirsch's hesitation in money matters and his scoffing at the idea of a Jewish State, and added: "Yes, one finds that tremendous amounts of Jewish money are available for a loan to China, for railways in Africa, and for the most adventuresome project—but it seems that there is none when it comes to the deepest, most immediate, and most torturing needs of the Jews." Taking exception to the Baron's doubt that a Jewish state could be established, he wrote: "Do you know how the German Reich has come into existence? It was forged out of dreams, songs, phantasies, and black, red, and golden ribbons—and it became a reality in a short time. Bismarck—the German Chancellor—only shook the tree that was planted by people of sheer imagination."

Despite the setback, Herzl continued to dream and plan for a Jewish state. He even devised new details, such as the establishment of an opera house and the uniforms of army officers.

An Undelivered Speech   *ignored but comes around later after the Basle Conference*

Then Herzl decided to turn to the financially most powerful Jewish group of his time, the Rothschild family. He spent two months preparing a speech he hoped to deliver before a council composed of members of the Rothschild family. But the council meeting never was held, and the speech remained undelivered. Yet the effort was not in vain. The speech served as the first draft of a book that later shook the Jewish world and shaped its future destinies. The book was called *The Jewish State*. Its content, as we will see later, was truly revolutionary.

Unanswered Letters   *ignored*

Was he on the right track? Was his idea really sound? . . . Herzl was tormented by such questions. He needed confirmation, encouragement. . . . He sent a letter to Otto Von Bismarck, the Iron Chancellor, who had once forged the many small German states into the powerful *Reich*. Bismarck never answered.

He thought of turning to the German Emperor himself. He drafted a memorandum but hesitated to put it in the mail. Instead, he wrote Baron Albert Rothschild, head of the Rothschild family, about the document and asked for aid in forwarding it to the Emperor. Again, there was no answer.

Herzl, who had set his ideas down in a small book, brought the manuscript to his oldest and best friend, and asked him to read it. What happened, as Herzl described later, was this:

When I had completed the book, I asked my oldest and best friend to read the manuscript. In the midst of the reading, he suddenly burst into tears. I found this natural enough, since he was a Jew; I, too, had wept at times during the writing of it. But I was staggered when he gave me an entirely different reason for his tears. He thought I had gone off my mind, and, since he was my friend, he was touched to tears by my misfortune. He ran off without saying another word. After a sleepless night, he returned, and pressed me hard to leave the entire business alone, for everyone would take me for a lunatic. He was so excited that I promised him anything in order to soothe him.

Herzl then came to a sad conclusion: "If this is the impression my ideas make on an educated and faithful friend, I shall give them up." But Herzl was not the person to give up. So, upon the advice of his friend, he decided to seek the council of Max Nordau.

Theodor Herzl.

As a Cartoonist
saw Herzl:
Day-dreaming
State Builder

Max Nordau:
Physician and
philosopher
Herzl's friend
and advisor

Von Sudermann hat er den Bart,
Die Ironie von Heine,
Doch sein Talent von starker Art
Gehört ihm ganz alleine.

Er sieht ein Ziel, ein Ziel so weit
Im Träumen, wie im Wachen:
Er denkt daran, in dieser Zeit
Mit Juden Staat zu machen!

Nordau Aids Herzl

Dr. Max Nordau was a physician by training, a writer by profession, and a politician by avocation. He had become a European celebrity. Herzl sought him out, and Nordau's reaction dispelled his doubts. He responded instantly and enthusiastically to Herzl's sweeping concept of solving "the Jewish question." They began a life-long friendship and close partnership in the service of the Jewish people.

It was Nordau who introduced Herzl to Israel Zangwill, the famous English Jewish writer. The author of *Children of the Ghetto* comprehended the magnificence of Herzl's project. Zangwill had long been one of the "Lovers of Zion," of whom there were a considerable number in the British Isles. And Zangwill had the very contacts that Herzl needed.

Among these was the Chief Rabbi of the British Empire, Dr. Herman Adler. Lukewarm to Herzl's idea at first, Dr. Adler later warmed to it and introduced Herzl to the "Maccabeans," an organization on whose membership roster were the leaders of the Jewish community in London.

There was Reverend Simeon Singer, editor and translator of the official Anglo-Jewish Prayer Book, and a leading member of the British section of the "Lovers of Zion." Another was Sir Samuel Montague, Member of Parliament, liberal in his party affiliation, but traditional in Jewish practice and deeply devoted to the Jewish colonization work in Palestine. Most important of all was another of "Zion's lovers," Colonel Albert Edward Goldsmith, commanding officer of a regiment in the British Army.

Goldsmith impressed Herzl most. The Colonel, commanding the British Army garrison in Cardiff, Wales, was passionately interested in Jewish affairs. Born in Bombay, India, as a Christian, the son of converted Jewish parents, Goldsmith only learned about his Jewish origin when he was a young lieutenant. He decided to return to the Judaism of his ancestors, and he lived as an observant Jew, bringing up his children, Rachel and Carmel, in an atmosphere of traditional Jewish living and with a deep love for the Hebrew language. Herzl was fascinated by the personality of Colonel Goldsmith, and the Colonel was set afire by Herzl's plan. His first reaction to Herzl's plan was to exclaim: "That's the idea of my life!"

These were some of the people Herzl met during his stay in London. He quickly made friends. Most important, his stay in London gave him the encouragement he so badly needed, and it gave him the decisive impulse to go ahead and publish his book, *The Jewish State*.

Remedy for Homelessness

We are more than a religion; we are a nation

The Jewish State was only a brochure, but its content was astounding. For what the author proposed was to end two thousand years of homelessness for a people that had been driven from its ancient land. It was a clarion call to bring together the Jewish people into a land of its own as a free and independent nation.

"We are a people, we are *one* people, regardless of where we live—whether in Austria, Prussia, France, Britain, Russia, or anywhere else," Herzl wrote. His words came in an age when many Jews considered themselves to be adherents of a religion only. It was the fashion of many Jews to call themselves followers of the "Mosaic persuasion." Accordingly, one spoke of "Germans of the Mosaic persuasion," or of their Hungarian, or Polish or French counterpart. Now Herzl came and proclaimed that being a Jew meant more than observance of the Jewish religion. Emphatically he declared: "We are a nation because we are a historic group of people whose belonging together is clear to see. We are a people, whether we like it or not—it's our common enemy that makes us a people, as it has been true through history. In the hour of crisis, we stick together and we suddenly discover our strength. Yes, we have the strength to create a state, and a model state at that. We have the human and material resources that are necessary for such ends." Herzl envisaged that the Jewish State would be created by a planned mass migration to a new "Promised Land" by all Jews who would not or could not live elsewhere.

Building a State

Herzl conceived of a democratic form of government with a free enterprise economy and safeguards for workers to prevent exploitation. All citizens would enjoy the benefits of education, health, and social welfare. Herzl's dream extended even to the idea of a seven-hour day for adult workers. In suggesting a design for a national flag, he wrote: "I think of a white banner, imprinted with seven golden stars. The white field stands for the new, pure life. The stars are the seven golden hours of our working day—for it is under the sign of work that the Jews go into the new land."

How could the mass movement of Jews from all over the world be financed? Herzl proposed that the entire Jewish people—the few rich and the masses of the poor—could do it together.

"The Jews who *will it*," he exclaimed in the closing paragraph of his book, "*will* have their State. . . . At long last, we shall live as free men on our own soil, and shall die in peace in our own homeland. . . . And what we shall try to do there for our own good will be a force for good and a blessing for all mankind."

Herzl and his Mother

They Try to Stop Him

While the printer was setting the type for Herzl's book, word had leaked out about its contents. There were some who, learning about it, earnestly worried over Herzl's sanity. To them, the idea of a Jewish state seemed so preposterous that only a madman could have proposed it. One high official of the Jewish community in Vienna, hurried into the editorial offices of the *Neue Freie Presse* personally to find out whether Theodor Herzl was well. "I knew him as an otherwise reasonable person," he remarked seriously.

The newspaper's editor and publisher were deeply afraid the book would cause the *Neue Freie Presse* to be laughed at. Herzl was a member of its staff and his scheme, they thought, was sure to result in embarrassment. So worried was the publisher that he attempted to bribe Herzl into stopping publication and abandoning the project. Herzl refused. The publisher pleaded, "At least don't sign your name to it." But Herzl remained steadfast.

The Book Appears

When the book finally appeared, it was met by rage, bewilderment and anxiety on the part of many Jews, especially the rich and timid. But the Jewish masses, along with many Christians, felt otherwise. A wave of enthusiasm engulfed the Jews everywhere. Overnight, Herzl and his book, *The Jewish State*, became the talk of Jews in thousands of towns, villages, and hamlets across Europe. It was the topic of discussion among Jewish millions in Vienna, Berlin, London, Warsaw, Lemberg, Kovno, as well as in the small settlements in Hungary, Galicia, Russia, Rumania, Bulgaria.

New hope suddenly entered lives that knew persecution, anguish, and despair. There were passionate demonstrations in Herzl's behalf, calling for immediate action. Jewish youth at the University of Vienna rallied to Herzl's support and proclaimed him their leader. Serbian Jews of Semlin, in what is now Yugoslavia, sent word that all were ready to leave for the new Jewish homeland. In Sofia, the capital of Bulgaria, the Chief Rabbi spoke of Herzl as a "messiah."

H

First Time   <u>1897</u>

ERZL'S first major achievement came in the summer of 1897 when the first <u>Zionist Congress convened in Basle, Switzerland.</u> There were 179 men and women from all parts of Europe, Africa, America, and also from Palestine, who came as members of a Jewish parliament called into existence after <u>2000 years of Jewish statelessness and homelessness.</u>

What had preceded the great event was a momentous decision taken by Herzl and a few of his friends to call such a Congress. Meetings dealing with "the Jewish problem" had taken place before in various places but without much result. This time the situation was altogether different. A worldwide gathering would openly confront political issues and enter into international negotiations under the banner of a new name—Zionism.

This was the program the Congress set for itself:

.. to create an instrument for dealing with all common Jewish needs
.. to create a meeting place for the aspirations of our brethren
.. to remove the Jewish problem from the private discretion of individual persons regardless of how well-meaning they may be and therefore
.. to create a body to which everyone may be held accountable for whatever he does in matters of the Jewish question.

The last two points aimed at objectives of highest importance—to effect a change in Jewish leadership.

People like Barons de Hirsch and Rothschild often, by virtue of their wealth and their personal influence, chose to be the spokesmen for the Jews. Now this leadership would become democratic.

The Opposition

Despite enthusiastic approval by many Jews throughout the world, the program met with terrific opposition, and some tried desperately to prevent the Congress from coming into being.

There were those who opposed the whole venture on strictly religious

Read to p 73. Skip p 73-82 (Tell about diplomatic failures)
Read: Uganda p 83 & Conclude
(We read on

CHAPTER 3   *Steppingstones to Reality*

tell chp 4)

grounds because they believed the Jewish people would have to wait for the arrival of the Messiah. No secular action, they held, should be undertaken to reconstitute the Jewish people.

There was another group among the *Hov'vei Tzion* who rejected the idea because not enough emphasis had been placed by Herzl on Palestine as the land of Jewish resurrection and on Hebrew as the most significant expression of Jewish culture.

And there were those who abhorred any independent political action by Jews because they felt that this would endanger Jewish security in the countries in which they lived by drawing attention to the Jews as a unique people. This was the most vocal and the most powerful group.

Hostility was expressed most sharply by the leaders of the Jewish community in Munich, Germany. That city had been selected as the site for the Congress, but the Jewish leaders demanded that it be held elsewhere.

The official association of German rabbis came out with widely publicized statements condemning the projected Congress in the strongest terms. "We protest," the statement read, "that sponsors of the Congress act as if they were the spokesmen of Jewry. We are convinced that no rabbi or leader of our German Jewish community will appear at the Congress, thus making it clear to the world at large that German Jewry has no part in any aspirations of the Zionists."

The move to hold a Congress, the rabbis declared, contradicts the religious concept of salvation through the Messiah. Futhermore, such a move seemed to be aimed at alienating the adherents of Judaism from the "fatherland to which they belong."

Herzl accepted the challenge at once. His reply was: "So, that they

ARBEITS-PROGRAMM

UND

GESCHÄFTS-ORDNUNG

DES

ZIONISTEN-CONGRESSES

IN

BASEL

AM

29., 30. und 31. AUGUST 1897.

VERLAG „DER WELT".
DRUCK DER „GESELLSCHAFT FÜR GRAPHISCHE INDUSTRIE".

Agenda for Redemption: A copy of the program of the First Zionist Congress

◂◂ *A High Moment in Basle: Herzl Greets Nordau after "State of the Jewish Nation" address*

Congress House in Basle ▸▸

shall not be confused with the good rabbis, we shall call the synagogue employees who oppose the salvation of their people—the Protest Rabbis."

The First Zionist Congress Is Held

This movement could no longer be stopped and the first Zionist Congress was called to order on Sunday, August 29, 1897. Jews the world over watched to see what would happen.

A streamer over the portal of the building announced, "The Congress of the Zionists," and a flag of blue and white with the Star of David in its center, fluttered over the entrance. The solemnity of the moment was summed up at the beginning when the eldest delegate intoned the age-old blessing of *Sheheheyanu:*

"Blessed art Thou, O Lord our God, King of the Universe, who has kept us alive and preserved us and allowed us to reach this season."

When Theodor Herzl ascended the rostrum to address the Congress, the pent up emotions of the assembly broke loose in a roaring acclaim. It seemed as if the hall were tossed about on waves of joy, as if the thunderous applause would never end. Herzl remained calm, even when there were shouts, *"Y'hi Ha-Melekh, Y'hi Ha-Melekh"*—long live the king!

Then Dr. Herzl began to deliver the keynote address of the Congress in cool and measured sentences. He declared:

"A people can be helped only by itself; if it cannot do that, then it cannot be helped. We Zionists seek to awaken the Jewish people everywhere to self-help."

Nordau's Speech

Then Herzl's friend Max Nordau arose and boldly portrayed the Jewish situation of his day. He spoke of Jews in various countries, who had gained civil rights but not real social acceptance. He analyzed the disease of anti-Semitism. Then he turned to those he called "the new Marranos," persons who tried to conceal their Jewish identity. And here is how Nordau described the Jews of many Western countries: "He is surrounded by strangers . . . he is suspicious even of the secret feelings of his friends . . . he exhausts his powers in an effort to suppress or conceal his real character . . . he never has the satisfaction of appearing as he is, in all his thoughts and feelings . . . he becomes an inner cripple."

Many Jews, he said, succumb to the impact of anti-Semitic propaganda and finally "imagine themselves in reality to be the physical and spiritual monstrosities which their mortal foes represent them to be." The fight against anti-Semitism is hopeless, Nordau declared. It cannot be waged with weapons of reason because anti-Semitism arises from deep-seated prejudices, aversions, and dislikes which are too ingrained to be uprooted.

The only answer appeared to be: Zionism.

The Basle Program

And what is Zionism? A definition, framed in the so-called Basle Program unanimously adopted by the Congress, stated: "Zionism aims to create a publicly secured, legally assured home for the Jewish people in Palestine!" With this, the Zionist movement officially came into being and the Basle Program became its birth certificate.

As Herzl had envisaged in his *Jewish State*, one of the main instruments of the Zionist movement was formally established at the Congress under the name of Zionist World Organization. To be a Zionist meant, from now on, to be a member of that organization. The requirements for membership were simple: one had to subscribe to the Basle Program, and give at least a small amount of money to the cause by purchasing a *shekel*, a token of the biblical coin. This was all one needed to have a voice in the democratically elected Congress that served as the central authority of the Zionist movement. The establishment of the Zionist World Organization was the most important accomplishment of the Basle Congress.

There was one painful issue that came up—the question of an "official" language for the Congress. The only practical solution was to use Ger-

"In Basle I founded the Jewish State"

man, since it was the language understood by most of the delegates. Why not Hebrew? Not enough delegates could speak it. Along with many other problems, that of language would have to await future attention. But the international meeting had opened a new phase of Jewish history. Summing up his feelings about the three exciting days of the First Zionist Congress, Herzl wrote in his private diary: "I shall beware of saying this in public, but in Basle I have founded the Jewish State."

The Russian Jews

It was in Basle that Herzl discovered a new Jewish world, that of Eastern Jewry, represented by delegates from Poland, Roumania and Russia. Until then, his entire acquaintance was with assimilationist-minded Western Jews. Of Russian Jews, he wrote, "These people are on the right track. They do not assimilate themselves to any other nation but they are striving to learn all good things from other people. That way they managed to be genuine and of upright character. And yet, they are ghetto Jews, the only ghetto Jews who exist in our times. Yes, in looking at them we understand what gave our fathers the strength for perseverance. . . . With strange, vibrant vitality, our history embodied itself in these people. I had to think of the argument that was made in the beginning, when people told me: you will *only* win over the Russian Jews to the cause—if this would be told to me again today, I would say: That · is enough."

The Zionist Congress had become the focus and the public platform of the Zionist movement. It became a continuing world forum for discussion of the Jewish problem. As the legislative body of the Zionist movement, it was the springboard for Zionist action and the mirror of the increasing growth of the Zionist idea.

In 1899 the second Congress was called in Basle. This time there were over 400 delegates who. represented 913 Zionist groups. Sixty of these groups were in the United States. In comparison with the first Congress, it was a ninefold increase of Zionists the world over.

Many Jews flocked into the Zionist camp in the intervening years. It attracted outstanding rabbis and intellectuals. One enthusiastic Zionist was Cesare Lombroso, famous Italian Jewish psychiatrist and a founder of modern psychiatry.

On the roster of delegates was a young man from Russia, Chaim Weizmann, who later became the first president of the State of Israel.

A little incident in front of the Congress building moved many to tears. A parade of Christian Swiss citizens marched past the Congress House. When they caught sight of the blue and white Zionist flag, one marcher shouted, "Long live the Jews," and others echoed the cry. Many carrying Swiss flags saluted the blue and white banner waving from the balcony of the Congress House. It was a new air Jews were breathing, an air of freedom and exultation.

A Financial Instrument

The "Jewish Colonial Trust," a bank that Herzl conceived of as "the Jewish company," was formally established by the Second Congress to be the financial instrument. Indefatigably, Herzl worked on this project, encountering many difficulties and obstacles. He negotiated with the mighty financiers of the day, with banks and bankers. But there were the barriers of silence, indifference, hesitation, and stalling. When Herzl's patience reached the exhaustion point, he looked for a different approach. What was needed was two hundred thousand pounds, about one million dollars.

He could not count on the rich, so he turned to the people. Shares in the venture were offered at one pound (five dollars) a piece and could be paid in installments. The response of the Jewish people was a tribute to his leadership. Modest people used their savings to invest in the future of the Jewish nation. Many bought single shares and paid for them on the installment plan. The first 100,000 pounds already were raised, when the Second Congress decided formally to establish the Jewish Colonial Trust. Herzl himself—certainly no man of means—purchased 2000 shares.

Thus started, the Jewish national bank transacted business—with varying success—for many years, until it was finally taken over by the Anglo-Palestine Bank in 1934.

The Jewish National Fund

Another, and by far a more significant instrument of the Zionist movement—the Jewish National Fund—had its beginnings in a brief telegram.

It was addressed to the first conference of the *Hov'vei Tzion* in Kattowitz in 1884 and was signed by Professor Herman Schapiro of the University of Heidelberg in Germany. The telegram proposed that the Jewish people establish a general fund for the purchase of land in Palestine. The message was read, filed and forgotten.

But thirteen years later the proposal turned up again. It was at the First Zionist Congress that Professor Schapiro again submitted his plan. Spelling out his idea in detail, Professor Schapiro proposed:

1. Money should be collected from Jews all over the world, from rich and poor alike, on the basis of a regular contribution to a general fund.
2. Two-thirds of the fund should be used for the purchase of land, while the remaining third should be devoted to its cultivation.
3. The land thus bought should forever remain under the control of the fund, and *not be sold to individuals. It should only be leased for a period of not more than forty-nine years.*

This last point was most important. It stipulated that land bought with public funds of the Jewish people would belong to the Jewish people forever. It might be leased to individuals or groups, but eventually must return to its owner, just as in biblical days land that changed hands had to be returned to its original owner after every forty-nine years. Though the proposal was received with great enthusiasm, nothing was done about it for four years. The plan finally materialized in 1901 when The Jewish National Fund (*Keren Kayemet*) was formally established by the Fifth Zionist Congress.

The Little Box

The Jewish National Fund depended on coins and small sums of money collected continuously throughout the Jewish world. Soon the small blue and white Jewish National Fund box found a place in millions of Jewish homes all over the globe. From coins dropped into these boxes, tre-

In a Niche of Honor in Jewish Homes around the world: The Blue Box of the Jewish National Fund

mendous amounts began to build up. They developed the Jewish National Fund into a most powerful instrument for the rebuilding of the Jewish homeland.

There were other means used by the Jewish National Fund to raise money. Jewish National Fund seals were sold, and the "Golden Book" was started for contributors to honor others.

The *Sefer Ha-Yeled*—the children's book of the Jewish National Fund —was organized along similar lines. A tree-planting program of gigantic proportions was inaugurated. Special drives were initiated by Zionist groups to acquire land for new settlements. The effort was the collective enterprise of a people who strove peacefully to redeem the soil of its ancestors.

"If You Will It, It Will Be No Legend"

Many difficulties and disappointments came Herzl's way as he tried to spread his idea of "The Jewish State" through writing, speaking, and negotiating, and through mobilizing a host of people for his cause.

Lack of understanding, opposition, and criticism came from many quarters. Yet, Herzl did not permit any obstacles to make him lose sight of his goal. He renewed his efforts with greater zeal, and popularized his plan in the form of a novel prefaced by the motto, "If you will it, it will be no legend."

Entitled *Altneuland (Old-New Land)*, the novel was almost a work of science fiction. Published in 1903, it tried to depict life in the Jewish State in 1925.

In a bold flight of imagination, Herzl takes the reader into the future Jewish State, into the old and yet new land, vibrating with a new spirit, a new culture, a new civilization. He writes of transforming a desolate wasteland into a thriving country of modern agricultural settlements and of great cities. The land belongs to the people, who find new and better ways of living and working together. Jews and Arabs strive side by side for a life of peace and brotherhood.

Herzl's novel was translated into many languages and of course into Hebrew, where it appeared under the title *Tel Aviv* (Hill of Spring). This served as inspiration for the name of the first all-Jewish city that was to emerge on the dunes of the Mediterranean.

Herzl's Diplomacy

Kaiser Wilhelm II & Sultan of Turkey

As Herzl saw it, the success of the Zionist program hinged on winning over two personalities—the Sultan of Turkey and the Emperor of Germany.

Turkey of those days, the Ottoman Empire, had been losing power and prestige for many years. The Empire was weak, as was its ruler, Sultan Abdul Hamid. He was physically sick, morally corrupted, and surrounded by a group of grafting courtiers.

Under Ottoman rule, Palestine had become an arid stretch of land, abandoned, neglected, and desolate. Perhaps Palestine actually could be bought from Turkey, Herzl thought. Turkey needed money. To buy Palestine would mean, in the very first place, to buy favors from the greedy courtiers that held sway over the Sultan. Herzl and his friends tried to penetrate the bribery-infested palace. They thought they might convince the Sultan, through a large scale financial transaction, to grant a charter for Jewish colonization in Palestine. But they failed.

Therefore Herzl had to shift his tactics. Now his efforts were directed towards enlisting the German Kaiser to influence the Sultan. An interview was arranged with the Grand Duke of Baden, who had become a Zionist-sympathizer and a regular reader of the Zionist weekly, *The World*, edited by Herzl. The Grand Duke prepared for the Kaiser a

Meets with little support

← *Planting for the Future*

from Kaiser, Sultan, Egypt, England, Russia

Can Skip pp 73-82

detailed report on the Zionist movement. The Kaiser was fascinated. He ordered the German ambassador in Vienna to explore the matter further and to report back without delay.

The Kaiser had been planning a trip to Turkey and Palestine. He was hoping to strengthen German influence in Turkey by visiting the Sultan. And there was another, stronger reason. The Kaiser wanted the Sultan's permission to search in Palestine for the Holy Ark, lost since the days of biblical antiquity.

Setting the Stage

To decide whether the Zionist idea fitted into German ambitions was a task the German Ambassador in Vienna was instructed to undertake. He wired Herzl for an appointment. The two met and were instantly impressed with each other. It was easy for Herzl to make his point: he would greatly appreciate an appointment with the Kaiser. Herzl said he would ask the Kaiser to persuade the Sultan to negotiate with the Zionists about granting Jewish autonomy to the land.

Herzl had succeeded in winning the Ambassador's good will. A dizzying sequence of developments brought Herzl face to face with the top dignitaries of the German Reich—among them with the Reich's Chancellor—and the stage was set for a most dramatic event—his meeting with the German Kaiser.

There were actually two meetings. The first one took place in Constantinople in the Sultan's palace with all the pomp and circumstance prescribed for such an occasion. Crowds waited outside the palace, state carriages moved up in solemn procession, guards of honor presented arms, and Herzl finally was ushered into a luxuriously furnished chamber, and stood in front of the Kaiser, one of the most powerful rulers of his time. The conversation began smoothly. Then the Kaiser asked, "Tell me with one word, what you want me to ask of the Sultan." Quickly Herzl retorted, "A chartered company—under German protection." "That's good—a chartered company," replied the Kaiser briskly.

The audience was over. But by agreement, it was to be continued soon on Palestinian soil. Here Herzl was supposed to make the request formally in a prepared address approved in advance by the Kaiser's advisors.

✔ Herzl and a Zionist delegation landed in Jaffa. They paid brief visits to the pioneer colonies of Mikveh Israel, Rishon L'Tzion and Yisrael. Meeting the colonists and their families, they encountered for the first time a new type of Jew—farmers, bound to the soil. Herzl and his fellow delegates were deeply impressed.

But they did not come to tour the country. Their purpose was to see the Kaiser.

The Meeting *falls through—*

On a road near Mikveh Israel leading past fields tilled by the farmers of that colony, German and Turkish cavalry officers in their colorful uniforms waited. Herzl stood in the blazing sun, his tropical helmet in his hands, leaning back on a plow. All of a sudden the Kaiser, high on a horse, galloped along. The children of the colony, who had been assembled and rehearsed for the occasion, broke into the singing of the German national anthem. The Kaiser led his horse toward Herzl. They greeted each other with a few words and the Kaiser departed.

But the two men met again in Jerusalem. By arrangement, Wilhelm II waited in a large oriental tent, for the entrance of the Zionist delegation. He wore a gray colonel's uniform, and held a horsewhip in his right hand. While cabinet members and German army officers stood by, the Zionist delegation, all in frock coats and high hats, entered. After all were formally introduced, Herzl stepped forward to read an address that, indeed, has become an historic document. He read: *Skip ↓*

"A delegation of sons of Israel reverently approaches the German Kaiser in the land our forefathers once owned, a land that belongs to us no longer. We are bound up with this land though we hold no valid title of property. Many generations have come and gone since this soil has been Jewish. If one talks about it, it is only like a dream of days of old. But the dream still lives, it lives in the hearts of hundreds of thousands. That dream was a comfort for our people in many sorrow-filled hours.

"Whenever enemies beset us with accusations and persecutions, whenever we were excluded from the companionship of our fellow citizens,

Sultan doesn't want an autonomous Jewish State — Kaiser, who would like to rid Germany of its Jews, drops the idea of support.

Steppingstones to Reality

whose destinies we were ready to share at all times, the thought of Zion rose again and again in our downcast souls.

"We have awakened the national consciousness of our dispersed brethren at our Congresses in Basle! The program of our movement has been formulated before the eyes of the entire world. It seeks for the Jewish people a publicly recognized, legally secured home in Palestine.

"Here is the land of our fathers, suitable for cultivation and colonization. Your Majesty has seen the land. It cries for people who want to cultivate it. And among our brethren are people who cry for a land to cultivate. . . . To satisfy these needs—of the people and of the land—we would like—in joint planning for both—to create a new welfare. We consider this cause so useful and so worthy of the support of the most generous that we appeal to your Majesty for your support of this work.

"We are honestly convinced that the implementation of the Zionist plan will also entail the welfare of Turkey. Human energies and material resources will flow into the country. It is easy to foresee the tremendous cultivation of these desolated areas. From all this, happiness and high standards will come to many people.

"We plan the establishment of a Jewish colonization company for Palestine to undertake this great work, and appeal to the German Kaiser for his protection of this company.

"An Emperor of Peace enters the Eternal City. We Jews greet Your Majesty in this great moment and from the depth of our hearts we pray that an age of peace and justice may come forth for all people—and also for us."

The Aftermath

When the reading was over, there was no response by the Kaiser. Only the Foreign Minister spoke. He asked how these arid stretches of Palestine could be properly irrigated. To this technical question there were answers given by an irrigation expert, a member of the Jewish delegation. What followed were a few polite platitudes by the Kaiser. Then the audience was over, and Herzl's and his friends' high hopes were shattered. It became clear that the Kaiser had no interest in intervening with the Sultan on behalf of the Jews, let alone in becoming their protector. The

disappointment was crushing for the Zionist delegation. Only Herzl remained undaunted. He said comfortingly to his friends, "I am neither
smarter nor better than you are, but I am not despondent. . . . In more
difficult moments, I have not lost courage. I have even made still greater
sacrifices."

Quickly, Herzl arranged for the departure of the delegation. He
wanted them to leave the country as fast as possible to avoid trouble with
the Turkish authorities. Years later the German Foreign Minister di-
vulged in his memoirs that, at first, the Kaiser had been quite enthusiastic
about the Zionist project as a way of ridding Germany of many of his
Jewish subjects. But when the Turkish ambassador told the Kaiser that
the Sultan would not tolerate an independent Jewish commonwealth on *Skip*
Palestinian soil, the Kaiser dropped the matter instantly.

The Sultan's Door Opens ~~and closes it~~ *Corruption in Turkish Court*

Still, Herzl continued to hope for the granting of a charter by the Sultan.
But how could one reach him? How could one get a hearing, unimpeded
by the corrupt courtiers who surrounded Abdul Hamid? Herzl hit upon
a new strategy. The key figure was Herman Vambery, an old man, a
professor of oriental languages at the University of Budapest. Born a
Jew, but no longer a professing one, he was the first European who, dis-
guised as a Moslem monk, had entered and traveled in Turkestan, Persia,
Samarkand, and other Asian territories. Vambery now wanted to help
the Jewish people he had once abandoned. "If I am helping you," he

*On the Ship of Good
Hope: Zionist
Delegation Enroute to
Palestine*

wrote to Herzl, "I am doing so for the sake of the cause." Vambery had many friends in the Sultan's Court. And he had been, since the days of his youth, a friend and personal advisor of Abdul Hamid, the Sultan. Through Vambery's efforts, one day in May, 1901, Herzl received a call to present himself to the Sultan. He waited while a glittering parade of pashas and princes in resplendent uniforms formed a processional and partook of solemn formalities. Herzl finally faced the Turkish ruler, an aged man with a dyed beard.

Abdul Hamid said to Vambery: "This man looks like a prophet, like a leader of his people." Herzl wrote in his diary: "My impression was that he is a weak man, a coward, but basically a good-natured fellow. I consider him neither malicious, nor cruel, but a deeply unhappy prisoner, in whose name a gang, an infamous and corrupted gang of robbers, perpetrates acts of utter shamefulness." It was the "robbers," the Sultan's advisors, who confronted Herzl with certain conditions before even considering the much coveted charter. First of all, Herzl should recommend a financial wizard to devise new taxes and open up new avenues of revenue for the bankrupt country. Then practical measures should be recommended to balance the budget of the Turkish Empire and wipe out immense debts Turkey owed if the Zionists really wanted to obtain the charter.

What this meant was to bail out the Turkish Empire from its total bankruptcy. And Herzl tried to raise the enormous funds needed. He traveled to Paris and London. He negotiated with financiers. He argued, pleaded, demanded. But his efforts came to nothing and the Sultan determined not to give up Palestine!

Shift to England

Again, Herzl shifted to England. Over the years, Herzl had assembled in the British Isles powerful allies for his cause. He had won personal friends who were men of great standing and influence. They now gave him their full support. Herzl came up with a plan for creating the Jewish State which was called "Egyptian Palestine." These were areas close to the real Palestine, in the vicinity of El Arish, in the Sinai Peninsula, and also on the Island of Cyprus. For these projects, particularly for a

Jewish settlement on the Sinai Peninsula, Herzl had finally won the approval and support of Lord Rothschild, the leader of British Jewry. Moreover, he aroused the interest of other members of the British Parliament and government. They had been deeply impressed by Herzl during his first "official" appearance on England's political scene.

This occurred when Herzl received an official invitation—through the intervention of his Jewish friends—to testify on the Jewish problem before a parliamentary committee. The British Alien Commission was holding hearings on the advisability of admitting foreigners, including poor Jews from Eastern Europe. These hearings marked the first time the Zionist movement gained wide political attention in Britain.

It was the editor of *The Jewish Chronicle*, England's oldest and most famous Jewish weekly newspaper, who had arranged for Herzl's appearance. "The Jews of Eastern Europe," Herzl said in his testimony, "cannot remain where they are now. Where are they to go? If they are not wanted here, then a place must be found to which they can emigrate. Otherwise the problem with which you are dealing here will continue to exist."

Questions followed. Herzl was asked about the aims of Zionism. He replied by quoting the Basle program. Then he added that the needs of oppressed Jews were so urgent that perhaps their temporary settlement outside Palestine might be accepted. On the following day, in a private conversation with the chairman of the Commission, Herzl presented his plan for a Jewish settlement in "Egyptian Palestine." Herzl visited Lord Lansdowne, the British Foreign Secretary, and he, in turn, entered negotiations with the Khedive, the Turkish ruler of British-dominated Egypt. The talks finally led to a major decision. Landsdowne advised Herzl that the Sinai Peninsula project would be considered, providing a commission of experts agreed, after a thorough study of the area, that the plan was feasible.

The Expedition to El Arish

Thus, the so-called El Arish expedition to the hot Sinai Peninsula got under way. Lord Rothschild, who not so long before had been opposed to all Zionist endeavors, underwent a complete change of heart. Now he promised far-reaching financial assistance. An English engineer was in charge of a group, which included representatives of the Zionist movement and the British government. Herzl journeyed to Cairo to join the commission upon its return.

But the commission finally reported that the area would hardly lend itself to colonization purposes. Too many difficulties would arise for European settlers unused to life under tropical conditions, it said. Besides, the Egyptian Government said it could not spare Nile River water needed for irrigation of that arid soil. The Egyptians also said the building of waterways from the Nile to El Arish would gravely impede the traffic on the Suez Canal and would lead to heavy economic losses. Thus the whole scheme collapsed.

Kishinev

A tragic event dictated the next move. In April, 1903, about fifty Jews in Kishinev, Russia, were killed, and their property plundered in a pogrom perpetrated by the officials of the Russian Government. A cry of horror and protest went up throughout the civilized world. Vienna, Berlin, Paris, London and New York became scenes of mass meetings ringing with condemnations and clamoring for political action. Herzl decided to go to Russia and deal with the man who actually was the instigator of the Kishinev pogrom, Count Von Plehve, the Czar's Minister of Interior.

Plehve was a ruthless anti-Semite, who was credited with the statement that "it is the task of the Russian Government to make life for the Jews in Russia a living hell." But he agreed to meet Herzl at St. Petersburg, the Russian capital. He said he would support a Jewish "emigration without return."

"The Russian Government, considers with the interest the activities of the Zionist movement as long as it is its aim to promote Jewish emigration from Russia," he said. He emphasized that "Russia has a definite interest in getting rid of those Jews who would not want to assimilate themselves completely to their Russian environment, and who would not want to give up their specific Jewish peculiarities. Therefore Russia would be willing to give active support to Zionism as an emigration movement that would contribute to an actual decrease of the Jewish population in Russia."

While Plehve behaved with calculating calm, a colleague, the Minister of Finance, Count Witte, displayed crudeness towards Herzl.

"So you want to take away the Jews?" he thundered. "Are you a Hebrew? And by the way, whom am I talking to?"

Herzl identified himself and presented his credentials. Then came another outburst.

"The Jews are of an arrogance that is characteristic of them. In addition, most of them are poor. And because they are poor, they are dirty and make a revolting impression. Also, they engage in all kinds of ugly deals, so that it becomes difficult for the friend of the Jews, to defend them." Yet, in spite of Herzl's dealings with these two Jew-baiters, his trip to St. Petersburg was a political success. He came back with pledges of support for Zionism as a movement of emigration, and with a written assurance that the Russian Government would be ready to further the work of Zionism. It would support Zionist representatives in dealings with the Turkish Government so that Jewish emigration from Russia be facilitated. Moreover, to maintain these activities, funds would be raised through special taxes imposed on Jews in Russia. To all appearances, the way seemed to have been paved for some sort of cooperation with even the Jew-hating government of the Czar.

Alas, these assurances paled into merest insignificance and turned to tragic irony in the shocking experience Herzl went through on his way back. It was an experience that shook him to the core of his innermost being. The occasion was a stopover in Vilna, where thousands of Jews thronged the streets to greet Herzl. It was past midnight, but the town was awake, when Herzl rode in his carriage to the railroad station. As the crowds surged closer to acclaim Herzl, Russian police went into action. It was a display of brutality such as Herzl had never seen before, and it indelibly imprinted itself on his mind. More than anything else, that

Scene of Devastation after a Pogrom

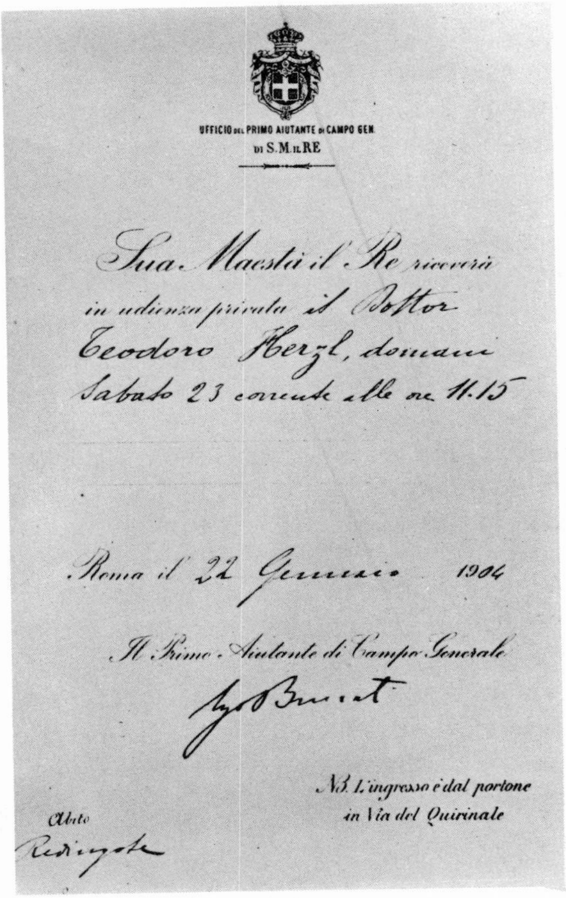

UFFICIO DEL PRIMO AIUTANTE DI CAMPO GEN.
DI S. M. IL RE

Sua Maestà il Re riceverà
in udienza privata il Dottor
Teodoro Herzl, domani
Sabato 23 corrente alle ore 11.15

Roma il 22 Gennaio 1904

Il Primo Aiutante di Campo Generale

[signature]

N.B. L'ingresso è dal portone
in Via del Quirinale

Abito
Redingote

Invitation to Herzl for an audience with the King of Italy night of horror brought home to Herzl the plight of Russian Jewry. It redoubled his resolve to leave no stone unturned to secure without delay some solution—if need be, even a temporary one—for the pressing needs of his people.

The UGANDA Project *6th Zionist Congress* *

Returning from an extensive trip to Africa, Joseph Chamberlain, the Colonial Secretary of the British Government, received Herzl and told him: "I have seen a land for you—Uganda. It's hot on the coastline, but if you go into the interior, the climate becomes excellent, even for Europeans. You can grow sugar and cotton there. Well, I thought, that would be a country for Dr. Herzl. But he only wants to go to Palestine or somewhere nearby." The idea of a Jewish settlement in Uganda came as a casual suggestion from Chamberlain. Herzl's reaction was a friendly, though decidedly firm "No."

But that was during the year before outbreaks at Kishinev. Later, the Uganda proposal came back to Herzl's mind. When Herzl reopened negotiations with the British Government, Chamberlain came back again to the idea of establishing a Jewish settlement in East Africa.

Though reluctant, Herzl finally agreed to consider the proposal and to submit it formally to the Sixth Zionist Congress, which convened in 1904.

New Palestine

A plan was drawn up quickly to establish a company that would organize Jewish colonization in Uganda. The company would own the territory which would be ruled by a Jewish governor. After a few years, it would enjoy complete autonomy and would be officially named "New Palestine."

Herzl insisted on quick action. The British Government approved the plan, announcing its offer in a letter signed by the head of the Foreign Office. The letter was an historic document. For the first time since the Jewish people went into dispersion, a world power gave formal recognition to the national aims of the Jewish people. When Herzl brought it before a small group of Zionist leaders meeting in a hotel room in Basle,

Steppingstones to Reality

one, a Russian Zionist, was so moved that he arose to pronounce the blessing, *Sheheḥeyanu*, for having been permitted to witness such a great occasion.

But that moment of exhilaration quickly passed when the Sixth Zionist Congress convened soon after. A debate on the Uganda proposal followed. It shook the Zionist movement to its foundations—and broke its leader's heart.

Why did Herzl take it upon himself to enter negotiations that led to the British offer? Why did he substitute Uganda for Palestine? Herzl, explained his reasons in a Congress address that introduced debate. He said:

"How great was our pain, when we learned of the historic occurrences of Kishinev, and how overwhelming our grief that Jews must live under such conditions.

"The bloody days of the Bessarabian city must not cause us to forget that there are yet other Kishinevs, not alone in Russia. Kishinev exists wherever Jews undergo bodily or spiritual tortures, wherever their self-respect is wounded and their possessions are damaged because they are Jews. Let us save those who can still be saved. . . .

"Zion it is not, and can never be; but it is . . . a temporary solution, founded upon a national and political basis. . . . It is and must be an emergency measure. . . ."

Herzl's faithful friend, Max Nordau, echoed the argument. With all his power of persuasion he cried out, "This means the establishment of an emergency structure for hundreds of thousands of our unfortunate brethren, who cannot wait, who are already wandering about, and who will perish if we don't do something for them to save them. For these hundreds of thousands we must, even before we are able to give permanent lodging, open up an asylum for the night."

Strange, but the Russian Zionists, who represented those who were in the most dire need of an "asylum for the night," would have no part in such a solution. Though living in the shadow of terror, they did not want to hear of any approach that would forego even temporarily, the claim to Palestine as the Jewish homeland. The Russian Zionists formed a formidable and solid opposition to Herzl and his advocacy of the British proposal. On the other hand, the delegates from Western countries, from England and America, sided with Herzl and Nordau.

A vote was taken, and the majority decided to send a commission of experts to Uganda to explore possibilities for the projected settlement. Then something unforeseen happened. Those who had voted "no" rose suddenly and walked out of the session in protest, and assembled in another hall.

Gloom settled over the group. It was a spirit of mourning. Some broke into tears and wept bitterly, some squatted down on the floor in that gesture of mourning customary on Tishah B'Av, the anniversary of the destruction of the Temple. There was such despair as if Palestine, Eretz Israel, were lost again.

Tempers had grown short. Charges of betrayal were raised in all seriousness. When Herzl was informed of what had happened, he went to visit those who had walked out of the session. Somebody shouted, "Traitor!" He was deeply hurt. But he gave assurances that the Basle program would remain untouched.

Such assurances—and Herzl repeated them—restored calm and order to the proceedings. The Russians rejoined the Congress and Herzl was re-elected president of the World Zionist Organization with all but three votes. But the hurt stung and came to the fore again in a scene of high drama when Herzl, in his concluding address to the Sixth Congress, passionately declared:

"When I thought that all hope was lost and might be gone for a lifetime, then I wanted to suggest to you an expediency of emergency. In the meantime, I have come to know your hearts. So, let me tell you in a word of comfort in the language of our fathers—and it is a word of commitment for me: *Im eshkaḥekh Y'rushalayim, tishkaḥ y'mini*—If I forget thee, O Jerusalem, let my right hand lose its cunning."

There he stood with his right arm outstretched as though he were transfixed in a pledge of majestic solemnity. He won back all the delegates, and the Uganda plan was all but finished.

Appointment at the Quirinal *Goes to Italy – sympathy*

Herzl turned next to the King of Italy, Victor Emanuel III. The King showed surprising knowledge of the struggles within the Zionist move-

Russian liaison utterly fail

? = Was Herzl a diplomatic failure

See next chapter –

Ans = Changed World Mind set –

The impossible could be accomplished.

85

ment and familiarity with Jewish customs. He even knew what a *Minyan* was, and told Herzl a story about one of his Jewish generals, Giuseppe Ottolenghi, who once could not assemble a *Minyan* in Naples. The King's interest in Jerusalem was sincere, and so was his interest in Zionism. Herzl sought Italian support for the Zionist position in negotiations with Turkey. Through Victor Emanuel's efforts, promises were given that the Italian Ambassador in Constantinople would act in concert with the Russian Ambassador in matters of the Zionist negotiations. This was good as far as it went, but the hoped for Russian support never came.

One more diplomatic attempt came when Herzl turned to the Pope for an endorsement. The attempt failed.

Did Herzl Fail?

Failure seemed to issue from the many diplomatic labors of Herzl. In terms of practical, tangible results, there was nothing that could be labelled as real achievement. At the end of his life, Herzl found himself blocked, his hopes for a Turkish charter unfulfilled. Yet, history was to prove that Herzl's tremendous exertions had prepared the foundations for genuine achievement.

The Herzl Family Grave in Vienna

LOOKING back on Theodor Herzl's sudden appearance on the scene of Jewish history, and the powerful impact he had on the course of events before his death at the age of 44, one may ask what it was that gave him the power to set hearts and minds afire.

The answer is that Herzl was endowed with such personal magnetism that he could attract, penetrate, and arouse people with enormous enthusiasm.

"Something touched him, a spark, a flash that came down from heaven. And in the heart of Herzl a sacred fire breaks out, unquenchable," was the way the writer Shmaryah Levin described Herzl's greatness.

Aḥad Ha'am, spoke of Herzl's "splendid visions," and of their power "to awaken a sense of national self-respect."

Years later, Chaim Weizmann, the first president of the State of Israel, reminisced, "If we throw our minds back to those far-off days, we realize how the naive faith in the unlimited power of our will to accomplish the well-nigh impossible set in motion hidden forces evoked by the genius of Herzl."

What these Jewish leaders felt and admired was shared by kings, princes, and statesmen, who were sought out by Herzl in his many attempts to arouse the great of the earth to the plight of the Jewish people.

"I still see before me that finely modeled head, with the dark, deep-set eyes, half brooding on a distant dream, half glowing with inner fire. . . . The manner of his speech showed at once that this was no fantastic dream, but a reality. And something more was irresistibly borne home by this man: his selfless love for his people . . . ," King Ferdinand the First of Bulgaria recalled of Herzl.

The Grand Duke Friedrich of Baden once remarked: "I consider it nothing less than a moral duty to assist a cause whose leader is a man like Theodor Herzl."

CHAPTER 4 *Herzl's Place in History*

"There was a breath of eternity in that man Herzl," Georges Clemenceau, France's famous statesman, related. "The burning bush and revolutionary Sinai took shape in his appearance . . . He was a man of genius."

For many years, the King of Italy had on his desk a picture of Herzl. "Scarcely," he told a visitor once, "have I ever met a man of such magnetic charm as this great Jew."

The end came for Herzl in 1904, the year of the Uganda dispute and many diplomatic frustrations. He had given every moment of the last nine years of his life to the Zionist cause and literally worked himself to death. His many labors affected a heart that already was weak.

News of Herzl's death left the Jewish world stricken. Jews were plunged into the deepest grief. Tens of thousands of Jews wept bitterly in the streets of Vienna as a black hearse with a simple coffin passed on its way to a grave Herzl had selected as his resting place "until the Jewish people will transport my body to Palestine."

That wish was fulfilled in 1949 when the Jewish people brought Herzl's remains to the State of Israel, his spiritual home.

Last Resting Place on Mt. Herzl near Jerusalem

UNIT THREE

Zionism Strikes Roots

THE GREAT leader had died and the movement was left without his steady hand to guide its destinies.

In Herzl's lifetime there was often strong, and even violent opposition. Yet, Herzl always knew how to rally his opponents when a situation called for unity in thought and action. With Herzl gone, sharp and deep divisions of opinion arose over the course the Zionist movement should take. Should Herzl's political efforts to obtain a charter be continued? Or should Zionists shift their attention to practical work in colonizing Palestine, regardless of political circumstances. Two major groups emerged—the "political" and the "practical" Zionists. And they became locked in a long and bitter struggle. Herzl's successor was a man who believed in a healthy combination of both methods. He was David Wolffsohn, who was selected president of the Zionist World Organization at its seventh Congress in 1905.

"How long have you been a Zionist?" Wolffsohn was once asked. "Ever since my infancy," he replied, "since the day that I first remember having seen my father weeping. I asked him why he wept and he answered: 'Because of the destruction of Zion!'"

Wolffsohn and Herzl had been intimate friends for many years. They shared big plans and minute details. They shared high hopes and bitter disappointments. And they shared one especially intimate moment when both first saw Palestine. Wolffsohn, who was a member of the Zionist delegation meeting the Kaiser, wrote this description:

"When our ship left Port Said, bound for Jaffa, it was evening. All of us knew that we should land in Palestine the following morning, and all of us, myself included, retired to our cabins for the night. Only Herzl did not think of resting, but remained on deck.

"I was sound asleep—for it was already long past midnight—when I heard someone calling: 'David are you sleeping, my friend?' I felt a hand

CHAPTER 1 *The Slow Decade*

pass gently over my face as the voice continued: 'Don't you want to see our mother, Zion, David? Get up—the light of morning is already shining on the towers of Jaffa. We can already see them gleaming.'

"Rising from my bed, I was amazed to see Herzl attired as for an audience with an emperor. His face, glowing, his eyes shining, he exclaimed: 'Come David, get dressed! Let us see our beloved motherland!'

"I dressed and we went up on deck, and we saw the pointed minarets of Jaffa beckoning to us. We fell into each other's arms, and tears rose to our eyes as we whispered softly, 'Our country! Our Mother Zion!' "

The two men remained inseparably bound to a cause that was sacred to them. Wolffsohn served indefatigably in all of Herzl's projects. He played a most important role in establishing the bank—the Jewish Colonial Trust—and it was here that Wolffsohn's talents shone most brightly. Wolffsohn, who had achieved great success as a businessman, displayed enormous skill in this highly complicated undertaking, and it justified his reputation as a financial genius.

As the years passed, the bonds of personal friendship grew stronger and stronger. No wonder Wolffsohn emerged as a central figure in Herzl's novel, *Altneuland*. After he had been elected by the seventh Congress to the presidency of the Zionist World Organization, Wolffsohn had the difficult task of keeping the Zionist movement intact despite many conflicts between "political" and "practical" Zionists. Time and again Wolffsohn tried to resolve these conflicts by keeping to a "middle of the road" course, though he personally favored Herzl's position of attempting first to find a political solution. He sought new negotiations with the Sultan

David Wolffsohn: Second President of the Zionist World Organization

and for a time it seemed that good results were in the offing. But in 1908, when "The Young Turks" staged their successful uprising against the regime, all prospects of an agreement ended.

The strains of his activities taxed Wolffsohn's health, and he withdrew from the leadership, yielding it to a spokesman of the opposition, Professor Otto Warburg, one of the champions of the "practical" approach.

Nevertheless, Wolffsohn's influence continued to be felt until his death in 1914. The Jewish people remain indebted to David Wolffsohn, whose memory lives on not only in the history of Zionism, but also in the blue-white flag of the Zionist movement and later of the State of Israel. It was Wolffsohn, who suggested the traditional blue and white colors of the *Tallit* for the flag.

Marking Time

The Zionist Congresses came and went. They were held every two years in various cities of central Europe. After the passing of Theodor Herzl, however, the movement lost much of its momentum. Herzl's successors to the presidency of the World Zionist Organization, like David Wolffsohn and later Professor Otto Warburg, of the University of Berlin, carried on, while the movement apparently marked time.

It was a difficult period. The political fortunes of Zionism were at their lowest ebb. The Uganda project had been abandoned, and all endeavors to obtain a charter from the Turkish Government had ended in frustration. The Young Turks, who had rebelled against their autocratic and corrupt government in 1908, decided upon a radical course of imposing Turkish culture on Palestine and their other Middle Eastern holdings, and they turned a deaf ear to national Jewish aspirations in Palestine. The new rulers were hostile towards the Jewish settlers. These events led Zionist leadership to intensify Jewish colonization efforts even without the charter and strengthened the hand of the "practical" Zionists.

Weizmann Enters

Most of the "practical" Zionists came from Eastern Europe, primarily from Russia. Most prominent among them was a young chemist, Chaim Weizmann, who was born in Motele, a small village in Russia, and became a teacher at the University of Manchester in England. His family, friends, and the teacher of his early youth all were "Zionists" long before Zionism became a political movement. When Herzl's call for the first Zionist Congress summoned Jewish leaders to Basle, young Weizmann travelled through Russia and from one Zionist group to another, to urge them to elect delegates.

Very quickly Weizmann stood at the center of the Russian delegation. He emerged as its most eloquent spokesman. Weizmann, unlike Herzl, came from a background of a living Jewish tradition. He felt very strongly that Zionism should be more than a political undertaking. It should embrace a rich cultural Jewish content. Weizmann and his followers demanded that Zionists be imbued with Judaism and speak the Hebrew language. They also stressed the necessity of doing practical work in Palestine. They demanded that more colonies be established, that more institutions be created, and that the Jewish resettlement in Palestine proceed, however slowly. It was their firm conviction that a Jewish homeland could be created only in Palestine—nowhere else. It was this passionate conviction that brought Weizmann and his friends into fiery opposition to Herzl when the Uganda proposal tore the sixth Congress asunder.

That controversy actually set the stage for the first meeting between Weizmann and a man who later played a most important part in British policies affecting the Jewish people. Arthur James Balfour, running for Member of Parliament from Manchester, tried to get the support of Jewish voters in that city while Weizmann was on the faculty of the University. Balfour sought out Weizmann, who commanded a large following of Zionists in Manchester. The two men talked about Jewish affairs and it was only natural that Britain's Uganda offer came up for discussion. Why did the Jews oppose this plan so violently, Balfour asked. Weizmann replied, "Supposing, I were to offer you Paris instead of London, would you take it?" "But, Weizmann—we have London," Balfour said, and Weizmann retorted, "Yes, that is true, but we had Jerusalem when London was a marsh."

The argument stuck in Balfour's mind many years later when he had become British Foreign Secretary—and it was a decisive factor in the fulfillment of the Zionist dream.

Splits and Parties

It was Chaim Weizmann who first organized a party within the Zionist movement. The Democratic Fraction was his creation, and as the name indicated, it strove for democratic methods in governing the movement. Weizmann and his followers became opponents of Herzl, who seemed to them to be somewhat dictatorial.

When the Congress, after Herzl's death, soon became divided between "political" and "practical" Zionists, Weizmann suggested a combination of both trends. He advocated a "synthetic" Zionism. "I regard," he once said, "political Zionism as the synthesis of all our activities. The practical work is a means to further the political objective."

On this kind of "synthetic" Zionism there was agreement, but various parties appeared on the scene, following the establishment of Weizmann's Democratic Fraction, and there were wide differences of opinion among them.

The Workers of Zion

There was another group that cherished two ideals—an independent Jewish State and an ideal social commonwealth for this Jewish State. At once fervent Zionists and dedicated Socialists, they called themselves *Poale Zion*, the Workers of Zion, or the Zionist Labor Party.

Poale Zion hoped for a land owned by all and inhabited by a new type of Jewish community, living differently from the way Jews lived in Europe as small businessmen and professionals. Palestine, they said, needed a class of Jewish farmers and workers.

They favored a socialist state free of both arrogant wealth and abysmal poverty. Their hopes were for better wages, better housing, and better living conditions than prevailed, for instance, in Russia. An unsuccessful revolt in Russia in 1905 spurred many young adherents of the Poale Zion to set out for Palestine. These youths belonged to the *Second Aliyah,* a new immigration wave that now surged over the shores of Palestine.

The Second Wave

A burning sense of idealism brought them to Deganya, in Galilee, and made them stay, stubbornly and doggedly defying almost unbearable heat and pitiless disease. Malaria exacted a murderous toll, but they would not give up.

A hardy group of young men and women, they settled in 1909 on soil purchased by the Jewish National Fund. When they came, it was fever-infested marshland, but it was their aim to make Deganya, a "place of corn," and they did. It took a rugged life of self-denial and sacrifice. But they were not unprepared. They had known hardship in Russia and through Jewish self-defense groups that had sprung up in response to pogroms, they learned how to survive.

Deganya B in the Jordan Valley

A Group of Pioneer Settlers

The Dignity of Work

It was the dignity of work that was closest to their hearts. They were determined to work the land by themselves, no matter how hard. There was to be no hired labor. They wanted to avoid conditions that had developed during the *First Aliyah*, when settlers hired Arab farmhands and began abandoning the land themselves or became mere foremen, who watched others do the work. Such conditions would not be tolerated in Deganya, nor in the other settlements established by the immigrants of the *Second Aliyah*.

The K'vutzah

Deganya set the tone for the new way of life. It became the model for the *K'vutzah*, a type of collective settlement where each member worked for all, where all property belonged to the entire community. The land was owned by the Jewish National Fund, which leased it to the settlers.

The Labor of Love ➡➡→

The Sage of Deganya—A. D. Gordon

Members shared all tasks—in the field and in the settlement, during the day and on guard duty against marauders at night. Hebrew was the language spoken.

It was a life of hardships and privations, of scarcities in food and of rugged accommodations. The standard menu was noodle soup and porridge. Their dwellings were shaky barracks and sagging tents. There was constant exposure to rain, storm, heat, cold, and disease. But in their struggle, they gained a new way of life.

A. D. Gordon   *A. D. Gordon*

As the first colony built on land acquired by the Jewish National Fund, Deganya was known as the Mother of the *K'vutzot*. Among its distinc-

"The Good Earth"

After the Day's Work

tions was that of having been home to the spiritual leader of the *Second Aliyah*, Aaron David Gordon, who emigrated from Russia to Palestine when he was nearly fifty.

In Russia, Gordon worked for a Jewish philanthropist as a minor official in an organization training Jews for agricultural work. But Gordon spent all his time in an office, and never worked in the fields himself. Nevertheless, he insisted that he must become a laborer on the land, for only through physical labor could the Jew recapture his lost identity. "The Jewish people has been completely cut off from nature and imprisoned within city walls these two thousands years. We have become accustomed to every form of life, except to a life of labor—of labor done for its own sake. It will require the greatest effort of will for such a people to become normal again."

A. D. Gordon quickly became the leader of the Jewish workers in Palestine. He led by example and was loved by settlers throughout the land. His preaching and writing won him a reputation as the "Sage of Deganya." Above all, he was a man who lived what he believed. And he believed deeply and religiously in the holiness of work, in the holiness of physical labor to which the Jewish people must return if it was ever to strike roots on its own soil. "In Palestine," Gordon wrote, "we must ourselves do all the work, from the least strenuous, cleanest, and most sophisticated, to the dirtiest and most difficult. . . . We who have been torn away from nature, who have lost the savor of natural living—if we desire life, we must establish a new relationship with nature; we must open a new account with it."

His ideas and work made A. D. Gordon a hero to those who called themselves *Ḥalutzim* (pioneers), and who banded together in a movement to live in *K'vutzot*. As a result, Gordon has been called "the father of the *Ḥalutz* Movement."

New Settlements

Deganya was only the first outpost of the *Second Aliyah*. Other settlements followed. What these settlers stood for was forcefully expressed by Ber Borochov, a native of Russia, who in his writings and in his speeches, had hammered out the platform of the Poale Zion. He soon found an eloquent companion in the person of Haim Joseph Brenner, a powerful Hebrew writer, who, through his magazine *Ha-M'orer*, tried to be an "awakener" of Jewish youth to the tasks and the blessings of labor in a Jewish state in Palestine. In the course of time the Poale Zion developed into a powerful party within the Zionist movement.

Religious Zionists *Mizrachi*

"*Eretz Yisrael L'am Yisrael Al Pi Torat Yisrael*—The Land of Israel for the people of Israel, on the basis of the Torah of Israel"—this was the slogan adopted by a party of religious Zionists called Mizrachi.

At Lida, a Russian town, the Mizrachi was formally established in 1902. Here a conference of religious Zionists was convened by Rabbi Isaac Jacob Reines, who had been an early follower of Theodor Herzl and an outstanding Talmudic scholar. He gathered a group of Orthodox Jews who were devoted to the building of a Jewish state on the principles of the Torah.

The Lida Conference was soon followed by other gatherings at which the basic principles of the new party were hammered out and brought to the attention of the Zionist movement. Mizrachi pressed for colonization and full observance of Jewish tradition within the Zionist organization. Strict observance of the Sabbath, of the dietary laws, and other Jewish observances ranked foremost in the program of the new party. It found its opponents among both non-observant Zionists and strictly observing anti-Zionists who rejected a Jewish state not founded by the Messiah. Mizrachi battled both with vigor and persistence and soon won a place of respect and influence within the World Zionist Organization.

The Territorialists *Skip*

Another party, known as the Territorialists, was led by the famous British Jewish writer, Israel Zangwill. With Palestine uncertain, it sought another territory for the Jews. Since the Uganda project had failed, the Territorialists looked elsewhere, but without success.

They were sharply opposed by those who had set their hearts on the ancient homeland and on that land alone. Calling themselves *Tzioney Tzion*—the Zionists of Zion—they rallied a majority at the 7th Congress for the defeat of the Territorialists' concept. Thus repudiated, the Territorialists walked out of the Zionist movement to form the Jewish Territorial Organization and continued the search for a Jewish territory. It was in vain, and in 1925, the organization disbanded.

United—on Hebrew *Skip & tell briefly*

While various parties brought diversity and division into the Zionist movement, they were united on one point, the importance of Hebrew.

The belief of Eliezer Ben Yehuda that Hebrew must be the bond linking together the Jews of Palestine and those of the world was shared by many others. Before long it was adopted by the Zionist movement, which spurred Hebrew creativity in Eastern Europe and elsewhere.

The First Zionist Congress fascinated a young man, Ḥayim Nahman Bialik, later to be acclaimed as the greatest Hebrew poet since the days of Judah Halevi. Bialik greeted the event in lines of sweeping exultation. The same chord was struck in the hearts of other Hebrew writers whose number and significance increased as the years passed. Soon Hebrew was used by a whole session of a Zionist Congress. To the delegates of the Congress Bialik could speak his spellbiding cadences in modern Hebrew.

Quite a large body of Hebrew literature had developed during the intervening years, owing its growth and influence to the Zionist movement. Besides Bialik a galaxy of Hebrew poets sprang up, among them Saul Tschernichovsky and Zalman Schneur. There were the novelists Samuel Joseph Agnon, Ḥayim Brenner, and David Frischmann. There was Aḥad Ha'am, in a class by himself as an analyst, critic, and stylist.

Ḥayim Naḥman Bialik:
Poet Laureate of the
Hebrew Renaissance ➠

And there were brilliant historians, writers, and journalists of a rapidly growing Hebrew press. Hebrew had rejoined the chorus of living languages.

Before the War

The years beween Herzl's death in 1904 and the outbreak of World War I in 1914 were a slow decade for the Zionist movement. These were the years of debate and inner conflict, of slow movement that sometimes lacked direction and produced little impact on the Jewish world.

In spite of Zionist drifting and Turkish misrule, however, the process of Jewish settlement continued, and not without considerable achievement.

By 1914, the total Jewish population in the Holy Land had reached 80,000, of whom 30,000 were new settlers living in a string of about fifty colonies. The rest were *Halukah* (charity) Jews who lived in Jerusalem, Safed, Hebron, and other cities, and led a dreary existence dependent on the charity of Jewish communities the world over.

Life for the new settlers was full of hardship and excitement as they fought against disease, stubborn soil, rocky hills and desert. They also had to fight against Bedouin marauders and their predatory night raids. Colonists joined a voluntary association of *Shomrim* (watchmen), who protected the settlements from their aggressive neighbors.

The Language Fight

For a time, a language struggle engulfed the *Yishuv*. The Hebraists, led by Ben Yehuda, were opposed by pious people who insisted on Yiddish for everyday purposes. At the same time, foreign Jewish charity organizations, such as the German *Hilfsverein* and the French *Alliance Israelite Universelle*, tried to force their sponsors' languages on the children of the new generation. But Hebrew emerged as the language of instruction in the schools. Some important schools also came into existence during these years. A Hebrew high school, started in 1904 in a private house in Jaffa, had developed into an internationally known *Gymnasium*. A few years later, a Jewish Technical Institute, the Technion, founded in Haifa, soon became the leading engineering school in the Near East. And the Bezalel School of Arts and Crafts, opened in Jerusalem under the leadership of Professor Boris Schatz, established itself in the world of arts.

Open Air Creativity at the Bezalel Art School in Jerusalem

Herzliah Gymnasium in Tel Aviv ➡

The Zionist movement played an increasingly important role in the *Yishuv*. A Palestine office was established in Jaffa. The Jewish Colonial Trust was set up. The Jewish National Fund began systematically to organize its land-purchasing operation. Land-development companies were founded, and stations for agricultural experimentation were placed at the service of the new settlers. Gradually a number of health services, so badly needed for combating and preventing disease, were installed.

Though the Turkish government approved Zionist plans for the creation of cooperative agricultural colonies, Turkish authorities on the scene were hostile. Unpleasantness was the order of the day on the part of the higher and minor officials, who did not miss any opportunity to create trying situations for the Jewish populations. That unconcealed enmity swept into full fury, when in 1914 the stormy waves of a world-wide war began to break on the shores of Palestine.

Jewish Immigrants from Russia at Collection Point

THOUSANDS of Jewish immigrants from Russia and other parts of Eastern Europe made their way to America during the latter part of the last century. They struggled bravely for a foothold in this new and strange country, crowding into tenements in New York's Lower East Side and into similar settlements in Chicago, Boston, Philadelphia, Baltimore, and other cities. While they were trying to eke out a livelihood and find a place in the sun that shone over America, the love for Zion was still aglow in many a heart. Quite a few Lovers of Zion had come over, and it was only natural that *Hov'vei Tzion* societies soon sprang up in New York, Chicago, Philadelphia, and other places. Small in numbers, these societies still took the lead in stimulating Zionist action, even before Zionism as an organized movement had entered the Jewish scene. One group, which purchased a piece of land east of the Jordan, called itself *Shavei Tzion*, Returnees of Zion.

At the First Zionist Congress in 1897, there was only one official delegate from America. He came from Baltimore. But a few other Americans also were present at Basle, and they returned with a determination to spread Herzl's word among American Jews to build an organized Zionist movement in the New World.

It was an uphill fight. The powerful leaders of the American Jewish community of those days, particularly the spokesmen for Reform Judaism, looked with utter disfavor upon the new idea and wanted to cut all ties with Zion. In fact, the Reform group left all mention of Zion out of their prayer books. Nor could the vast mass of new immigrants from Eastern Europe, so beset with the problems of earning a livelihood in the new country, pay much attention to Zionism. In its very early days, Zionism in America was confined to a small minority of enthusiastic idealists.

Slowly the movement began to gain ground. Zionist societies started to form and to arouse attention. As years passed, Zionist activity increased throughout the United States. By 1898, the various groups banded to-

Read at home

CHAPTER ② *The New World*

gether in a Federation of American Zionists. Its first president was Richard Gottheil, professor at Columbia University, and its first secretary was a young man, who later on was to be one of the great men in American Jewry, Rabbi Stephen S. Wise.

Herzl and America

Theodor Herzl was deeply interested in the growth of Zionist energies in America. It was upon his personal initiative that one of his English friends, Jacob de Haas, came to the United States to help organize the Zionist movement. As if he had foreseen the role American Jews were to play in the development of Zionism and Israel, Herzl once said prophetically, "Our strength lies with the Jews in America. I hope they will not fail us."

They didn't. More and more rallied to the blue and white colors of the Zionist movement. Zionists took the initiative in arousing American Jews to the fate of their brethren in Russia, particularly after the Kishinev calamity. They organized help for the victims of the Russian terror. They began to move into the forefront of the Jewish community.

When Herzl died, mourning swept the Jewish ranks in America. Memorial meetings were held in many cities. In Chicago a funeral procession of thousands, led by a bereaved Reform Rabbi, Bernard Felsenthal, followed an empty black coffin carried through predominantly Jewish residential sections.

Fighter and Spokesman for American Zionism: Rabbi Stephen S. Wise

The Challenge

Younger men enlisted in the cause of Zionism. There was Rabbi Stephen S. Wise, outspoken foe of anti-Zionists, whose views caused him to turn down the pulpit of Temple Emanu-El in New York, the leading Reform congregation in the United States. There was Judah L. Magnes, who later became the first Chancellor of the Hebrew University. And there was Abba Hillel Silver, who, decades later, was to plead the cause of the Jewish State before the United Nations.

Solomon Schechter Speaks Out

Conservative Judaism was just beginning to make its entry on the American scene. Its founder, Dr. Solomon Schechter, president of the Jewish Theological Seminary of America, emerged before long among those who took a fighting stand for Zionism. Time and again, though, he differed with some Zionist leaders over the question of religious emphasis. Echoing a famous utterance of Theodor Herzl, Schechter declared, "The rebirth of Israel's national consciousness and the revival of Judaism are inseparable."

Among the Orthodox, an old Lover of Zion, Zvi Hirsch Masliansky, who came from Russia, preached Zionism to the Jewish masses. Unsurpassed as a preacher, he brought large audiences to a high pitch of enthusiasm. The great Yiddish "orator of the people" became one of the most powerful influences for Zionism in America.

New Groups

Yiddish-speaking immigrants from Eastern Europe formed the bulk of Zionist followers. All in all, the Zionists in America numbered only a few thousand. What they lacked in numbers, however, they abundantly made up in idealism and devotion. New goals beckoned to the young and to the women in the American Jewish community. Young Judea, a children's

Zionist organization, came into being. Clubs for boys and girls sprang up throughout the country fostering enthusiasm for Judaism, the Jewish people, and Zion.

The Women

Hadassah, ZOA

At a meeting in New York in 1912, a women's Zionist group, named the Daughters of Zion, changed its name to one that later became famous throughout the United States—Hadassah. The members worked to bring Zionism to the Jewish women of America, and to bring modern medical care to those who had returned to Zion.

The founder and leader of that group was a remarkable woman, Henrietta Szold, daughter of a Baltimore Rabbi and a Jewish scholar in her own right. She lived to see Hadassah grow from a small group of devoted Daughters of Zion into the powerful Women's Zionist Organization of America. Hadassah brought healing to their people in the Jewish homeland through a large system of medical services. And they gave Jewish womanhood on the American continent a new and deep sense of dedication to the cause of Zion.

Henrietta Szold

Justice Louis D. Brandeis

Slow Progress

For years Zionism in America made only slight inroads into the Jewish community. Some thought of Zionism only as an immigrant's concern.

Then American-born leaders began to come to the fore. In addition to Professor Gottheil, there were Dr. Harry Friedenwald of Baltimore and Louis Lipsky of Rochester. The latter quickly made a name for himself as the fighting editor of *The Maccabean*, the first Zionist publication in America. But many leaders of American Jewry still kept aloof or took an openly hostile attitude. A decisive change, however, took place when a new, vigorous personality entered the American Jewish and Zionist scene—Louis Dembitz Brandeis.

The People's Lawyer

The annals of jurisprudence in America record Louis D. Brandeis as the "people's lawyer," who defended the interest of the "little man" against the big and powerful. Kentucky-born Brandeis was almost estranged from his Jewish background. He knew little about the Jewish people, its faith, its life.

But in his late middle years he served as an arbitrator during a garment industry strike and came to know the Jewish cloakmakers of the New York garment district. He learned about their living conditions, their problems, their background. All of a sudden, a new world opened up for him. The immigrants, who worked in the garment industry and lived in the tenement ghetto of New York's Lower East Side, were poor in worldly possessions but rich in Jewish heritage. Brandeis was first intrigued, then moved by these people, and finally felt an awakened sense of kinship with them. He started out as an arbitrator and ended up as a Jew. His next step was to become a Zionist.

The Decision

Yet this did not happen overnight. Brandeis turned to Zionism as a direct result of a personal association with Jacob de Haas, who had come to America at Herzl's behest to help organize the Zionist movement in this country. De Haas, while editor of the *Boston Jewish Advocate*, sought out

Brandeis to explain the essence and the purpose of Zionism. Brandeis was fascinated by Herzl's concept of a Jewish State. He was deeply stirred by the dramatic and tragic story of Herzl's life, and was vividly impressed by de Haas' personal account of his own dealings with Herzl.

Brandeis ascertained the facts, analyzed them, and tested them against his own conscience. He found Zionism a necessity. It was the expression of a deep-seated and yet unfulfilled desire for the freedom of the Jewish people in its own land! That land "where the Jewish life may be naturally led, the Jewish language spoken, and Jewish spirit prevail . . . is our father's land; it is Palestine!" What had disturbed quite a few, the question of whether one could be a Zionist and a good American, left Brandeis perfectly at ease! To him Judaism, Zionism, and Americanism, seemed to be one world. As he put it in one of his telling essays, "The twentieth century ideals of America have been the ideals of the Jew for twenty centuries." He developed this thought further by saying, "To be a good American, we must be better Jews, and to be better Jews, we must become Zionists."

These were the insights that determined Brandeis' decision to become a member of the Federation of American Zionists. His affiliation with the Zionist movement was made public at a convention in Cleveland in 1912.

"In Flight Before the Furies of War"

Use headings, notes & underlinings & quickly relate WWI sequence of events

AGAIN a fateful Tishah B'Av had come up in the Jewish calendar. On the <u>Ninth of Av</u> of the year 5674, corresponding to <u>August 1, 1914</u>, the Jews of Palestine heard the news that war had come to Europe. Germany and the Austro-Hungarian Empire—the Central Powers—were ranged against France, England, and Czarist Russia—the Allied Powers— in a struggle that was to last four years and was to become world-wide. The war affected Palestine when its master, Turkey, joined the Central Powers. Suddenly the *Yishuv* was plunged into serious crisis. The ports were closed, cutting off all imports so badly needed by the country. Also stopped was the flow of money from various countries to support the *Halukah* Jews, who were completely dependent on donations, particularly those from Eastern Europe. Money, foodstuff, and all commodities of daily living became scarce. Prices went up quickly. It was a grim picture. The *Yishuv* was in peril.

Turkish Persecution

Political repercussions set in almost immediately. The Turks, already hostile to Zionism, began to persecute the Zionists as enemies of the Ottoman Empire. False rumors were planted that arms were hidden in Jewish villages. Searches were instituted, and arrests were made. Zionist emblems like blue-and-white flags, Jewish National Fund stamps, and Shekel certificates were confiscated. Finally, Zionist leaders were rounded up and expelled from the country. Some were ejected as individuals, some were deported in groups. Many were sent to places in Asia Minor.

The Turks' purpose was clear—to create confusion and panic among the Jews, to impose hardships, and eventually to drive them off the land. Yet, the morale of the *Yishuv* proved to be sturdy. Settlers stood by their land and steadfastly refused to abandon it. To make sure that the fruits of their labor should not be lost, many who still were citizens of the

CHAPTER 3 *Engulfed by War*

lands of their origin became naturalized Turkish citizens so that they would be legally entitled to remain.

Still the situation was critical, not only for the Jews of Palestine, but also for the entire Zionist movement.

Zionist fortunes were at their lowest ebb, and all its achievements in Palestine were in jeopardy. Fulfillment of its objective seemed more remote than ever. Its leadership was dispersed all over war-torn Europe. At this critical moment, Zionism looked westward to the United States, which had not yet entered the great conflict.

Turning to the U.S. *Herzl hopes in U.S. & Eng*

A conference that took place on August 30th, 1914 in New York City marked the beginning of a new phase in American Zionism. It had a profound effect upon the fate of the *Yishuv* and of the Zionist movement as a whole.

One hundred and fifty delegates, representing all Zionist groups in the United States, responded to a call issued by Louis Lipsky in behalf of the American Zionist Federation and by Dr. Shmaryahu Levin on behalf of the World Zionist Organization. Shmaryahu Levin was a brilliant writer and speaker, and a one-time member of the Russian Parliament in Czarist days. A few weeks before the war broke out, Levin had come to America to represent the Zionist World Organization at the convention of the American Zionist Federation. The war made his return to Europe impossible; so he remained.

For Levin and his American associates, there was no doubt that American Zionists had to assume the initiative and responsibility in Zionist affairs. They knew that the first task was to come to the aid of the hard-pressed *Yishuv* in Palestine. A committee was established to direct the activities of the Zionist movement from America. Contacts were made with Zionist leaders and agencies in England, in Turkey, and later in neutral Denmark, where a Zionist Bureau had been set up. An emergency fund was established to give financial aid to Jews in Palestine.

The wheels for a gigantic fund-raising drive began to turn without delay, and the sums available for Zionist work in America jumped from $14,000 in the beginning to the millions by the end of the war. Such

Because of W.W.I, Bazl was ant for conf. as was Palestine. U.S. became new focal pt.

achievements were only feasible because the masses of American Jews were deeply stirred by a sense of solidarity with their brethren in Palestine. This tremendous task was carried forward by a leadership team that included Stephen Wise, Louis Lipsky, Henrietta Szold, Jacob de Haas, and Justice Julian W. Mack. Its captain was Louis D. Brandeis, whom destiny had placed at the helm of American Zionism.

Brandeis Heads Effort *Brandeis*

Brandeis plunged into Zionist work with every ounce of his boundless energy. Himself a convert to Zionism, he converted many thousands of indifferent American Jews. Many who often had mocked Zionism now flocked into its ranks.

When President Wilson appointed Brandeis to the Supreme Court in 1916, it was a matter of course that the Associate Justice had to withdraw from the political arena and forego the many involvements entailed in Zionist work. But this meant only a change of roles for Brandeis, because he continued to play a part of inestimable importance behind the scenes.

Through his intimate contact with the President and other administration leaders, Justice Brandeis paved the way for a thorough understanding of the Jewish problem by the American Government. Thus, he became instrumental in bringing about the American endorsement of the Balfour Declaration, that momentous British statement which later ushered in a new era in Jewish history.

The English Effort

While Zionist efforts in America were stepped up, a simultaneous attempt was launched in England. Here a diplomatic front was opened up for Zionism by a group of Zionist leaders, such as Naḥum Sokolow, Aḥad Ha'am, and most important, Dr. Chaim Weizmann, who had become a British citizen. These men felt that the time had come to negotiate with the British for a Jewish Palestine under British auspices. After all, the British had long displayed great sympathy for a Jewish State, as the Uganda offer by Foreign Secretary Chamberlain demonstrated in 1903. On the other hand, Turkey, as an ally of Germany, had become Britain's enemy. What the Zionist leaders were aiming for was that the British should include the liberation of Turkish-dominated Palestine and its designation as a Jewish territory as a British war objective.

With this in mind, the Zionist leaders began their contact work. After many years, Dr. Chaim Weizmann and Lord Arthur Balfour, now a member of the War Cabinet, met again. The old sentiments were still alive. "I believe, Dr. Weizmann, that when the guns stop firing, you may get your Jerusalem," Balfour remarked.

"Nothing for Myself—Palestine for My People" *Dr. Chaim Weizmann*

Indeed, Weizmann made a most valuable contribution to the British war effort. As a chemist, he discovered a method for speeding up the production of acetone, important to the manufacture of high explosives, and gave the formula to the British government. When Lloyd George, the British Prime Minister, asked Weizmann how the government might reward him, his answer was: "Nothing for myself, Palestine for my people!"

The Zion Mule Corps *Jabotinsky*

In Palestine, meanwhile, masses of Russian-born Jewish settlers and others, who were citizens of allied states, were expelled. Some—including Yitzhak Ben-Zvi and David Ben-Gurion—found asylum in the United States. The majority fled to Alexandria in Egypt, which was under British domination. There they lived in camps, waiting for the day when they could return to Palestine.

Among them was a young man, who came from an assimilated Jewish family in Russia. He was Vladimir Jabotinsky, at one time the only Jewish officer in the Russian Army. Convinced of the necessity for Jews to take an active part in the war, he proposed to the Zionist refugees in Alexandria that they form a military unit of Jewish volunteers to fight along with the British against the Turks. Jabotinsky wanted to form a regular fighting group, but the British authorities consented only to the setting up of a service unit that would bring supplies and ammunition to the front. A unit called the Zion Mule Corps was formed, and despite the British plan, it was soon in the thick of battle, going into action around Gallipoli, Turkey, where the British had sent an expeditionary force to try an attack on the Turkish heartland through the Dardanelles. The at-

Recruitment for the Jewish Legion in New York ➤➤

tempt failed, but the Jewish Battalion, as it was also known, was commended for its bravery by the British commander-in-chief. When the Gallipoli operation ended, the Zion Mule Corps was dissolved and Jabotinsky hurried to England to press for the formation of a Jewish army.

The Jewish Legion *2700 American*

Out of Jabotinsky's efforts came the Jewish Legion. Its members wore the Star of David on their battle dress. Hebrew was the language they used. The blue-and-white Zionist flag and the British flag were their standards. At first, about 900 men belonged to the unit, organized as the 38th Battalion, Royal Fusiliers, under the command of Colonel Henry Patterson. An old hand at taking charge of a Jewish unit, he had been the commander of the Zion Mule Corps.

Battalions 39 and 40 were formed shortly after. The three battalions making up the Jewish Legion were dispatched to Palestine, where British General Edmund Allenby had started a major military campaign against the Turks. Commanded by Jewish officers, these outfits drew their main strength from Jewish volunteers from America. The Zionist Organization engaged in a major recruitment drive among those who were not drafted into the American army because they were not

citizens. For, in the meantime, America had also gone to war—to swing the pendulum of victory in favor of the Allies.

A total of about 2700 volunteers from the United States signed up for the three battalions of the Jewish Legion. They were joined by volunteer groups from Russia, Argentina, South Africa, Mexico, and elsewhere.

Theirs was a glorious record which was gratefully acknowledged by the British field commanders. Their burning zeal was enthusiastically acclaimed by South Africa's Prime Minister, General Jan Christian Smuts, who declared: "It's the finest idea I have heard in my life that the Jews should themselves fight for the land of Israel."

General Smuts was not the only one who felt this way. There were many in England whose sympathies for the Zionist cause were aroused by the performance of the Zion Mule Corps. Such sentiments, later reinforced by the establishment of the Jewish Legion, were of considerable value in bringing about the Balfour Declaration.

The Balfour Declaration

[handwritten annotations: "Recognition of Jewish homeland", "at end of W.W.I 1917", "Before it"]

It took the Zionists about three years of intensive diplomatic endeavors in Great Britain, France, Italy, and the United States before the British Government issued its statement on the future of Palestine after the end of the war. The consent of the other Allied powers was needed. Opposition had come from various government circles, and also from Jewish anti-Zionists in England. They feared that a Jewish state in Palestine might endanger the Jews of Great Britain by raising a question of dual allegiance. British Jews, they argued, could not be loyal citizens of England and at the same time sympathizers and supporters of a Jewish State. A stormy public debate ensued in the English press and within the Anglo-Jewish community. It ended with the repudiation of its anti-Zionist leadership and its replacement by men of pro-Zionist attitudes. The approval of the United States was secured through the labors of

Arthur James Balfour

Foreign Office,
November 2nd, 1917

Dear Lord Rothschild,

I have much pleasure in conveying to you, on behalf of His Majesty's Government, the following declaration of sympathy with Jewish Zionist aspirations which has been submitted to, and approved by, the Cabinet

"His Majesty's Government view with favour the establishment in Palestine of a national home for the Jewish people, and will use their best endeavours to facilitate the achievement of this object, it being clearly understood that nothing shall be done which may prejudice the civil and religious rights of existing non-Jewish communities in Palestine, or the rights and political status enjoyed by Jews in any other country".

I should be grateful if you would bring this declaration to the knowledge of the Zionist Federation

*The letter
that made
Jewish History*

ionist leaders like Stephen S. Wise and Louis D. Brandeis. Finally, on November 2, 1917, the day came when the British Foreign Secretary, Arthur James Balfour, wrote the following letter to Lord Walter Rothschild: "I have much pleasure in conveying to you, on behalf of His Majesty's Government, the following declaration of sympathy with Jewish Zionist aspirations which has been submitted to and approved by the Cabinet.

"His Majesty's Government view with favour the establishment in Palestine of a national home for the Jewish people, and will use their best endeavours to facilitate the achievement of this object, it being clearly understood that nothing shall be done which may prejudice the civil and religious rights of existing non-Jewish communities in Palestine, or the rights and political status enjoyed by Jews in any other country.

"I should be grateful if you would bring this declaration to the knowledge of the Zionist Federation."

A wave of rejoicing swept through the Jewish world. Everyone felt that a turning point in Jewish history had been reached. The establishment of the Jewish State seemed to be at hand. Now apparently, Jewish history was on the threshold of a third Commonwealth. The pulse of the Jewish people beat faster. Five weeks after the Balfour Declaration, Jerusalem was liberated from the Turks by a British expeditionary force aided by troops of the Jewish Legion. When General Allenby triumphantly entered the Holy City, Jewish hopes rode with him.

To persuade various governments to endorse the Balfour Declaration was the assignment of Nahum Sokolow, leading diplomat of the Zionist movement. He accomplished his mission successfully, even receiving an expression of sympathy from the Pope, who felt confident that the Jews would provide proper protection for the interests of all religious groups in the Holy Land.

The roster of endorsing states was impressive. It embraced France, Italy, Greece, and Holland, as well as Siam, Japan, China, and others.

China was far away and may have found it easy to endorse the Declaration. But what about the Arabs nearby—in Palestine and in neighboring lands? Theirs was a story of swiftly changing attitudes.

Arab Nationalism

Before World War I, the Arabs and Jews of Palestine lived together rather peacefully. From time to time clashes occurred, usually as the result of marauders raiding Jewish settlements. Generally, the culprit was the Arab nomad, the Bedouin, for whom looting and robbing had been a way of life for centuries.

But for Arabs living in cities and villages, there came advantages when Jewish immigration began to develop. Landowning Arabs sold wasteland to the Jews at high prices. Arab farmers found new markets for their foodstuffs. Arab laborers found work. Almost all found opportunities that did not exist before large-scale Jewish immigration. While the Turks were masters of the Middle East region, the Arabs seemed to entertain few political ambitions. In the wake of the war, however, an Arab nationalist movement began to awaken all over the Arabic-speaking world. Leaders of Arab tribes and states became interested in the idea of welding the entire region into one Arab nation. In such an empire as they hoped for, there would be no room for a Jewish State as envisaged by the Balfour Declaration. There was one highly influential Arab leader, the Emir (or Prince) Feisal, son of King Hussein of the Hedjaz, who approved of the Declaration after a dramatic meeting with Dr. Weizmann in June 1918.

General Allenby, the British Commander-in-Chief, had suggested the meeting as a means of winning over to Zionist aspirations a man whose word carried great weight in the Arab world. Weizmann undertook a long wearisome journey by train, boat, car, and camel to meet the Emir near Amman, in what is now the Kingdom of Jordan.

Meeting in the Desert *With Feisel 1918–1919*

When Weizmann arrived at the Emir's encampment, there were Arab officers on camels to welcome him with gifts of fruit. On hand were many sheiks in picturesque garb, joined by Colonel T. E. Lawrence, the British soldier and adventurer, better known as "Lawrence of Arabia." Then, Dr. Weizmann was ushered into the Emir's tent, where, with the aid of an interpreter, and over cups of tea, a two-hour long conversation en-

very favorable agreement which was ultimately cancelled out by influence of other powerful Arab states

119

sued. Dr. Weizmann explained to the Arab leader the purposes and aims of the Zionist program. Weizmann encountered sympathy and understanding.

The meeting with Feisal marked the beginning of a life-long friendship that resulted finally in an agreement signed by both in London in January 1919. That agreement spoke of "the most cordial good will and understanding" of both parties, pledged "fuller guarantees for carrying into effect the British Government's declaration of the 2nd of November 1917," promised "all necessary measures to be taken to encourage and stimulate emigration of Jews into Palestine on a large scale, and to settle Jewish immigrants on the land," with the understanding "that the Arab peasant and tenant farmers shall be protected in their rights, and shall be assisted in their economic development."

Yet Feisal's favorable sentiments towards Zionism soon came to naught. Feisal dreamed of uniting the Arab world under his leadership. But rival Arab leaders would not let this happen. The Emir was forced to yield to other Arab chieftains, who sought to nullify the Balfour Declaration.

A Zionist Commission Arrives

In 1918, while the war in Palestine entered its final stage, a Zionist commission, formed at Britain's behest under Weizmann's leadership, arrived in the Holy Land. It had many tasks. First the Commission had to deal with the plight of the Jewish settlements. It sought to bring back those who had fled when Palestine was engulfed by the war. Then came plans to put the ports in working order, prepare roads, provide communications, create water supplies, install medical facilities, and take care of many other requirements of day-to-day living.

Looking far beyond the needs of the hour, the commission, consisting of Englishmen, Americans, and Italians working closely with the British military authorities, also surveyed the possibilities for future Jewish immigration and settlement. It projected ideas for the political and administrative organization of the country, and for the future of its cultural life. One of the first public demonstrations of the commission's work came while the rumbling of guns could be heard from a distance. Dr. Weizmann, on July 24, 1918, laid the cornerstone of the Hebrew University on Mount Scopus at Jerusalem.

"A Great Act of Faith"

It was rather difficult to arrange for this event though Weizmann had such a step in mind prior to his leaving London and had obtained Lord Balfour's approval. The war was still on, and at this particular time was going badly for the Allies. On the Western front the Germans had broken through and were rapidly approaching Paris. The Palestine campaign was rather fluid, following a see-saw pattern, and full of grave uncertainties. Understandably, General Allenby balked at the idea. "We may be rolled back any minute! What is the good of beginning something you may never be able to finish?" To this Weizmann replied: "This will be a great act of faith—faith in the victory which is bound to come, and faith in the future of Palestine!"

"The Act of Faith" came to pass on the afternoon of the 24th of July, 1918, and was witnessed by General Allenby, his officers, the representatives of the Christian, Moslem, and Jewish communities of Jerusalem, and of Jewish colonies throughout the land.

1918 — Heb. U. at Mount Scopus
(while war was still
brewing)

Balfour Declaration ultimately
becomes sympathic "paper"
rather than tangible physical
support.
British troops hostile:
favor Arabs

Engulfed by War

Naḥum Sokoloff:
"*Ambassador of Zionism*"

Menaḥem Mendel Ussishkin:
Pioneer and protagonist of Zionism

Chaim Weizmann:
President of the World
Zionist Organization
and First President
of the State
of Israel

THE GUNS of World War I fell silent on November 11, 1918. Governments and nations began to prepare for the peace conference that was to convene at Versailles, near Paris. Among those who hurried to Versailles to lay their national claims were the Zionists.

A Zionist bureau was set up in Paris to serve as a center of communications. A Zionist delegation came to plead the cause of the Jewish people before the tribunal. It demanded that the Balfour Declaration be endorsed by the Peace Conference, that Great Britain be appointed by the League of Nations as the mandatory power for the establishment of the Jewish national home, and that the nature of the Jewish national home be clarified before the world.

Before the Allies' Supreme Council of Ten, Naḥum Sokolow telescoped twenty centuries of Jewish homelessness into six minutes of brilliant narration. Then Dr. Weizmann followed and eloquently underscored one single fact—that at the war's end, the Jewish people was finding itself, more than any other nation, in a situation of extreme danger. And to illustrate this point Menaḥem Ussishkin, another leader of the Zionist movement, spoke on behalf of the Jews in the Ukraine, where, after the war, wild outbreaks of anti-Semitic atrocities swept that part of Russia. Ussishkin addressed the Council in Hebrew. It was the first time in 2000 years that Hebrew, as a living language, resounded from the halls of international diplomacy.

Consensus of Statesmen

The Council listened attentively and responded. The representative of France, André Tardieu, summarized its feelings by saying, "There is not the slightest difference of opinion among the Great Powers on the establishment of a Zionist state nor on giving Great Britain the Mandate."

Such an opinion was fully shared by the President of the United States, Woodrow Wilson, when he declared: "I have, before this, ex-

CHAPTER 4 *Towards a New Dawn*

pressed my personal approval of the Declaration of the British Government regarding the aspirations and historic claim of the Jewish people in regard to Palestine. I am moreover persuaded that the Allied nations, with the full concurrence of our own government and people, are agreed that in Palestine shall be laid the foundation of a Jewish commonwealth."

Dr. Weizmann thus could sum up the achievements at the Peace Conference by saying, "We have obtained full recognition of the historic title of the Jewish people in Palestine and of the Jewish right to constitute a national home there."

Was it any wonder that the delegates to the Zionist Conference held in London after the war, when hearing these reports, rose as a man, to pronounce the traditional blessing of "Sheheḥeyanu!"

Early Disillusionment

When the members of the Zionist Commission had first arrived in Palestine, they came full of anticipation, expecting the Balfour Declaration to be put into effect. What they found most disturbing was the attitude of the British Military Government.

The behavior of the British army officers who governed various parts of the newly occupied territory was plainly hostile towards the Jews. The British Army acted as if they never had heard of the Balfour Declaration. They were apparently determined to ignore these solemn assurances altogether. Outspoken anti-Jewish feelings seemed to animate the British field commanders and many of their subordinate officers. They showed open contempt for Jews, but for Arabs undisguised sympathy and favoritism.

Dr. Weizmann and the other members of the Zionist Commission were taken aback by these signs of hostility. They complained and protested—but to no avail. The Arabs, on the other hand, became quickly and keenly aware of this partiality and took advantage of it.

Tragedy was to set in soon. It was enacted in different places, but it always showed the same pattern. Agitators drove the Arabs into a frenzy of religious and political hatred against the Jews. There was the cool, studied indifference of the British military, sitting unconcernedly on the sidelines, and doing nothing to prevent outbreaks that were sure to come.

In short: Britain turns into arch enemy. Arab states become more determined w. Hidden Eng. support.

The result was bloodshed again and again. The first major clash occurred in upper Galilee in an area next to the Syrian border where three Jewish colonies, Metulla, K'far Gileadi and Tel Hai, were located. British troops had been in that region but were withdrawn.

French in Syria

The French, given the mandate of neighboring Syria, claimed that strip of land for themselves, but actually left it as no-man's land. The settlers in these three Jewish colonies decided to take matters into their own hands. Despite French claims, they wanted to see to it that this piece of land remained part of British-mandated Palestine. They resolved to stay.

What was coming could clearly be seen. Large groups of armed Bedouins closed in. They followed directives of an Arab National Committee in Damascus that aimed at a "Greater Syria," to include Palestine, which would be free from either French or British overlords.

In these critical circumstances the Jewish settlers rallied for self-defense. Their leader was Joseph Trumpeldor. *settlers under siege*

Trumpeldor *Hero settled in Palestine*

Read 2.

Trumpeldor had joined the Mule Corps—as a cripple. He had lost one arm while fighting with the Russian Army against the Japanese at the fortress of Port Arthur in 1904. Refusing removal to the rear, he continued fighting, and when the fortress fell, Trumpeldor became a Japanese prisoner of war.

In prison, he organized a school for his Jewish fellow prisoners and taught them two major subjects—the love of Zion and a desire for a better social order in the world. It was then that Trumpeldor and a few of his friends decided to go to Palestine and establish a communal settlement, where the new social order they advocated would be practiced. And so it happened. Trumpeldor, after his release from captivity, was received as a war hero by the Empress of Russia and given an artificial arm as a gift. He could have made a career in the Czarist Russian Army, but he remained true to his resolve. With some of his friends he went to Palestine and founded a settlement. But it failed. They then moved to Deganya, where Trumpeldor became a farm hand. But soon after, he met

Vladimir Jabotinsky, and during their exile in Alexandria in the First World War, the two organized the Zion Mule Corps.

After the Corps was dissolved, Trumpeldor was again at Jabotinsky's side to help organize the Jewish Legion. Ironically, he could not serve in the British unit because he was Russian-born and a cripple.

But Trumpeldor could not remain idle. In 1917, when the Czarist Empire collapsed, Trumpeldor hurried to Russia—with a scheme to bring into existence a Jewish Army of a hundred thousand. He wanted to lead the army through the Caucasus, Armenia, and Mesopotamia to conquer Palestine and claim it for the Jewish people. But the Communist Revolution of October, 1917 put a speedy end to this plan. Trumpeldor returned to Palestine alone.

At Tel Ḥai, Trumpeldor commanded a small force for the defense of the three colonies on the Palestinian-Syrian border. They repulsed waves of marauding Arab attackers and then, on March 1, 1920, they became victims of treachery. The Arabs, incapable of breaking through, sent a "peace mission" to Tel Ḥai. The Arab emissaries were received into the colony and suddenly turned into an assault force, spraying bullets among the settlers. Five of Trumpeldor's comrades, including two women, were killed instantly. Trumpeldor was fatally wounded but survived long enough to utter: *"Ein davar! Tov lamut b'ad artzenu"*—"Never mind! It is good to die for our country."

Tel Ḥai and K'far Gileadi were taken by the Arabs, but shortly afterwards were recaptured by the Jews. Trumpeldor's heroic stand helped to keep them part of Palestine. The tragedy at Tel Ḥai proved to be the first episode in a design of violence, prepared and executed by the Arab National Committee. Riots in Jerusalem in April, 1920 were next.

Even before it happened, the *Yishuv* knew that trouble would break out on the first day of Passover, which coincided with Easter and the Moslem festival of Nebi Musa, "the Prophet Moses."

On that day, Arabs customarily assembled in Jerusalem for a procession to a hill where Moslems believe Moses is buried.

At the Dome of the Rock on Mount Moriah, popularly called the Mosque of Omar, thousands of Arabs converged to begin the celebration. They listened to sermons that turned out to be open calls to acts of violence against the Jews. When the customary procession formed, it made its way to the Jewish Quarter of the old city and rapidly disintegrated into riotous mobs, racing through the streets, attacking and killing Jewish residents and plundering Jewish property. Though many British troops were in the city, none came to stop the outbreaks, about which they had known long in advance. They appeared only to arrest Jabotinsky, who, with a group of young men, had rushed to the defense of the Jewish quarter.

Nothing could demonstrate more clearly the partiality of the British military. They added to the injustice by sentencing Jabotinsky to a fifteen-year prison term. Later he was granted amnesty and released.

"The first pogrom under the British Flag," as Dr. Weizmann, in a moment of bitterness, called the outbreaks in Jerusalem, was the result of a political calculation on the part of the Arab leaders. They knew that very shortly the Allied Powers would hold a conference in San Remo, Italy, to deliberate on the future fate of defeated Turkey. They correctly guessed that the Balfour Declaration would come up for consideration and thought that a show of force in Palestine would work against it.

The attempt failed. The Allied Powers refused to be pressured. Instead they acted to confirm the Balfour Declaration, making Great Britain the mandatory power and incorporating this decision into the peace treaty with Turkey.

Another highly important decision resulted. The military rule in Palestine came to an end. In its place a civilian administration was named to take over. A High Commissioner was appointed, and the man selected was a Jew and pro-Zionist, Sir Herbert Samuel, who had previously held various high positions in the British Government.

Sir Herbert Samuel *Jewish High Commissioner who favored Arab*

The news from San Remo caused even more rejoicing among Jews than did the Balfour Declaration. When Dr. Weizmann returned to London, a crowd surged to greet him with a Torah scroll in their arms.

The new High Commissioner brought Jewish and Arab representatives together to hear an official pronouncement of his mission. The task of the mandatory power, he said, was "to secure the gradual establish-

in attempting to be "fair".

late ally 27-135

ment of a National Home for the Jewish people." And this promise was coupled with the solemn assurance that all safeguards would be taken "to protect the rights and the interests of the Arab people of Palestine."

"Comfort Ye, My People . . ."

On the Sabbath following Tishah B'Av, the High Commissioner made his way through Jerusalem's ancient quarters to join his fellow Jews in prayer at one of the city's oldest synagogues. Excitement gripped the worshippers as he was called up to the Torah as *Maftir*, to chant the scriptural reading for the day. Wrapped in his *Tallit*, the British High Commissioner read with a firm voice the words of the prophet Isaiah, "Comfort ye, comfort ye, my people, saith your God."

But there was little comfort for the *Yishuv* to draw from Sir Herbert Samuel's administration, as the record of his five-year term of office proved.

The Record

Some measures were taken towards creating the National Home. Hebrew was proclaimed, along with Arabic and English, to be one of Palestine's official languages. New roads were opened. A network of telephone and telegraph lines was established. Hospitals were built. Jewish hands planted forests on a landscape that had lain barren for centuries.

In his effort to demonstrate his impartiality because he was a Jew, the High Commissioner had a tendency to lean over backwards and sup-

Sir Herbert Samuel:
"A Modern Nehemia"

port the Arabs. He retained in his service most of those British officials who were notorious for their anti-Jewish feelings and pro-Arab inclinations. He permitted the release from prison of those Arab ringleaders who had been responsible for the bloody outbreaks in Jerusalem. One of them who escaped imprisonment and fled abroad was even permitted to return to Palestine. More amazing still, he was appointed by the High Commissioner to the post of Grand Mufti in Jerusalem, a position of extraordinary power and influence in the Moslem world. Herbert Samuel was apparently determined to win the Arabs' favor at all costs. This became strikingly clear when he ordered all further Jewish immigration stopped immediately after the Arabs had staged—this time in Jaffa—another bloody riot. Instead of punishing the guilty and crushing the disturbances, he clamped down forcefully on the development of the *Yishuv*, while yielding to Arab threats of terror. The more he tried to court the Arabs, the more insolent they became and the more insatiable were their demands. Though Herbert Samuel was not responsible, it was during his *but* regime that Palestine was drastically reduced in area. Its largest part, the territory on the East bank of the River Jordan, was given away to an

Arab ruler by the British Government in a deal with the politically ambitious Hashemite family. They set up Prince Feisal as King of Iraq and his brother Abdullah as Emir of what became known as Transjordan, later the Hashemite Kingdom of Jordan. Thus Palestine, which had included land on both sides of the Jordan since ancient times, was now dismembered.

Hebrew University

Sir Herbert's tenure as High Commissioner was crowned by one event of historic splendor, the solemn opening of the Hebrew University.

More than 7000 people filled the natural amphitheatre on the northeast slope of Mount Scopus on April 1, 1925 to share in an unforgettable experience. In a colorful academic procession, representatives of universities from all parts of the world saluted the new school. The central figure was Lord Balfour, now seventy-seven, who had made a pilgrimage to the Jewish National Home. There were many other great men,

Samuels, in trying to be fair, "allows" palestine" to be reduced in size —

East Bank of Jordan River becomes Trans-Jordan (later Jordan)

Towards a New Dawn

including Aḥad Ha'am, the prophet of cultural Zionism, and Ḥayim Naḥman Bialik, the poet, and, of course, Chaim Weizmann, who said this would be "the university of the future."

Against the Declaration

The battle for the abolition of the Balfour Declaration was waged by the Arabs with increasing intensity. The League of Nations formally confirmed the Declaration in 1922 and made its substance the content of an internationally affirmed covenant.

But in Palestine, outbreaks of violence by the Arabs were kept up to terrorize the Jewish population and to intimidate the British government so that it would submit to Arab demands.

In Great Britain, the Arabs found powerful helpers among some influential politicians and newspaper owners. A propaganda barrage was

laid down demanding that the Balfour Declaration be
deed, a motion to repeal the Declaration was carried by a
House of Lords. However, in the House of Commons, the
legislative body of the British Parliament, the motion was d

An Arab delegation made its way also into the fore
Paris and Rome and also into the Vatican. They found willi
pathy, and encouragement. Political counter-pressures mour
British Government was caught in the dilemma of keeping fa   with the
Jews while simultaneously keeping peace with the Arabs. Finally it came
out with a statement signed by Winston Churchill, then Colonial Secre-
tary. Known as Churchill's White Paper, it was published in June 1922.
It marked the beginning of the end of the Balfour Declaration.

The White Paper stated that it was not the intent of the Balfour
Declaration to make Palestine the national home *of* the Jewish people,
but rather to give the Jewish people a national home *in* Palestine. Therefore, the immigration of Jews would be limited to what was called "the
economic absorptive capacity" of the country. Only such a number of
immigrants would be permitted to enter as was deemed economically
feasible. The statement recommended that a Jewish Agency and an Arab
Agency take care of the needs of their respective people. Churchill's
White Paper was presented to the Zionist Executive for approval. The
Zionists, though most reluctantly, approved it. But the Arabs rejected it.
Though it was for their sole benefit, the Arabs would have no part of it.
But the British went ahead anyway and proposed to impose immigration
restrictions based on the principle of "absorptive capacity."

This presented a real challenge to the Zionist movement. If the "absorptive capacity" could be increased, if more capital flowed into the
country, if more opportunities for development were created, and if
more land was in Jewish hands, there would be more "absorptive capacity."

The Challenge and the Movement

Was the Zionist movement ready to pick up this challenge? The last
Zionist Congress before World War I took place in 1913 in Vienna.
Then seven fateful years followed, during which the work of the World
Zionist Movement continued in various countries, but without a Con-

← *The Hebrew University
Opens on Mount Scopus*

Towards a New Dawn

ow the time had come for the Zionist World Organization to
up where it had left off. However, the disruptions caused by the
ar and its aftermath presented too many obstacles for the convening of
a Zionist World Congress. Instead, a preliminary conference was held in
London during the summer of 1920.

Here the Zionist leaders of many countries met once again. Many
oldtimers, including the aged Max Nordau, were among them, and there
were also many new faces. The United States sent a delegation of forty,
headed by Justice Louis D. Brandeis.

The London Conference reflected a wide difference of opinion between European and American Zionist leaders on the course of action to
follow.

The American delegates, deeply influenced by Brandeis, soon found
themselves at odds with many of the European delegates, who felt that
the Zionist movement should pursue vigorously its political efforts.
Brandeis and his friends saw it differently. For them the political work
now assumed secondary importance, since the Balfour Declaration had already provided a political solution. They wanted all energies to be devoted to Jewish colonization in Palestine. They also felt strongly that
the Jewish National Home, aside from all its publicly owned enterprises,
should make room for private enterprise—with businessmen investing their
own money for their own profit. And they believed that not only Zionists should have a voice in the Zionist World Organization, but also non-
Zionists.

These views were sharply opposed by European delegates for whom,
in spite of the Balfour Declaration and the San Remo Decision, the political struggle for the establishment of the Jewish National Home was
far from over. In addition, they firmly believed in the priority of Zionist
convictions over all economic considerations. What was needed first was
more believers in the Zionist ideal, and not investors in the land reclaimed
and regained by Zionism. The economy of the country, to be sure, was
of paramount importance. Precisely for that reason, they held, Jewish
Palestine could only be economically secure if its economy were guaran-
teed by funds raised by the Zionist movement throughout the world and
if those funds were spent according to a budget planned and adopted by

*Two movements at Zionist Congress
of 1922 in London*
1. European — Political Struggle for homeland
*2. Investment in land
& expansion*

the World Zionist Organization. Therefore, the functions of this body should be increased to meet the demands of the new situation.

The spokesman for these views was Dr. Chaim Weizmann. He was elected at the London Conference President of the World Zionist Organization. His political associate, Naḥum Sokolow, was elected Chairman of the Executive.

Weizmann and Sokolow became the key leaders of an administration in which the Americans were conspicuous by their absence. The clash of views had produced a rift that widened a year later into a far-reaching breach.

What had brought this clash to a head in London was the question of setting up a central fund from contributions to be raised from Jews everywhere. This fund was to be known as the Keren Hayesod or the Foundation Fund. The monies raised were to assure the financial foundations of the *Yishuv* for the next five years. Notwithstanding the opposition of the American Zionists the plan was adopted and every Jew was called upon to contribute to the Keren Hayesod. The purpose of this new fund was to take care of the "religious, cultural, social, economic, agricultural, and general welfare of the Jewish settlers and inhabitants in Palestine." In other words, everything pertaining to the development of the Jewish National Home was to be financed by the Keren Hayesod, except the purchase of land, which was left to the Keren Kayemet, the Jewish National Fund.

Taking the Issue to America

The success of the Keren Hayesod would depend mainly on the response of the American Zionists. Their leaders had opposed the plan; the movement, however, had adopted it. What to do now? Dr. Weizmann, as President of the Zionist Organization, felt that he had to bring the Keren Hayesod into existence everywhere. He decided to journey to America.

Weizmann came in illustrious company. Albert Einstein, already famous for his Theory of Relativity, had joined a group of Zionist leaders participating in Weizmann's trip to America. However, Einstein was mainly interested in gaining support for the Hebrew University not yet built.

[handwritten annotation:] ...t faction truggles for next 10 years

Enthusiastic acclaim greeted Weizmann and Einstein on their arrival in New York. Thousands lined the streets to give them a rousing welcome as they began a cross-country tour. While the Zionist masses were jubilant over Weizmann's arrival, the leaders of the American Zionist organization adopted a rather reserved attitude. They proceeded to negotiate once more on those matters that had been left unsolved in London. Again, there was no accord. The negotiations failed.

Storm in Cleveland

The whole conflict came up for debate at the next national convention of the Zionist Organization of America, held in 1921 in Cleveland. So passionate was the debate that it lasted three days, and the administration led by Brandeis' friend, Judge Julian Mack, was overwhelmingly defeated. Judge Mack resigned from the presidency. Other officers who were members of the Brandeis group followed suit. The Justice himself resigned as Honorary President.

Thus, all of what was known as the "Brandeis Group" withdrew from the activities of the Zionist Organization, staying away almost a decade, until in 1930, again at a convention in Cleveland, that group returned to full participation in the movement.

Brandeis severed all official ties with the organization he had brought

to new life and new heights of achievement. However, he plunged himself into a variety of efforts to help in the upbuilding of the Jewish land. The Palestine Cooperative Company, the Palestine Economic Council, the Palestine Endowment Funds, and the Palestine Development League all were his creation. He did not forsake his love for Zion.

A New Regime

When the Zionist Organization of America was split asunder in Cleveland, a group of new and younger men stepped into the breach to take over. A new standard-bearer emerged in the person of Louis Lipsky, the leader of the victorious opposition.

It was Lipsky's powerful personality that now shaped the course of American Zionism and of the Zionist Organization. It grew in numbers, in strength and influence. Indeed, a major political victory was achieved when the United States Congress adopted a resolution endorsing the Balfour Declaration in 1922.

Under the new regime, the Keren Hayesod was firmly established. Its director was Emanuel Neumann, a founder of Young Judea who was later to become one of the leading figures in American Zionism.

The achievements of the Keren Hayesod in America surpassed all expectations. Millions of dollars were raised without which the development of Jewish Palestine would have been virtually impossible. The American Jews gave willingly, regularly, and generously. Thus, the Keren Hayesod developed into the main financial instrument of the Zionist Movement. A steady stream of dollars flowed into the *Yishuv*, which steadily expanded. But dollars alone were not enough to rebuild the Jewish land.

← *Zionist Mission to America:*
from left to right:
Menaḥem M. Ussishkin, Dr. Chaim Weizmann,
Mrs. Weizmann, Professor Albert Einstein,
Mrs. Einstein, Dr. Ben Zion Mosensohn, on
arrival in New York on S.S. Rotterdam, 1921

135

Series of Aliyot

1st Aliyah in
1800's —
2nd - Herzl —
      new
      Nationalism
$ 4th 3rd - Aliyah —
             1920's
             Halutzim
             (pioneers)

5th - Hitler 1933

UNIT FOUR

How the Jewish Homeland Developed

"THE land is dear, but when we speak of Palestine there is something dearer still—Time!"

Thus argued Menahem Mendel Ussishkin from the platform of the 12th Zionist Congress. He was defending the purchase of 30,000 Dunam (about 7500 acres) of land in the eastern Emek, the valley of Jezreel, in Palestine. Since the days of the prophetess Deborah, every inch of the valley was drenched with memories of Jewish glories and disasters. This land now returned to Jewish ownership. Ussishkin and Dr. Arthur Ruppin, the Zionist movement's architect of agricultural development, were the prime movers in this transaction. It was approved by the Congress, the first to meet after World War I, which convened in Karlsbad in Czechoslovakia.

Ussishkin spoke about time because time had been running out in Palestine and in Europe. In Russia, terror, pogroms, and persecution stalked the Jewish communities while civil war raged. The Czarist forces engaged in wholesale destruction of Jewish life and property. The victorious Communists brought new agonies upon Russian Jewry. And they made it difficult for Jews to leave the country.

But many escaped, using all possible routes of flight across borders, rivers, and mountains. Those who went to Palestine formed the backbone of what was called the *Third Aliyah* (1920–1924) of about 48,000 immigrants. They were young and determined.

Challenging the Wilderness

In a patch of wilderness surrounded by malaria-ridden swamp, a group of 35 young men and women arrived in September, 1921 to do battle with the forces of nature. They pitched tents and started draining off the

CHAPTER 1 *Advances and Setbacks*

swamps as a first step towards making the area livable. On the following day they were joined by another group of forty. A camp sprang up with thirty-five tents fenced off by wire. The face of the wilderness was changing.

Such were the beginnings of a settlement that one day became a flourishing village called Ein Ḥarod.

A Kibbutz

It was founded as a *Kibbutz*, a type of settlement in which the inhabitants own alike and share alike everything they possess. Working together, the settlers till the soil, tend vineyards and beehives, grow vegetables and fruits, breed chickens, and nurse flowers and trees. They also do carpentry, repair agricultural machinery and run a smithy and a printing press, thus combining agriculture and industry. In time, Ein Ḥarod developed rich cultural activities, including a special art center for painters and sculptors, and an open-air theatre for concerts and drama. For Ein Ḥarod became the cultural center of the eastern part of the Valley. It is also the seat of Ha-Kibutz Ha-M'uḥad, the United *Kibbutz*, an organization of the large *Kibbutzim*, whose purpose is joint planning.

Ein Ḥarod was first to be wrested from the wilderness by the men and women of the *Third Aliyah*. In the very same year six other settlements were established in the Emek, and many more followed in future years.

A New Type of Jew—the Ḥalutz

The original settlers all came from *G'dud Ha-Avodah*, the Labor Legion, organized by Joseph Trumpeldor, whose name lives on in Tel Yosef, another *Kibbutz* in the region. Trumpeldor rallied men and women willing

to work under dangerous and difficult conditions in order to achieve a new social order. A new type of Jew, the *Ḥalutz* (pioneer) came into being. Jewish youth all over the world flocked in tens of thousands to the banners of an organization whose members dedicated themselves to pioneering in Palestine. The organization, *"He-Ḥalutz,"* became active in many countries and held its first convention in Danzig in 1924. A sense of burning zeal had brought Jewish youth into the ranks of the *Ḥalutz* movement. But hardships of *Ḥalutz* life in Palestine soon made it clear that enthusiasm alone was not enough. Needed most urgently was practical training for the pioneering work ahead. An intensive program of preparation and training (*Hakhsharah*) was therefore launched in many countries. *Hakhsharah* farms were established to prepare young people for the communal living that awaited them in Palestine. City-bred youngsters learned how to farm and work with their hands. They learned the meaning of Zionism and, of course, the language of daily living was Hebrew.

While the main strength of *He-Ḥalutz* was concentrated in Europe, primarily in Poland, the movement soon reached across the Atlantic. In the United States, David Ben Gurion and Itzḥak Ben Zvi tried, during World War I, to stimulate interest in *Ḥalutz* life. But it was only after the war was over, that *He-Ḥalutz* gained a foothold in America.

Hakhsharah gave Jews a new appreciation of physical work. It helped abolish prejudices against manual labor held by many Jews who felt that only business and the professions were worthy occupations.

*"Kibbutzniks"
on the way
to work*

◀◀ *Ein Ḥarod:
A Kvutza in
the Plains of
Jezreel at the
Foot of Mount
Gilboa*

The Fourth Aliyah

From the Polish middle-class came a new wave of immigration, the *Fourth Aliyah*, in 1925 and the four years that followed. Old-timers in the *Yishuv* tended to look down on these newcomers because they were mainly businessmen who shunned the hard life of the *Halutz* and wanted to continue in Palestine the type of life they had left in Poland. In the first year alone, 36,000 new immigrants came to Palestine. It was not sheer idealism that moved many to turn to the *Yishuv*. Poland had adopted a policy of anti-Semitism, and many Jews went to Palestine simply because they could not enter the United States. From the beginning, most of these middle-class immigrants flocked to Tel Aviv.

The First All-Jewish City

Tel Aviv, the first all-Jewish city, almost doubled its population during the first year of the *Fourth Aliyah*, nearing a population of 50,000. It had its beginning in 1909 when a small group of Jewish residents of Jaffa decided to build a suburb to the north on sand dunes near the Mediterranean. The group consisted of sixty people, most of whom were doctors, lawyers, teachers, and businessmen. Among them was Meir Dizengoff, who was to become the first mayor of Tel Aviv.

A row of houses went up on property acquired with the aid of a loan from the Jewish National Fund. New houses were added rapidly. After

"Building on Sand": The founding of Tel Aviv in 1909

A view of the city today ➡

five years there were 2000 inhabitants, and soon a Hebrew high school, "Herzliah," the first Jewish secondary school in the country, was started.

But Tel Aviv suffered during the war. It was totally evacuated by the Turks because its people were considered sympathetic to the Allies. By 1919, however, the population had returned and soon reached 3000. It continued to climb rapidly and constantly, becoming the pride of the *Yishuv*, and of Jews throughout the world with its Jewish mayor, a police force, court, fire brigade, and other municipal institutions. On the Sabbath all communal life came to a standstill. Purim and other Jewish holidays were public occasions.

Boom and Bust

The newcomers invested their money in business and real estate. All over the city, houses went up, factories were constructed, and large investments were made in orange groves and other property. A real boom was on.

Soon a depression set in. Many businesses were lost. The value of real estate fell. Houses in the process of construction were abandoned. Many lost their jobs. Soup kitchens had to be set up to feed the hungry.

As a result, immigration almost stopped. And many emigrated from Palestine and turned to other countries, some even returning to Poland.

As bad as conditions were in the cities, the agricultural settlements felt little of the severe economic crisis. The Keren Kayemet and the Keren Hayesod both continued to operate effectively. Now *Halutzim* arrived and were promptly settled on J.N.F.-owned land. The Keren Hayesod advanced money. Compared with previous settlement efforts on the land, the process was slow, but it was sound and solid.

The Keren Hayesod also helped new industries to develop, and aided schools and hospitals in cooperation with Hadassah, the Women's Zionist Organization of America.

Not for Zionists Alone

Weizmann felt that the time had come when the rebuilding of the Jewish land should cease to be the responsibility of the Zionists alone, but of all Jews. Palestine deserved the support of all, whether they believed in a Jewish state, as did the Zionists, or whether they saw it only as a great humanitarian effort for homeless Jews, as did non-Zionists opposed to the idea of Jewish nationhood, but in favor of a cultural homeland. To win the support of all Jews was now the object of Zionist leaders.

The League of Nations, in entrusting the Palestine Mandate to Great Britain, urged the setting up of a "Jewish Agency" representing *all* Jews willing to assist in the establishment of a Jewish national home. The British Government agreed to recognize the World Zionist Organization temporarily as "The Jewish Agency for Palestine."

How to broaden the Jewish Agency to include all Jews and gain their financial support was the problem. Negotiations with the non-Zionists were to be undertaken.

The issue aroused much debate. There were many who feared that Zionism would be "watered down" if such a plan would be put into effect, and that the non-Zionists possibly would gain domination over developments in Palestine. Before long, Dr. Weizmann was confronted by a formidable opposition.

Revolt Against Weizmann

[handwritten: Remember! Weizmann had fought against Herzl / Uganda idea]

As if history had repeated itself, Weizmann, leader of the "democratic faction" that revolted against Herzl, was now challenged by a group that first called itself "democratic" and later changed its name to "Radical Zionists." They bitterly opposed Weizmann's plan for an enlarged Jewish Agency. So did another new party that had appeared. The "Revisionists," led by Jabotinsky, pressed for a "revision" of Zionist policies. Striving for what was called a "Maximum Zionism," the Revisionists demanded a Jewish state on *both* sides of the Jordan under the "auspices of a Jewish majority," and also pressed for the setting up again of the Jewish Legion as a special unit of the British military forces. They wanted no part in a Jewish Agency composed of both Zionists and non-Zionists.

The debate went on for eight years and came to a head at the 15th Congress in Basle in 1927. An overwhelming majority decided to proceed with Weizmann's plan and to organize a Council of the Jewish Agency that should consist of an equal number of Zionists and non-Zionists. But there were a number of conditions: Non-Zionists would have to agree to increasing immigration, purchasing land as public property of the Jewish people, adopting the *Kibbutz* system for settlements, and recognizing Hebrew as the language of the country. Also, the President of the World Zionist Organization would serve as the president of the Jewish Agency. The non-Zionists agreed.

[handwritten margin notes: Parties: / Weizmann – Democratic / Radical Zionists / Revisionists → / a. Palestine (both sides of Jordan) / b. wanted no part of Jewish agency of non/zionists / c. Jewish legion]

Soldier, Writer, Leader:
Vladimir Jabotinsky

143

With non-Zionists participating, the newly enlarged Jewish Agency was convened for its first session in Zurich in August, 1929. It was a great moment for Jewish unity. Among those participating were Louis Marshall, a leader of American Jewry at that time; Lord Melchett, one of the outstanding representatives of British Jewry; Albert Einstein, the great scientist; Léon Blum, leader of the French Labor Party and future Premier of France; and Oscar Wasserman, one of the prominent personalities of German Jewry. It was a brilliant array of talent and wealth.

But the Zurich assembly proved to be merely a brilliant assemblage, and its promise remained largely unfulfilled. What primarily caused the collapse of those great expectations was, first of all, the death in quick succession of Louis Marshall and Lord Melchett, prime movers among the non-Zionists, and secondly, the onset of the great depression in the United States. These were the main reasons for failure. The new agency produced neither new money nor manpower. Still, it was a brave and, to a certain extent, successful attempt to unite all Jews in a common cause.

A Non-Zionist
in the leadership
of the Jewish Agency:
Louis Marshall

ALMOST at the very time the enlarged Jewish Agency held its first meeting in Zurich, Arab riots broke out in Palestine.

It began at the Wailing Wall, sacred to Jews throughout the ages as a remnant of the ancient Temple, and claimed by the Arabs as a Moslem holy place. According to Moslem tradition, Mohammed stopped in Jerusalem on his way to heaven and tied his horse to the Wailing Wall.

A dispute over the Wall's rightful ownership had been the source of frequent incidents between Jews and Arabs. Jewish religious services often were disturbed. As more and more incidents occurred, Arab leaders began to arouse their followers with all sorts of fantastic charges. Wild rumors were afoot—that the Jews planned to attack the famous Dome of the Rock near the Wailing Wall, or other Moslem holy places, and were trying to drive the Moslem faith out of Palestine. As such rumors spread, they stirred up fanatical hatred among the Arabs, and created deep anxiety among the Jews, who knew a showdown was at hand. *Arab uprising*

On Tishah B'Av, in August, 1929, many pious Jews gathered as usual at the Wailing Wall to chant the ritual lamentations. In addition, Jewish youth turned out in great numbers for a peaceful demonstration of the right of Jews to pray there. The following day, Arabs gathered at the Wall for a counter-demonstration. Arab agitators stirred them to action. Infuriated, the Arab mob seized a large number of Jewish prayer books and tore them to pieces, littering the holy place.

During the next few days, the British authorities failed to act, although they must have known what was to follow. Finally, the blow fell. One week after Tishah B'Av, an Arab uprising shook the country. In Jerusalem heavily armed Arab bands terrorized the Jewish population and struck down a number of people in murderous assaults. Bloody riots enveloped the old Jewish quarters of Safed, claiming a toll of forty-five Jewish lives. Haifa and Jaffa became the scenes of murder, arson, and looting. Rural settlements were attacked and six were completely de-

including Hebron

CHAPTER 2 *Upheaval From Within and Without*

stroyed. The worst was in Hebron, where more than sixty men, women, and children were victims of mass murder. Here, like in Safed, the old and weak Jewish inhabitants could offer no resistance. Casualty figures were lower in other places only through the efforts of Jewish self-defense units, which organized to become the Haganah.

Too Little and Too Late

And the British—where were they when the whole Yishuv seemed to go up in flames? They were either absent or utterly ineffective. At long last, when the situation had gotten completely out of hand, the British authorities called for reinforcements from Egypt. But the troops took about a week to arrive and failed completely to deal with the turmoil. The British countermeasures were too little and too late.

Before the riots ended, there were one hundred and thirty-three dead and three hundred and sixty-seven wounded among the Jews. The Arabs counted one hundred and sixteen dead and two hundred and thirty-two wounded. Property damage was enormous.

The British Government finally acted, not against the Arabs, but the Jews. Three thousand certificates providing for the entry of new Jewish

Arabs Demonstrate—1929

settlers, and already approved by the High Commissioner, were revoked. Though the High Commissioner held Arab leaders responsible and some were brought to trial for the riots and convicted, few death sentences were carried out. More important, the ringleaders who actually had instigated the bloodshed were left untouched. This was not all. It was declared that Jewish immigration and colonization were indirectly responsible for the outbreaks. Though the Arabs had attacked first, their leaders, and among them the ill-famed Grand Mufti of Jerusalem, were absolved of guilt and complicity by a British commission of inquiry.

Commissions and Papers

This investigation was the first in a series of British commissions, with their reports and white papers, that had the effect of restricting the development of the Jewish National Home, limiting the scope of the Jewish Agency, and nullifying the Balfour Declaration. In fact, one white paper asserted "that the Jewish National Home is not meant to be the principal feature of the Mandate." This led to a complete break of the World Zionist Organization with the Mandatory Power. Dr. Weizmann, known as a staunch supporter of England, felt called upon to resign as president of the World Zionist Organization and of the Jewish Agency.

In 1931, Prime Minister Ramsay MacDonald announced a change of heart and promised that Jewish immigration into Palestine would be resumed. Weizmann returned to office, but he was forced out again by vigorous opposition from within the Zionist ranks. Composed of a number of parties at the Congress, the opposition was sparked by the Revisionist Party, which denounced Weizmann for his moderation. The Revisionist Party had increased more than tenfold in numbers since it first entered the arena of Zionist politics at the Congress in Vienna in 1925. Its leader was Vladimir Jabotinsky.

The Zionist Parties

The Revisionists hammered away at the leadership of the Zionist movement for not moving more quickly and more forcefully to secure Palestine for the Jews. They fought bitterly with the spoken and printed word, and sometimes with their fists. It was a bewildering variety of parties that made up the movement in those days. There were the General Zionists, divided between liberals and conservatives. There were the religious Zionists, organized into the Mizrachi Organization and the religious workers group, the Hapoel Hamizrachi. Strongest of all was the Zionist labor movement, the Poale Zion, chief opponent of the Revisionists. Thus, the political pendulum of the Zionist Movement swung from the extreme right of the Revisionists to the extreme left of the Socialist group within the labor party.

Histadrut

Organized Jewish labor had developed a powerful voice over the years. Histadrut came into being in 1920 in Haifa, when about forty-five hundred members banded together into the General Federation of Labor. Their expressed aim was to form "an organization of Jewish settlers who live by their own labor without exploiting others and who aim to establish a Jewish Commonwealth in Palestine."

Histadrut regulated working conditions. It called for equal rights for women and between Jews and Arabs. It organized a bureau of immigration to train and place workers in settlements. It maintained a labor exchange. It handled wholesale buying and marketing for all settlements. It built cooperative apartment houses in the cities, and developed industries. It set up a bank and an insurance company, and a system of medical care for all its members. It established schools for children and adults. It published a newspaper, and founded a theatre and sports organization.

As Histadrut grew to a commanding position within the *Yishuv*, it attracted a wide membership of varied political beliefs. Soon, separate parties developed within the organization. One, the Palestine Labor Party, or *Mifleget Poalei Eretz Yisrael*, better known as the Mapai, was most important. Its leaders included David Ben-Gurion, Moshe Shertok (Sharett), and Yitzḥak Ben-Zvi.

Partisan Passions Explode

Antagonism and hatred marked the rivalry between the Labor Party and the Revisionists. This exploded into violence one night in June, 1933, when a Labor Party leader, Dr. Chaim Arlosoroff, was struck down by assassins' bullets while strolling with his wife on the beach of Tel Aviv. Dr. Arlosoroff, head of the political department of the Jewish Agency, had been assailed by the Revisionists for what they called a "lack of national spirit." They condemned him for his mild attitude towards Great Britain, and bitterly accused him of inaction.

Not only the Yishuv, but the entire Zionist Movement, was thrown into turmoil by the murder. Two young men, pointed out by Mrs. Arlosoroff as the attackers of her husband and identified as members of the Revisionist party, were arrested and brought to trial. Finally, the defendants were acquitted for lack of evidence, but the conflict continued. Partisanship exploded time and again in riotous exchanges of charges. As the violent hostility between the two camps shook the Yishuv and the Zionist Movement, the Jewish Agency flatly denied immigration certificates to Revisionist applicants. Eventually the Revisionists withdrew entirely from the World Zionist Organization and formed a group of their own, the *New* Zionist Organization, headed, of course, by Jabotinsky.

Design for Annihilation

A few weeks before his death, Dr. Arlosoroff had been in Europe for the Jewish Agency on a highly controversial mission. Hitler had come into

Delegates to the Founding Convention of the Histadrut, Haifa, 1902

Automation of Horror:
The Crematorium at
Dachau Concentration Camp

power in Germany and the persecution of the Jews had begun. Whether the Zionists should try to negotiate with the Nazis was the hotly disputed question.

The Nazi horror, visited on every European country conquered by the Germans during World War II and responsible for the death of six million Jews by 1945, started in Germany with the enactment of the Nuremberg laws. These did away with all political, economic, and social rights of the Jews in Germany. The Jew practically ceased to be a citizen. He was classified as an inferior person and an enemy of the state.

The Fifth Aliyah

Many German Jews thought the terror would pass. Others lacked the means to leave. But some escaped, seeking shelter all over Europe, across the ocean in the New World, and large numbers turned to Palestine. Over fifty thousand found a haven in Palestine in 1933 and 1934. They became part of a new powerful immigration wave, the *Fifth Aliyah.*

Jews who left Germany were not permitted to take money out of the country. But under what was called a Transfer Agreement, worked out between the Zionists and the Nazis, Jews could trade their property for German machinery and other products that would be shipped to Palestine. There, a bank, the Anglo-Palestine Company, gave them money for the products.

To many Jews the very idea of Zionists making a deal with the Nazis was intolerable. Better to lose all than negotiate with a government that outlawed its Jewish citizens and deprived them of their possessions. Nevertheless, this arrangement made it possible for refugees to get some funds out of Germany in order to build a new life. Goods with a total value of about eight million pounds ($40,000,000) were transferred. This exchange was indeed of considerable benefit to the Fifth Aliyah, which had started in 1929, and which was greatly stepped up by the advent of the Nazis.

Over one hundred thousand immigrants came with the *Fifth Aliyah* from 1933 through 1935. This number increased to three hundred thousand mostly from Germany at the outbreak of World War II.

"We should thank God several times a day that there is Palestine to take in the German Jews," stated James G. MacDonald, who was appointed by the League of Nations as High Commissioner for German Refugees. Palestine became an asylum for tens of thousands of youngsters, rescued by the *Youth Aliyah*, whose parents had to stay behind. This project was catalyzed by Henrietta Szold, Hadassah's great lady, who had settled in Palestine and had played a major role in the work of the Jewish Agency. Youth Aliyah, with a splendidly organized study-work-play program, was her crowning achievement. It brought healing, health, and strength to more than fifty-five thousand youths.

With the influx of the immigrants from Germany, new energies poured into the country. Business and professional men brought new resources into the Palestine economy, and introduced new skills, new methods, and a new sense of enterprise. They brought a new economic boom across the country which created many new opportunities for Jews and Arabs alike. In fact, many Arabs from areas outside Palestine were so attracted that they slipped across the borders into the land.

Mother of Youth Aliyah: Henrietta Szold

Youth Aliyah from Berlin and Teheran

These were years of high prosperity and of peace, punctured occasionally by incidents of Arab hostility. By and large, the process of building the Jewish National Home was on the upswing.

In three years alone the Jewish population had jumped by one hundred and thirty thousand. Tel Aviv passed the hundred thousand mark. Jerusalem's new city teemed with urban development and the energies of modern civilization. Haifa, in surroundings of breathtaking natural beauty, had become, the country's new port, its gateway. Pioneers continued to fire the imagination of their fellow Jews. The Huleh Swamp District in upper Galilee was purchased and soon was dotted with new colonies, and bursting with new life. All over Palestine things began to look up for Jews and Arabs.

For the Arab masses, a new life was in the making to replace the dreary existence they had known for centuries. Many began to enjoy better work and pay, better health and housing, and decent living conditions. But Arab leaders became ill at ease with the prospect of losing their hold on the Arab masses. The peasants and Bedouins were used to living in abject poverty, exploited by feudal overlords and rich landowners. Social changes brought by Jews might stir them to claim their own basic rights to a better existence. The Arab leaders decided to act.

Arab Ally—Italy

The Arab leadership carried forward its plans by carefully planting rumors and promises of plunder. It found a highly interested partner and powerful ally in a European power, Italy, which was ruled by the dictator Mussolini and his Fascist Blackshirts. Mussolini, having vanquished Ethiopia, dreamed of Italy as a colonial power of first order. Seeking to drive the British out of their colonial position in the Middle East, he sent money and agents to foster propaganda for an Arab rebellion. Day after day, a powerful radio transmitter in southern Italy beamed broadcasts in Arabic to Palestine. Radio sets and loudspeakers in village huts, Arab cafés, and other public places blared with rumors, distortions, and hatred. Native and foreign agents whipped up the masses, and finally, in April 1936, riots broke out all over Palestine.

From Riots to Rebellion

A wild rumor set off the first explosion in Jaffa, where Jews were set upon in the streets and killed in cold blood. In many other localities the

*After an
Arab Riot
at Tel Aviv
City Line
in 1936*

154

pattern repeated itself. Unlike the uprising of 1929, there were no concentrated large-scale disturbances, but there were isolated flare-ups and guerilla raids throughout Palestine. Arab guerillas came mostly from Syria, where they had been enlisted for good pay for banditry. Crossing into Palestine, they suddenly would swoop down on towns, villages and settlements, leaving behind a trail of death and destruction. They would ambush settlers at work, set fire to fields and forests, mine roads, shoot at busses, bomb homes and public places, cut telephone lines, attack factories, blow up installations, and create havoc with life and property all over. The terrorism was aimed not only against the Jews, but also against the British and even against some Arabs. Armed Arab gangs held up many of their own kinsmen and forced them to give money or shelter. They proclaimed a general strike and forced peace-loving Arabs to participate. This seriously affected the citrus industry, and forced thousands of Arabs to be thrown out of work. Shipping in Jaffa came to a complete standstill. In the end, the strike was disastrous for the Arabs, and it collapsed because it brought ruin to thousands.

The upheaval, with its acts of terror and destruction, was primarily the work of the Mufti of Jerusalem. But the British administration was slow in reacting, even though Arab bands dared to attack British army units and installations. True, reinforcements were sent to Palestine, bringing the number of British troops to twenty thousand, but the British administration still hesitated to take drastic action. It still sought to win the good will of the Arab leaders, fearing that a strong course in restoring order might drive the Arabs into the arms of the Axis powers.

The British policy of vacillation continued, until one day they awoke to reality with a jolt. The British District Commissioner for Galilee and a number of officers of his entourage were murdered.

Then the British moved against the Arab guerillas in the northern hills of Palestine. These were combed and cleaned out. Arab leaders were rounded up and deported. But the Mufti fled across the border into Lebanon. Though removed as head of the Supreme Moslem Council, the Mufti still continued to direct the uprising. Amply supplied with German and Italian money and arms, he kept throwing the British into a state of turmoil. The terror went on for three years more.

The Haganah

How did the Yishuv react to the Arab rebellion? Gone were the days when Jews were helpless. No longer did they lack arms, training, and means to defend themselves. This time the story was altogether different. Haganah, the self-defense corps of the Yishuv, met the assault bravely and effectively. Haganah fighters fended off attacks on settlements. It protected convoys on highways. It guarded fields and factories, and provided armed escort for workers. Haganah organized defense patrols to rove through the country day and night. The watch over the Yishuv involved a running battle with bands of marauders and individual infiltrators.

New and ingenious methods were tried to accelerate the process of settlements. The prefabricated *Kibbutz* became the new model of colonization. Ḥanita, an outpost in the north, was so built. Early one day, armed trucks and workers rumbled into the territory. By nightfall the *Kibbutz*, with all its installations, was firmly set up, from houses to chicken coops. A tower in the center of the settlement became the trademark of this kind of community building. Powerful searchlights played over the area for protection.

Soon more than fifty watchtowers dotted the countryside. Neither the *Kibbutzim* nor the Haganah managed to end the Arab surprise attacks. Yet the Yishuv kept calm. However strong its temptation to exact revenge on the Arab community, the entire community, with but few exceptions, exercised iron self-restraint. Palestine's Jews felt they had no quarrel with the Arab people. They did not want to harm those who were innocent. They blamed only certain Arab leaders for the violence and knew the Arab masses were forced into line through terror and intimidation. The Jews refused to retaliate. The Yishuv's policy was *Havlagah*, self-restraint.

Shopworn Remedies

The British continued to fall back on their shopworn remedies. Again commissions were appointed to investigate, explore, and report. Diplomats drew up more papers.

Haganah in Training ➤➤

A royal commission under the chairmanship of Earl Peel was sent to Palestine. It held seventy sessions with Jews and Arabs. Finally, in 1937, the Peel Report was put before the British Parliament. The finding was that the Mandate was unworkable.

The Peel Report acknowledged that there had always been close ties linking the Jewish people with its ancient homeland and that Palestine on both sides of the Jordan River had been considered as the National Home of the Jewish People in the Mandate given to England by the League of Nations. It also conceded that Jewish efforts greatly helped the Arabs in their economic development. In addition, it held that the Zionist leaders had been friendly to the Arab people, regardless of the hostile attitudes of Arab leaders. It also found that Great Britain had shown undue favoritism towards the Arabs and could have stopped the 1936 disturbances.

Yet Arab and Jewish interests were so irreconcilable, the Commission found, that it could recommend only one course—to end the Mandate

and to divide Palestine into three parts—a Jewish state, an Arab state, and a permanent mandate territory under British control.

The Peel Partition plan envisaged the Jewish state to include Galilee, the Emek, and the Coastal plain; the territory adjacent to Transjordan would go to the Arabs. The British mandate would comprise Jerusalem and other holy places.

The plan was immediately and unanimously rejected by the Arabs. Among Jews, it brought sharply divided opinion, causing sharp clashes at the Twentieth Zionist Congress in Zurich in 1937. In the British Parliament, it met a heated reception. It was clear to most members that the proposed scheme was unfair to the Jews and also constituted a severe setback for Great Britain.

Nevertheless, the British Government proceeded with measures to carry out the partition proposal. Another commission was sent to Palestine to draw boundaries.

The new commission could not agree among its own members, whereupon the British Government dropped the plan. It was found entirely impractical. That was in November 1938.

London Conference

A round-table conference of Jews and Arabs was called in London in an attempt to solve the Palestine problem. But the Arabs refused to sit down with the Jews. So the British had to hold separate meetings with each side

Round Table Conference in London in 1939

and act as intermediary. In addition, the Arabs broke up into factions that would not deal with each other. One group insisted that the infamous Mufti, proven to be the chief instigator of the trouble in Palestine, be invited as an Arab representative. The British refused him a seat but accepted four other Arab leaders, known for their complicity in the uprisings. The conference by its nature could only end in failure.

The White Paper *1938 Harrison* *Read p 159 + 165*

The height of disgrace was still to be reached. The moment came when the British Government decided to go it alone and settle the matter once and for all. It issued a new White Paper that struck the heaviest blow to Jewish aspirations. Published in May, 1939, the White Paper seemed to kill all hopes of making the Jewish national home a reality.

The paper declared that all Jewish immigration was to cease after five years, during which a maximum of seventy-five thousand Jews could be admitted. Afterwards the Jewish population could not exceed a third of the total Palestine population. The Jews would thus be permanently

Balfour 1920 (1917-18)
Churchill's
White paper 1922
Peel Commission 1937
Mandate
Unworkable
White paper 1938

*At the 21st
Zionist Congress
in Geneva:
Weizmann Speaks*

159

held to a minority in the land. Within ten years Palestine was to become an independent Arab state allied to the British Empire.

This was abject surrender to Arab violence, crowning a long standing British policy of breaking promises. Surprisingly, the Arabs were displeased. For them this was not enough. They wanted still more.

British public opinion recoiled with shame in the face of this incredible reversal. The League of Nations uttered a feeble protest. The Jewish world was stunned.

In an atmosphere of gloom the Twenty-first Zionist Congress convened in Geneva in 1939, on the eve of World War II. The shadows of catastrophe moved across the hall, as the Zionist representatives rallied behind Dr. Weizmann in his solemn protest against the latest British move. He delivered a soul-stirring indictment of the White Paper. And yet it was clear that the Jewish people had to cooperate with England in the coming world struggle.

What irony! The war came, but the Chamberlain Government went ahead, in 1940, to carry out the policy it avowed in the White Paper. In Palestine regulations were enacted which almost entirely prohibited the purchase of land, except for a minute bit of property. It was a brutal measure. Nevertheless the Jewish people had no choice but to support England. They remembered Weizmann's parting words to the Zionist Congress when he spoke of England and its allies, and declared: "Their concern is ours. Their fight is our fight."

As Night Descended

With the outbreak of war, night descended upon European Jewry. It was a night of horrors that never can be told fully.

Wherever Hitler's armies reached, as they crashed across most of the European continent and beyond, Jews were trapped. They were rounded up and driven into trains that carried them to points of their final destination—death by mass extermination.

Auschwitz, Buchenwald, Dachau were only a few of the extermination camps where, during six years, six million Jewish men, women, and children were murdered by the efficient Nazis. Hitler and his henchmen were determined to "solve the Jewish problem" through forced labor camps, and finally, gas ovens, and crematoria.

The horror stirred Jews in free nations to action. They tried desperately to seize any chance to save the lives of their brethren. Rescue teams were organized. Tremendous sums of money were raised.

Palestine again became a beacon of hope and promise. Yet, while the Hitler terror tramped steadily on, the British stood firm on their resolve to let only a limited number of Jews enter. Under the pressure of desperation, there came a determination to defy regulations, ignore personal safety, and crash through the gates of Palestine. Aliyah Bet, the movement for illegal immigration, was formed to penetrate the Palestine fortress. *Battle against the White paper*

It was what amounted to real warfare. The British army and navy fought illegal immigrants trying to land on Palestine's beaches in rickety ships. Many "illegals," as they were called, did scurry ashore and remain undetected. Others were not so lucky. After an extensive manhunt, about fifteen hundred refugees were rounded up and packed into a prison camp at Atlit; finally they were deported to the island of Mauritius. Britain's navy prevented the landing of a chartered ship, the *Patria*, which was blown up by its own passengers in desperation and sank off the Palestine coast with a loss of two hundred and sixty lives. It forced another, the *Struma*, out to sea, and seven hundred and sixty-five refugees from the Balkans drowned. Refugees on other ships, many unseaworthy, lost their lives in wrecks, fire, and through interception by the British.

Still many evaded the vigilance of the British sea and coastal patrols. Their boats dropped anchor offshore in the darkness of the night, and the refugees waded through shallow waters into the arms of Haganah groups waiting for them. They were transported into hiding with lightning speed. It was a battle of wits, with the leadership of the *Yishuv* masterminding a risky underground rescue operation of tremendous proportions. It was an unequal struggle with the British, but the *Yishuv* succeeded to such an extent that during the years 1939–1948 at least seventy-five thousand Jews were saved.

It was ironical, but the same *Yishuv*, which, by bitter necessity, had to combat the intentions of the British, rallied all its forces to help

England in the war effort. In contrast, some leading Arabs, and the Mufti in particular, collaborated with the Nazis. When the British prepared to move on Syria and Lebanon, occupied by the Nazi puppet regime of the Vichy French, only the *Yishuv* gave aid.

Immediately after the war broke out, the *Yishuv* conducted a voluntary registration for national service, and over one hundred and thirty-six thousand men and women responded. The *Yishuv* put all its resources— agriculture, industry, and medical services—into the war effort at England's disposal. The Jewish Agency offered an army of forty thousand young Jews to serve in Jewish units as part of the British Army. The offer, however, was rejected because England did not want to antagonize the Arabs.

The Jewish Brigade

Five years later, in 1944, the British were hard pressed for troops and finally consented to the formation of a Jewish Brigade. Even this was grudging. The Brigade was not permitted to function as a Jewish entity. It was formed as merely a Palestinian regiment, and it was decided that Jewish battalions should be no stronger than Arab battalions to be organized. But almost no Arabs came to the British colors, and the unit thus was in fact a Jewish brigade.

"We shall never yield": Moshe Shertok (Sharett) addressing Jewish military unit

The Jewish Brigade: Returning from forced march »»

The British were more than eager to put individual Jews from Palestine and even auxiliary Jewish units into uniform. About twenty thousand Jews from Palestine joined the British army and saw action in battles from France to Tripoli. They fought with distinction in Greece, Crete, Malta, Abyssinia, Eritrea, and in North Africa. They played a large part in the battle of El Alamein in the British Eighth Army and helped to roll back the Nazi tide that almost had reached Alexandria in Egypt and threatened Palestine.

"Blessed Is the Match"

The *Yishuv's* part in the war went even further. Their eagerness to aid the doomed Jews in Nazi-overrun countries moved a number of immigrant youths to deeds of extraordinary heroism as members of a volunteer group of parachutists trained by the British to be dropped behind enemy lines. They were to make contact with resistance groups in their native countries, collect information, and help Allied prisoners of war to escape. For most, it was a chance to aid their own people. One young parachutist was Enzio Sereni, son of the one-time personal physician to the King of Italy and an ardent Zionist, who had come to Palestine as a *Halutz* and had been one of the founders of Givat Brenner. Captured behind German lines in northern Italy, he was killed at Dachau.

Another was a budding writer and poetess, Ḥannah Senesch, formerly of Budapest, and later of K'vutzah Sdot Yam. Her aim was to attempt to get Jewish children out of Nazi-occupied Hungary and save her own mother, who had stayed behind when Hannah left for Palestine five years earlier as a girl of eighteen. Dropped over Yugoslavia in 1944, she made her way to Hungary. She was captured, tortured, and executed by a firing squad. But for the Jewish people she became the symbol of heroic resistance. A line in one of her poems reads: "Blessed is the match consumed igniting the flame."

IN 1945 the war was over and the mighty Nazi empire was crushed. A dazed humanity stumbled into the light of a new day, only to be overwhelmed by shock at the realization of the war's toll. Among the Jewish people, almost one-third of its sons and daughters had been killed.

The world shuddered at the sights of concentration camps and crematoria, at the piles of bodies unburied, and the pathetic spectacle of the survivors! They were called DP's—Displaced Persons. With no place to go, they had no choice but to stay in the tents and shacks of DP camps until some solution would be found for them to mend their broken lives.

The overwhelming majority of survivors wanted to go to Palestine. They wanted to live among their own people, and to build a new life. A fanatical passion to go to the land of Israel gripped the camps. *Aliyah* could not come fast enough! But the gates of Palestine remained closed. The pre-war White Paper still was in effect and enforced more strictly than before. Though the British had ended their war against the Axis, their war against the Yishuv continued unabated.

Yishuv War Goes On

The British Empire deployed its land, air, and naval forces against the Jews of Palestine as against sworn enemies. And this was done by the newly elected Labor Government, with which the *Yishuv*, with its own strong labor party, had felt a special sense of kinship. Soon it became painfully clear that the new Foreign Secretary, Ernest Bevin, was a new oppressor, bent on the destruction of the Jewish national home.

A small group of hotheaded Jewish youths reacted violently. The Irgun Zvai Leumi (National Military Organization) proclaimed that only ruthless force was the method of dealing with the British. To drive the British out was the avowed aim of the Irgun, whose members stemmed mainly from the ranks of the Revisionists. A rifle raised for action became its symbol.

CHAPTER 3 *Shadows and Agonies*

Guerilla warfare was carried on by the Irgun, and another extremist group, the Fighters for the Freedom of Israel, better known as the Sternists, after their leader, Abraham Stern, a Hebrew University student who had been killed by the British. The two groups attacked government buildings and other installations, blew up police stations, and raided arms depots. An abortive attempt was even made to assassinate the British High Commissioner. Emotions ran high among the people of the Yishuv as to what tactics should be employed in resisting the British. In its overwhelming majority, the Jewish community of Palestine recoiled at the terror practised by the Sternists and the Irgun. This was not the way. It made a mockery of Jewish ethical behavior. The way was to combat the British administration, but with decency. But *Havlagah*, self-restraint, became next to impossible as the British stepped up their measures to seal off Palestine against illegal immigration and paralyze the *Yishuv*.

Blockade Running

Running the British blockade off the Palestine coast developed into a major effort on the part of the *Yishuv*. It was a gigantic effort, fraught with innumerable hardships, carried out with cunning and courage. There were spectacular successes and hopeless failures. For years a human cargo fleet was on the move, winding its way from Black Sea and Mediterranean ports to the shores of the Promised Land. Leaky boats maneuvered to the Palestine coastline, often intercepted by the British Navy within sight of land. Once caught, the helpless passengers were assaulted by boarding parties using rifle butts to silence their sounds of distress. Then the armed escort led survivors to new concentration camps in Palestine, on the island of Mauritius, or later, in Cyprus.

Exodus 1947

An agonizing episode occurred when an American-built excursion boat, renamed *Exodus 1947*, set sail in July of that year from southern France. With a normal capacity of seven hundred, it was packed with forty-five hundred refugees. British Naval Intelligence detected the *Exodus* and set a cruiser and three destroyers on its trail. They followed the passenger ship on a zig-zag course across the Mediterranean for

"The Illegals"
on the "Exodus"

Memento of Shame:
"Illegals" are
returned to camp
in Germany

almost a week. While it remained at sea, the British craft could do nothing. Then the refugee boat, with all lights out, tried to make for the shores of Palestine under the cover of darkness. The British craft closed in and rammed the *Exodus*. A boarding party came on the stricken ship and met with turbulent resistance. In the struggle three persons were killed. Many others were wounded before the resistance was quelled. Captured, the *Exodus 1947* steamed into Haifa, and its passengers were herded onto three British prison ships that sailed back to France, anchoring at Marseilles.

But the refugees refused to land. The French extended hospitality and promised to help them rebuild their lives. But the inmates of the prison ship refused. They resolved to set foot only on the soil of Palestine.

They stayed aboard in the harbor of Marseilles for almost a month in conditions of unspeakable horror. The British stood condemned before the civilized world. Then came worse fortune. Orders were given to move the victims of Hitler's tyranny to Hamburg, Germany, of all places. Hamburg was in the post-war British zone of occupation. The returnees finally disembarked, submitting to savage conduct on the part of British soldiers, who ruthlessly pushed them down the gangplank and shoved them behind the bars of concentration camps.

While the British Navy battled the coffin ships, the British Army pursued those who had managed to get ashore. A search went on for years to track down the *Ma'apilim*, as the illegal settlers were called. A dragnet was thrown around the country, but it was pierced so often and in so many places that the results were negligible in comparison with the number of successful landings. The successes were due to the Haganah.

Target: Haganah

The Haganah had grown considerably in numbers and strength during World War II. Since the days of the Arab insurrection in 1936, it had been

In search of victims: The scene after an explosion in Jerusalem's business district

clear that no reliance could be placed on the British to safeguard Jewish lives and property. The British always failed to take action needed to repulse Arab aggression. Their security forces came on the scene only to turn against homeless Jews trying to reach the Promised Land.

On the other hand, the British would not tolerate the development of Jewish defensive strength. They tried to counteract it with every means at their disposal. For them, the Haganah was an illegal army whose striking power had been demonstrated on a number of occasions. The British embarked upon a determined campaign to disarm the Haganah and eventually dissolve it.

Extensive searches for arms and ammunition were carried out. Regular raids were staged against a great number of Jewish settlements to uncover weapons and arrest the suppliers. Possession of arms was made a criminal offense to be punished severely. The law was invoked against Jewish and Arab offenders alike.

There were many trials for illegal procurement and possession of arms. And invariably, Arab offenders got away lightly, while the full severity of the law was brought against the Jews. The *Yishuv* could not fail to take note of British justice.

The Haganah thus came to abandon its ideal of self-restraint and adopted a complete change of tactics. It went on the offensive—in defense of the *Yishuv*.

The Haganah staged a surprise raid on the British detention camp at Atlit and liberated several hundred refugees awaiting deportation. It attacked and destroyed a network of radar stations that were screening the ocean for approaching refugee ships. It dynamited bridges and railroad installations to interrupt British troop movements against the Jewish Agency.

The upheavals that shook the country notwithstanding, the *Yishuv* expanded. New settlements came into being despite the government's repeated measures to prevent new colonization by force. Time and again British troops moved in on new colonies, demolished installations, and drove out the settlers. As often as the colonists were dispersed, they returned to rebuild.

There were sit-down strikes and sympathy expeditions from other colonies. Volunteers would accompany the ejected newcomers on their way back and help them begin anew. With perseverance that no British Government could break, pioneers moved into the barren southland of Palestine, the Negev, in 1946 and created eleven new settlements with lightning sped.

A Letter From President Truman

With violence shaking the country, British statesmanship had no other choice but to come to grips again with the Palestine question. It was prodded into action by the United States government, and particularly by a letter President Truman had sent to the British Prime Minister.

That was in the late summer of 1945. A personal representative of the President had toured the DP camps, had spoken to many survivors, and reported that the majority insisted on settling in Palestine. On the basis of this report, President Truman addressed to the British government an urgent request that one hundred thousand DP's be admitted to Palestine.

There was no immediate reply. Two months later, however, the British government, through its Foreign Secretary Bevin, proposed the formation of a joint Anglo-American Committee of Inquiry, the recommendations of which would be followed through, but only if they were unanimous. Meanwhile, the British would permit the admission of fifteen hundred Jewish immigrants per month.

"Behind the Silken Curtain"

The Joint Committee, consisting of six Britons and six Americans, visited DP camps in Germany and Austria, conferred with officials in Washington, London, and Cairo, and went to Palestine. Finally it issued a massive, unanimous report with the conclusion that the doors of Palestine should swing wide open for a hundred thousand immigrants without delay.

Now all eyes were on Britain. It had solemnly promised to accept the unanimous recommendation of the committee. Prime Minister Clement Attlee told the House of Commons, however, that Haganah first must be dissolved prior to the admission of "so large a body of immigrants," and that the United States must supply funds to support the immigration. Bevin cynically declared some time later that the Americans advocated the immigration of one hundred thousand Jews into Palestine because they did not want "too many of them in New York." The Yishuv was shocked into the sharpest realization that its survival was still at stake. Acts of British oppression continued without let-up. Small wonder that British force was answered by organized resistance on the part of the Haganah, and terror on the part of the Irgun.

The country reverberated with increased violence. Both camps, British and Jewish, shared in outbursts and outrages. In July, 1946, the Irgun set off dynamite charges in the fashionable King David Hotel in Jerusalem, seat of the British Chief Secretary. It was a reprisal against the outlawing of the Jewish Agency and the mass arrest of its leadership. While detonations rocked the city, a whole wing of the hotel went up in smoke and rubble. The blast killed about one hundred persons, forty of them Jews. Stern measures of retaliation followed, together with an outbreak of bitter indignation in the *Yishuv* against the Irgun. Its acts of terror almost led to civil war within the *Yishuv*.

Though the Irgun may justifiably be condemned for its violent methods, its acts should not be studied without some understanding of the reasons behind them. Many members of the Irgun felt that the Haganah did not work quickly enough to be able to take advantage of all opportunities. They thought the Haganah ineffectual because it compromised, waiting for the proper time to strike. The Irgunists were believers in immediate action. Theirs was a policy of desperation born out of intense impatience with the slow-moving process of diplomacy. And they demonstrated a talent for decisive action and skillful improvisation.

British atrocities in November, 1946, brought on a new wave of terror. British soldiers and policemen raced through the streets of Tel Aviv and Jerusalem firing wildly and wounding many bystanders. When a member of the Irgun was publicly flogged by the British, the Irgun replied in kind. It kidnaped and flogged British soldiers! Violence begat violence in an ever widening circle. Police stations were blown up. Troop trains were derailed. British officers' clubs were destroyed. When Dov Gruner, a leader of the Irgun, and three of his comrades went to the gallows for participation in an attack on the British, the Irgun kidnaped and executed three British sergeants. These were only a few of the crimes perpetrated by both sides. Finally, the British proclaimed martial law in Palestine. The *Yishuv* was paralyzed and so was the British regime. Things had gotten completely out of hand. The whole British policy had collapsed in failure.

Faced with disaster, the British government decided upon a drastic solution—to take the problem to the United Nations.

United Nations Special Committee meets in Jerusalem

IN the shadow of chaos in Palestine, the Twenty-Second Zionist Congress convened in Geneva in December, 1946. It was the first post-war assembly of the World Zionist movement. Dr. Weizmann, in his autobiography, *Trial and Error*, wrote: "It was a dreadful experience to stand before that assembly and to run one's eyes along row after row of delegates, finding among them hardly one of the friendly faces which had adorned past Congresses."

"Polish Jewry was missing, Central and Southeast European Jewry was missing, German Jewry was missing. The two main groups represented were the Palestinians and the Americans. Between them sat representatives of only fragments of European Jewry, together with small delegations from England, the Dominions, and South America."

Yet the presence of three hundred and eighty-five delegates demonstrated the great strides the Zionist movement had made in the intervening years. They represented two million one hundred thousand persons, each of whom had bought a token shekel. Clearly, Zionism had become the most powerful movement in the world Jewish community. The nations of the world were deeply conscious of this, as evidenced by the presence of diplomats of many countries. But one power was absent, Great Britain. England, that once had championed the Zionist cause, had now become its bitter enemy. Open war raged in Palestine. And on the political front, a stalemate had set in.

A number of proposals were put forward, but they were rejected by one side or the other. There was the Morrison plan, advanced by a member of the British Cabinet. It proposed a bi-national state on the order of Switzerland, with separate Jewish and Arab cantons. There was one hitch—the one hundred thousand Jews, whose admission was at issue, were to be crowded into an area that comprised fourteen hundred square miles. Rejection also sealed the fate of a plan advanced by Foreign Secretary Bevin, who suggested that the hundred thousand should be ac-

CHAPTER 4 *Road Blocks to Fulfillment*

cepted gradually over several years, while Palestine was to be split into a Jewish zone and an Arab zone, with both enjoying "partial" independence. A British bid for another round table conference in London was turned down.

Weizmann Withdraws

The decision of the Zionist movement to reject participation in the proposed round table conference was taken at the Twenty-second Congress. Weizmann had been in favor of accepting, and had staked his leadership on it. After a long and bitter debate, he was rebuffed by a majority vote. A general council emerged, with David Ben-Gurion, of Palestine, serving as chairman, and Rabbi Abba Hillel Silver, of Cleveland, Ohio, heading the American Section of the Jewish Agency. Deeply hurt, Weizmann withdrew to his home and laboratory in Reḥovot, in Palestine. The Congress did not elect a new President, but reaffirmed the so-called "Biltmore Program" demanding Palestine as a "Jewish Commonwealth." At the Biltmore Hotel in New York this program for Zionist action was adopted in May, 1942. It greatly influenced the destinies of Zionism in America.

A New Effort

The Zionist Organization of America, with men like Stephen Wise, Abba Hillel Silver, and Emanuel Neumann at its helm, led the way. By the same token, other Zionist groups, such as the Labor Zionists (Po'ale Zion), the Religious Zionists (Mizrachi), and the Women Zionists (Hadassah), had made great progress in the American Jewish community. Zionism had become a potent factor in American Jewish life. From a small minority at the century's turn, Zionist ranks swelled in the 1940's into the hundreds of thousands, almost reaching the million mark. Besides, there were masses of sympathizers, deeply stirred by the great tragedy that had befallen European Jewry and moved to give Zionist aspirations their moral and financial support. Giving for the cause of a Jewish Palestine reached peaks unsurpassed in all philanthropic endeavors. The United Jewish Appeal had become American Jewry's most powerful financial instrument and the Yishuv's truly life-saving source of economic strength and stability.

But of even far greater importance than this gigantic fund-raising effort—and it reached into the hundreds of millions of dollars—was the moral and political influence exerted by American Zionism. That influence was mightily brought to bear when the decisive political battle over the Jewish future in Palestine began to unfold at the United Nations.

UNSCOP—The Last of Commissions *UNSCOP*

The United Nations, at a special assembly in 1947, decided to set up a United Nations Special Committee on Palestine (UNSCOP). Now a new investigation was in the making with new hearings, new reports, new discussions, new delays.

Yet there was one encouraging note. Soviet Russia advocated consideration of a division of Palestine into Jewish and Arab states. The United States also was in favor of the division—which also would provide an international zone under the auspices of the United Nations.

An eleven-man committee, led by a Swedish chairman and including representatives of the major powers, and delegates from Australia, Guatemala, India, Iran and Yugoslavia, began an inquiry. It turned first to the dark miseries in the displaced persons camps in Europe. It perceived the lack of cooperation of the Palestinian Arabs and the opposition of the Arab states. Most important, it illuminated the terrible ordeal through which the Yishuv was passing.

As the committee was touring Palestine, bloodshed was again sweeping the country. Members of the United Nations mission saw the terror from close range. The UN probers, moving through the crossfires of violence, interviewed British officials entrenched in barbed wire fortresses. They even contacted the Irgun and met with its leaders in secret hideouts.

The committee took extensive testimony from leaders of the Yishuv. They studied its structure, got acquainted with its parties, came to know the Haganah, and met many people. Their most prominent witness was Weizmann.

He appeared before the committee not in any official capacity, but at the request of the Vaad Leumi or the Jewish National Council. No longer was he president of the World Zionist Organization or of the

Jewish Agency, but he felt that he "spoke the mind of the overwhelming majority of Jews everywhere," and that he "could without immodesty, after more than half a century of activity, claim to speak for the spirit of the Zionist movement."

The UNSCOP made public its report in August, 1947. It unanimously agreed that the British Mandate should come to an end as quickly as possible.

A majority of the committee declared that Palestine should be partitioned into three parts—a Jewish state, an Arab state, and an international zone in Jerusalem and its surroundings, under the auspices of the United Nations, to embrace the places holy to Judaism, Christianity, and Islam. Each zone was to be completely independent, but for practical purposes, the three would use a common currency, and employ the ports of Haifa and Jaffa. The Jewish state would embrace the greater part of the coastal area, eastern Galilee, the Emek, and the Negev.

There were more hearings before the UN, and the General Assembly called to its table representatives of Jews and Arabs. Pleading the Jewish case was Abba Hillel Silver. The principal Arab spokesman was a cousin of the former Mufti, still in exile for his crimes. On behalf of the Arab

*United Nations
Special Committee
at the Wailing Wall*

High Committee, he threatened that blood and fire would follow if partition were voted. Other representatives of the Arab states followed suit with threats and intimidation.

The issue seemed to be decided when the United States, and a few days later Soviet Russia, came out in favor of the partition plan. In spite of this there were still hesitations and vacillations on the part of the United States about a number of very important details, each of which was an issue in itself. The tension mounted day by day, giving way to renewed excitement, and leading to behind-the-scenes negotiations. Public opinion in America was overwhelmingly on behalf of the Jewish cause. The Zionist movement in America mobilized all its forces, and all its friends among the Jews and non-Jews.

The Roll Call

YEH!

Finally, the day came when the roll call of nations brought the struggle of five decades to its climax. After hours, and minutes, and seconds ticked off, the counting of votes on the partition plan was complete. The United States, the Soviet Union, and France headed a list of thirty-three nations declaring themselves in favor of independent Jewish and Arab states. Thirteen nations were against it, and eleven, including Great Britain, did not participate in the voting. It was a definitive consent, exceeding by two votes the requirement of a two-thirds majority. The vote heard around the world by radio sealed the agreement of the nations, and brought outpourings of thanksgiving by Jews everywhere.

"The Day the Lord Hath Made"

In exaltation, Jews danced in the streets of New York and Jerusalem, on the squares of Tel Aviv and Haifa, in the Kibbutzim of the Emek, and in the lonely outposts of the Negev. They danced in the stockades of Cyprus, and in survivor camps of Germany and Austria. They danced, and sang, and rejoiced, saying this was "the day the Lord hath made!" The day was November 29, 1947.

Arab Defiance

Though the nations of the world had spoken, it was clear that the Arabs would not bow to the decision. Immediately after the voting, the representatives of the Arab states left the assembly hall in protest. The next day, and for two days after, the Arabs in Palestine staged a general strike on orders of the Arab Higher Committee. Under its command, a wave of looting and bloodshed rapidly expanded into widespread guerilla warfare. Armed Arab gangs prowled the countryside. And a no man's land between Jewish Tel Aviv and Arab Jaffa became the scene of marauding, sniping, and fighting.

The British were still the masters of Palestine, and were still charged with the responsibility for maintaining law and order. But they did not do this. What they did was to permit or create as much chaos as possible to aid the Arabs. A full scale war was now engulfing the country, and it was unmistakably clear that Britain was an ally of the Arabs.

British troops stood idly aside or flatly refused to protect Jews against Arab attacks. They deprived Jews of means of self-defense by confiscating weapons. They continued to enforce their stringent measures preventing the landing of immigrants and deporting to Cyprus those who were caught.

British military assistance to the Arabs was directly extended through the Arab Legion, the militia of neighboring Transjordan. Nominally an independent kingdom, Transjordan was in fact politically dominated and financially subsidized by Britain, and its army was trained, maintained, and commanded by the British. The Arab Legion was brought into Palestine by the British for what was called police duty, but it un-

◄◄◄ After the U.N. decision: Celebration in Tel Aviv

abashedly attacked the Jews, and later played a key role in the full-scale war the Arabs started when the British Mandate came to its end.

The Undeclared War

During the half year before the Mandate ended in 1948, Palestine became a large battleground for an undeclared war of the Arabs against the Jews.

Those were trying days with never-ending challenges to the *Yishuv*. Its courage, bravery, and ingenuity were constantly put to the test as the Arabs tried to drive a wedge of terror between the main parts of the *Yishuv*, and to cut off one section from another. The aim was to destroy or starve into submission the Jewish settlements, particularly, the new city of Jerusalem. At every turn of the highway, cars, trucks, and convoys, carrying food and supplies, guarded against ambush. The road connecting Tel Aviv and Jerusalem was under fire for weeks and conditions in Jerusalem became critical.

The Battle for Jerusalem

The population of Jerusalem of one hundred thousand underwent a siege that reduced food, water, and fuel supplies to a catastrophic low. The new city was subjected to a disastrous ordeal, and Jews suffered even more in the crowded quarters within the walls of the old city, surrounded by a sea of Arab hostility. Their trials came to an end when a detachment of Palmach, the shock troops of Haganah, overran an Arab guerilla nest from which much disaster had come. The road to the coast was opened and the blockade of Jerusalem was lifted.

There were many other ordeals created by Arab snipers, and there were crimes committed by Jewish extremists acting in retaliation. Arab gunmen attacked a Jewish convoy moving up the road to the Hebrew University and the Hadassah Hospital on Mount Scopus with medical supplies and killed over seventy doctors, nurses, and teachers. A combined force of Sternists and Irgunists moved in on an Arab village and mowed down its population without mercy.

The undeclared and unhampered war between Arabs and Jews spread with ever-growing intensity. The Haganah lacked sufficient arms and ammunition, and was greatly outnumbered by its Arab adversaries.

*Arab Volunteers
receive
rifle instruction*

*Haganah convoy
relieves
hard pressed
New City
of Jerusalem*

Arab ranks had been swelled by outsiders who infiltrated into Palestine by the thousands from Iraq, Syria, Lebanon, and Egypt, to join what was called the Arab Army of Liberation. It was commanded by the same rebel leaders who had directed the uprising of 1936 and the ensuing guerilla war. Against tremendous odds, the Haganah stood fast, or rather, moved fast. Lacking manpower and equipment, it developed a spectacular mobility and strategy. It handed the Arabs a decisive defeat in a key battle for the Emek in April, 1948.

"Leave Your Homes"

A mass flight of Arabs set in about the middle of April 1948. It was mostly a voluntary evacuation from places with a mixed Arab-Jewish population, and was in part Arab strategy in anticipation of the full scale war planned by the Arab states for the moment the British Mandate was to terminate.

The Arab strategists were convinced it would be a short war. With Arab civilians out of the fighting zones, the Jews could be attacked more easily, they thought. "Leave your homes," the Arab masses were urged, and they were promised that within a few weeks they would be back very soon to reap the fruits of an all-out Arab victory.

The Arab leaders told this to their people through word of mouth, newspapers, and radio. The argument sounded convincing. The masses followed their leaders.

Thus Arabs by the tens of thousands left their homes. In a number of cases the mass exodus followed on the heels of a successful surprise operation of the Haganah. Determined to remove once and for all the dangers to the safety of the *Yishuv*, the Haganah's shock troops had in quick succession overrun Tiberias and Safed, victoriously battled with Syrian Arabs

Panic on wheels: Arabs on the move in self-imposed flight from Haifa

in Haifa, and attacked Jaffa, the base of daily and nightly assaults against adjacent Tel Aviv. For a time, British troops served as a buffer between Arabs and Jews in Jaffa. Then they pulled out, and the Jewish forces, including some Irgunist units, readied themselves for an assault. The Arabs offered to surrender. When the Jews entered, they found the Arab port city almost deserted. The population had fled, only a small minority staying on. The total number of the self-evicted Arab refugees went into the hundreds of thousands streaming in haste across the borders.

British Exodus

The British exodus from Palestine left Palestine in a state of anarchy. There was little doubt about where the British stood in the Jewish-Arab controversy. In the closing days of the British administration, the Arab Higher Committee or its associates were given large quantities of arms and ammunition, barracks and camps.

The British openly sabotaged the orderly transfer of authority to the Jewish and Arab authorities as envisaged by the United Nations decision. A five-man United Nations commission, appointed to serve as trustees during the change-over, was denied permission to enter Palestine earlier than two weeks before the end of the Mandate. When the UN team did arrive, it could not function effectively because of British obstructionist tactics. The Commission demanded that a port be designated as a receiving point for Jewish immigrants, but the British refused. When the Commission urged that Jewish and Arab security formations be organized to maintain order in their respective areas, this was denied. Against this background of chaos the Union Jack was hauled down on the twelfth of May, 1948 in Haifa harbor, and the last British soldiers boarded a ship to take them home. The Jews and Arabs were left alone to fight it out.

UNIT FIVE

How the Jewish Homeland Became the State of Israel

MAY 15, 1948, the date on which the British Mandate was to expire, fell on the Sabbath, so the schedule for the beginning of Jewish statehood was moved up to Sabbath eve of the 5th of Iyar, 5708, corresponding to Friday afternoon, May 14, 1948. At a simple, yet majestic ceremony in a small lecture hall of the Tel Aviv Art Museum, the *Sheheheyanu* blessing was pronounced: "Blessed art Thou, O Lord, our God, King of the universe, who has kept us alive and preserved us, and enabled us to reach this season." Those present—thirty-seven members of the Vaad Leumi, the National Council, and about fifty other representatives of the Yishuv—heard David Ben-Gurion read the proclamation of the establishment of the Jewish state. Standing on a dais under a huge portrait of Theodor Herzl, Ben-Gurion declared: "We, the members of the National Council, representing the Jewish people in Palestine and the Zionist movement of the world, meet together in solemn assembly today, the day of termination of the British Mandate for Palestine, and by virtue of the national and historic right of the Jewish people and of the resolution of the General Assembly of the United Nations, hereby proclaim the establishment of the Jewish State in Palestine to be called Israel."

The first act of the new government was to do away with the White Paper of 1939.

The War Begins

The next day air raid sirens shrieked through the Sabbath quiet of Tel Aviv, and Egyptian bombers rained death and destruction from the skies. During the days that followed, Egyptian columns advanced from the south, heading towards Tel Aviv. From the north came Syrian and Lebanese invaders, while from the west, on the Mediterranean, the Egyptian navy stood poised to strike. From the east, troops of Iraq and Transjordan moved towards Jerusalem. The Transjordanian Arab Legion, stationed in Palestine by the British long before the outbreak of hostilities,

CHAPTER 1 *A Nation Restored*

started from its base on the road to Jerusalem. Saudi Arabia sent a token number of troops to join the Transjordanian army.

The situation was desperate. With insufficient and outmoded weapons, Israeli fighters had to face armies equipped with tanks, heavy guns, and planes. Yet Israel had one powerful weapon—the will to survive. Drawing heavily on their underground experience, former Haganah units became the backbone of Israel's army, and continued to operate with daring and ingenuity. Within three-quarters of a year, the invasion was turned into a complete rout, and Israel's weak and poorly equipped militia proved itself a first-rate fighting force.

The Spirit of the Haganah

This victory was the result of training and tradition. The tradition of defense can be traced to biblical times when a small people living in an area coveted by great empires had to learn to exploit their limited manpower and to utilize the element of surprise. Successful strategy called for small, lightly armed, mobile units. The victory of David over Goliath serves as an appropriate symbol of this kind of fighting.

During the latter part of the nineteenth century, the European Jews who began to resettle Palestine learned to guard their villages against attack. In 1909, these watchmen organized themselves into a group called *Ha-Shomer* (The Guard). Subjected to recurrent Arab riots, and failing to receive support from the British mandatory government, the Jewish population developed its own underground defense, the Haganah, which replaced *Ha-Shomer*.

The Haganah trained its members to use small arms and to fight as small independent units. The experience gained by the 30,000 Jewish volunteers who fought with the British army against Hitler was later put to good use in Haganah's battles with the Arabs.

One of the most fascinating military heroes of modern times, Orde Wingate, played an important role in the preparation of the Haganah for its future successes. Wingate, a British staff officer, was sent to Palestine in 1936. Within a month, he became so ardent a Zionist that many people found his enthusiasm hard to understand. Some insisted that he was a Jew, but, in fact, Wingate was descended from a long line of Scottish

Preparing for action:
An Arab Legion armored
car moves into position

Christians. Someone once asked him why he so zealously supported the Zionist cause. He replied, "When I was at school, I was looked down on, and made to feel that I was a failure and not wanted in the world. When I came to Palestine I found a whole people who had been treated like that through scores of generations. . . . I felt I belonged to such a people."

Wingate favored the organization of a Jewish defense force. He spent a full year gaining a thorough familiarity with the geography of the land. He read every report on military operations which had taken place there, and even became moderately fluent in Hebrew. He envisaged a frontier militia which could defend itself in case of Arab attack. This became the basis for the formation of his famous night squads. Wingate would lead a patrol out at night in order to discover the routes used by Arab infiltrators. "There are two ways to do a job," Wingate said. "One is to sit down and write a report, and the alternative is to go to the spot and obtain results."

Captain Orde Wingate, a great British soldier who loved Zion, is still affectionately spoken of by Israelis as *"Ha-Y'did,"* "The Friend." The reprisals his squads undertook against Arab terrorists contributed enormously to the safety of the country, and the training which Wingate's men received was to prove invaluable to the future development of Jewish military strength.

The Israeli army had the advantage of a coordinated master plan and unity of purpose. This helps to explain the victory of a small improvised force over six regular armies. The social gap between the Arab officer and his men was so great that he made no attempt to appeal to their intelligence or patriotism. For the Jewish people, the defense of the new homeland was a matter of life and death. The Israeli soldier knew that if he lost the war, he lost everything of value to him—his country, his freedom, and his right to independence. Thus the Israelis said that their commander was named *"Ein B'rerah,"* "No Alternative."

UN Intercedes

The United Nations tried repeatedly to end the fighting but its many calls were ignored by the Arabs. But from time to time, UN teams were able to arrange temporary cease-fire agreements between the two sides.

*A Westpointer helps to defend Israel:
Colonel Mickey Marcus* ➡

Again, as it was during the undeclared war of 1947, Jerusalem was cut off from the rest of the *Yishuv*, and faced a massive attack by Transjordanians and Egyptians. There was merciless shelling by the Arab Legion. The Israelis tried desperately to dislocate the attackers from their dominating positions on the main road from Tel Aviv, but they failed. Another way had to be found before the Jewish population of Jerusalem fell for lack of food, weapons, and supplies. Under cover of darkness, a ten-mile detour was marked out through the hilly countryside. Every night men came to build the road until the connecting link was completed. Over this trail moved men, animals, and jeeps laden with supplies that enabled Jerusalem's Jewish defenders to hold out. Its defense was directed by an American-Jewish volunteer, Colonel David Marcus.

Colonel Marcus, a West Pointer who had a distinguished record in World War II, died trying to open the road to Jerusalem. Though not a life-long Zionist, he believed that Jews must have their own homeland. In 1948, he answered the call for professional soldiers to help the Haganah. To this job, David Marcus brought thirteen years of army experience. He had served with MacArthur in the Pacific and parachuted into Normandy on D-Day.

Mickey, as he was known in the American Army, was smuggled into Palestine in January, 1948. He posed as a foundry worker, using an

assumed name, but was soon affectionately known as "The American." David Marcus was one of the great leaders of the Haganah. He planned the strategy in the Jerusalem front, he organized officers' training schools, and he wrote basic field manuals for the Israeli forces. All admired his courage and his sense of commitment. This American soldier who gave his life for Israel will not be forgotten by her people.

The Jewish quarter in Jerusalem's old walled section withstood for half a year the constant bombardment to which it was ruthlessly subjected. But in the end, after severe street-to-street and house-to-house fighting, its defenders had to surrender.

The Battle of Deganya

In the North, soldiers of Iraq and Syria attacked settlements throughout the valley. Israeli troops counter-attacked, and some settlements changed hands frequently. A crisis came when Arab tanks penetrated deeply into the valley and almost overran Deganya. Almost at the gates of the settlement, the defenders rallied, and after a furious battle, the Arab armor was completely destroyed.

Israeli representative signs Armistice Agreement at Rhodes

← *After the recapture of their Kibbutz in the Negev: Settlers at Nitzanim dig for the bodies of their fallen comrades*

Prime Minister Ben-Gurion hands General Yigal Yadin commission as "Rav Aloof" (General)

Trap in the Negev

The barren spaces of the Negev seemed inviting for a quick Egyptian breakthrough to Tel Aviv. There were only a few small Jewish outposts in the area. But the Jews were one step ahead of their enemies. When the Egyptian invaders advanced, they were greeted by a hail of fire bursting forth from dugouts and subterranean installations prepared long in advance. Many Egyptian tanks and guns were trapped and destroyed or captured. Bombing by Egyptian planes was largely without effect. The settlers were able to blunt the thrust of the invading forces and fight them to a standstill.

The Tables Turn

With every passing week the fighting strength of the Israeli army increased, though there were some severe setbacks. In the beginning only guts and ingenuity stemmed the Arab onslaught. Later, with arms from various countries, mainly from Czechoslovakia, Israeli forces could take the offensive. Equipped with tanks, heavy artillery, and planes, Israel struck back with such force and skill that the attackers reeled back. Only the intervention of the United Nations, striving for a truce, helped save them from complete collapse.

At Long Last: Armistice

Egypt, which had been badly mauled by Israel's army, indicated its willingness to stop fighting, and after weeks of negotiation, an armistice with Israel was signed on the Greek island of Rhodes on February 25, 1949.

The Egyptian-Israeli agreement, negotiated by the UN mediator Dr. Ralph Bunche, was the first in a series of armistice agreements he arranged between Israel and its enemies. The original concept of an Arab and a Jewish state and an internationalized zone in Jerusalem was altered by the military realities that emerged at the end of the fighting. Accordingly, the Jewish state was assigned the major part of the Negev it had won by force of arms, and Israel gained access to the Red Sea, through Eilat. What has since been called the Gaza strip on the coast remained in

Egyptian hands. Some parts of what should have been the Arab state under the partition arrangement fell to Israel. The bulk of it, however, went to Transjordan, as did the old city of Jerusalem.

The other Arab parties to the war against Israel—Lebanon, Syria, and Saudi Arabia—also signed armistice agreements during the following months. Only Iraq, which had no common frontier with Israel, refused to sign and theoretically remained at war.

Peace—and No Peace

The armistice agreements brought an official end to hostilities. But the hostility of the Arab states towards Israel continued unabated. They called for revenge, and throughout all Arab lands a "second round" of the war against Israel was promised.

An uneasy peace settled over Israel's frontiers, punctured time and again by countless incidents of sniping, marauding, and raids. Israel's five hundred miles of frontier remained in a state of tension.

Ingathering of the Exiles

On the day the State of Israel came into being, its gates swung open for every Jew who wanted to enter. Israel's Declaration of Independence stated emphatically: "The State of Israel will be open to the immigration of Jews from all countries of their dispersion." Now *Kibbutz Galuyot*, the Ingathering of the Exiles, had begun.

An influx began that dwarfed all previous immigrations. Jews came from no fewer than fifty-two countries. They came from Germany and Austria, from France and Italy. They returned from Cyprus. They streamed in from the Balkans, with whole communities often moving together. They struck their tents in Ethiopia, left behind their dwellings in Morocco, Tunisia, and other parts of North Africa. They abandoned their homes in India, Pakistan, and Afghanistan to reach the shores of Israel.

On Eagles' Wings

From Yemen, the most primitive of all the Arab countries, came the most unusual exodus of modern times. Yemen is a country isolated from the world—a land of nomadic tribesmen and poor peasants. Its population cannot be accurately counted because people are afraid that the census takers will give them the "evil eye." There are no newspapers and no real need for them, since 90% of the population is illiterate. The Jews of Yemen worked in the towns as silversmiths, tailors, and shoemakers. In the villages, the Jewish blacksmiths made plows and weapons for the Arabs.

The harshness of Jewish life in Yemen is reflected in the proclamation issued to the Jews in 1906 by the reigning Imam (ruler):

"In the name of Allah, the Merciful, the All-Compassionate. This is my command to the Jews—that they should be subservient to my laws and pay the tax without any modifications.

"The Jews shall live in peace and feel sure of their lives if they pay the *jizyah* (poll tax) as prescribed.

"Jews are forbidden:

Operation "Magic Carpet": Yemenite Jews lining up to embark on plane

*In the driver's seat:
A Yemenite Jew
operating his tractor*

1) to raise their voices in front of Moslems;
2) to build higher than the houses of Moslems;
3) to touch a Moslem passing on his way;
4) to engage in the traditional trades and occupations of Moslems;
5) to curse the prophets;
6) to discuss religion with Moslems;
7) to ride an animal cross-saddle;
8) to study their books outside the synagogue;
9) to raise their voices when praying;
10) to lend money on interest, which leads to the destruction of the world;
11) Jews must always stand up in the presence of Moslems and show them honor and respect on all occasions."

Thus the Jew had none of the rights of a citizen. Moreover, not only did the Jew suffer from legal restrictions, but he was "put in his place" in the course of his daily life. He was forced to do the lowliest forms of work and, since he must always feel inferior to the Arab, he must salute him first. When a Jew passed an Arab on the street, he had to pass on the left of him . . . for on the right side of the Arabs walk the angels.

The Jews of Yemen lived by the Bible and Talmud and made it an essential part of their day-to-day existence. They had no printing presses so that scribes carefully copied the text letter by letter. In their daily life, they spoke Arabic, but they learned the Bible in Hebrew and knew large portions of it by heart. Religion played a significant part in maintaining the hopes and dreams of this Jewish community. They longed for the Messiah to deliver them from exile and restore them to the Promised Land. Though they had little knowledge of the world, they believed all the words of the Bible and spoke of a return to Palestine. When the Redemption came to them, it came with all the wonder of a miracle— the miracle of transporting a barefoot Yemenite Jew to the world of the twentieth century.

They came from the far north of Yemen, travelling across the mountain ranges from the Saudi Arabian border and for three hundred miles across the whole length of Yemen. They came from the desert of the west and from the remote regions outside Yemen, from the most primitive cultures in the modern world. They came from places where no one had suspected Jews existed. For most of them, the journey on foot took four to six weeks. At the end of the journey was a camp organized to prepare them for their flight to Israel.

"And thus we came to Aden as long as there was breath in our nostrils, bruised and robbed, weary and bereft of everything. There was not a penny with us nor any possession. Also the rich among us came, most of them without money, in the same position as we. . . . And they gathered us into the great camp which was near the city and it was on the sands of the desert, and the place was too small for us all, and we lay in large numbers on the sand under the bare sky, each family together, and mighty sandstorms raged about us, and in our heart was a prayer for *Aliyah*, to fly 'on eagles' wings' to our country. And we went up." (From a letter written by a Yemenite Jew.)

The air-lift carrying the Yemenite Jews to Israel became known as "Operation Magic Carpet," reflecting the astonishment of these Jews when they saw their first airplane. Truly, they thought, the Redemption was at hand, for it is written:

> . . . *They shall mount up with wings as eagles;*
> *they shall run, and not be weary;*
> *and they shall walk, and not faint* (Isaiah 40:31).

The newcomers had to be housed and fed. They had to be given work. They had to make tremendous adjustments to each other. Many immigrants had to be taken to hospitals for immediate attention. How a former lawyer from Germany could make common cause with a peddler from Yemen, for example, was a problem that had to be solved. Not all those able to work could do so immediately. Housing was scarce. Many hardships had to be borne by the new settlers, who first had to live in tents, and in tent camps (*Ma'abarot*) until homes could be built. Most accepted these hardships willingly and with understanding. What sustained them was the knowledge that theirs was a future of freedom.

The tremendous influx of new immigrants presented the young state daily with new and most intricate challenges. There were Yemenites who had never seen bread made with yeast. They were wary of touching it and would eat it only if it were cut into small pieces for, according to Yemenite tradition, when only a little could be had of a thing, it became more desirable. The Israelis had to demonstrate that one slept on a bed, and not under it, and that a chair is often more convenient than the floor.

It was in the matter of family relationships that the new conditions most drastically clashed with the old Yemenite values. In Yemen, the roles and responsibilities of the husband and wife were clearly defined; men were the unquestioned masters and women were restricted to the home. Now Yemenite women saw their Israeli sisters do army service and occupy positions of equality with men. Such assaults against the accepted values of the past left many families in a state of bewilderment.

The gigantic financial burden never could have been coped with if American and other Jews had not displayed unprecedented generosity and a sense of responsibility. The United Jewish Appeal raised staggering sums to meet the enormous needs of Israel. American Jews also invested substantial sums in State of Israel bonds.

Other sums came in the form of loans from the United States Export-Import Bank and outright grants from the United States Congress.

Israel's Melting Pot

With immigrants coming from so many different countries and speaking so many different languages and dialects, the teaching of Hebrew became one of the first big tasks. Children would pick it up at school, but what about adults? A massive effort was needed. Thousands of volunteers went into the transit camps and private homes to teach Hebrew. Hebrew courses were conducted on the radio and through the newspapers. And

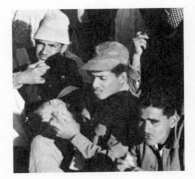

From India: It's a long way from Cochin

From Egypt: A family in their new home

From Iraq: Their first meal in Israel ➠

concentrated study of the language was provided by Ulpanim, special training centers, for acquiring skill in the language.

The most effective results were achieved by the Israeli army. Along with military training, young men and women underwent rigorous schooling in Hebrew and Israeli citizenship. Within a short time, a refugee became a Hebrew-speaking citizen-soldier of Israel. At the same time, immigrants added to the strength of Israel's army and provided manpower for building new settlements. In one year, 1950, no fewer than ninety-four new settlements sprang up on Israel's soil.

The First Million

The Ingathering of the Exiles assumed amazing proportions, and on the first day of Ḥanukah, 1950, the one-millionth person entered the land. It became a national holiday. The event was celebrated with song and dance in the streets of the cities, in the *Kibbutzim*, in the army camps, and in the tent cities. Israel hoped more would follow.

Party system formulated & understood

I N a Tel Aviv hall that once had been a movie house, the first parliament of Israel convened in 1949. It was the first parliament of the Jewish state after almost two thousand years. One hundred and twenty members of the Knesset took their seats and recalled the forty-five years that had passed since Theodor Herzl and the First Zionist Congress met in the Town Hall in Basle. Israel's first regular government, with Prime Minister Ben-Gurion at its helm, was formally and solemnly sworn in and presented to the country and to the world.

On the basis of what was called the Little Constitution, adopted shortly after the state had come into being, the rights, privileges, and functions of the Knesset were determined, the government was formed, its powers defined, and the president of the state was elected.

President Weizmann

The election of Chaim Weizmann as president was almost a foregone conclusion, just as his election as president of the Provisional Council of the state had been, two days after the declaration of Israel's independence had taken place.

President Weizmann was a great personal symbol of Israel's independence, but his office was a purely ceremonial one. According to Israel's governmental arrangements, the president of the republic is the formal head of the state, but in name only. He is present at all occasions of state; affixes his signature to laws and treaties; appoints and receives ambassadors; and can grant pardons. As in Great Britain, the real power is vested in the Prime Minister, who is the chief executive.

First Election *21 parties*

When the first general election took place in January, 1949, no fewer than twenty-one parties competed for the favor of the voters. After an election campaign marked by meetings, parades, speeches, promises,

CHAPTER 2 *Building the New State*

charges, and countercharges, and all the other features of campaigning, Israel went to the polls for the first time. The turnout of voters was extraordinary compared with the voting habits in other free countries. Out of more than five hundred thousand persons entitled to cast their vote, eighty-eight per cent voted, an indication of how deep a personal interest the citizens of Israel took in shaping the destinies of their country.

Politics

When the votes were counted, twelve parties gained enough votes to be represented in the Knesset, and four emerged as the leading groups. No party won an absolute majority. A coalition government was formed, composed of representatives of the four major groups.

With thirty-five per cent of the votes, the strongest party was Mapai (abbreviation of *Mifleget Poale Eretz Israel*), Israel's labor party, the backbone of which were the labor unions organized as the Histadrut, powerful through its political organization and its network of economic and cultural institutions.

In second place with fifteen per cent was Mapam (the United Workers Party, *Mifleget Poalim M'uḥedet*). While Mapai championed a moderate socialist program, Mapam was more radical. There were differences in foreign policy, with Mapam leaning more towards Soviet Russia, while Mapai felt closer to the United States. Mapai and Mapam were seated on the left side of the House in keeping with modern political practices in Europe. The other two coalition parties, each with twelve per cent of the vote, sat on the right. They were the Religious Bloc (composed of Mizrachi, the religious Zionists, and the even more Orthodox Agudat Yisrael).

President Weizmann takes the oath of office

Added up, these parties, now forming the coalition government, represented a majority of seventy-four per cent. It was a strange combination, this partnership of parties that had actually little in common, but were welded together—after difficult negotiations—into a workable government by Ben-Gurion through his great gifts of leadership, diplomacy, and iron will.

The major opposition parties were the General Zionists, who favored a system of free enterprise common in the United States and other parts of the western world, and the Herut or Freedom Party. The latter was the successor of the Irgun, and stood broadly for the principles of Revisionism and its founder, Vladimir Jabotinsky. The General Zionists, who had played a dominant part at Zionist Congresses, were a minority in the first Knesset. Their political lot and influence improved over the years as many new immigrants turned to their standards.

Arabs in the Knesset

Among the minority groups in the Knesset were Israel's Arabs with three seats. The Arabs participated freely in the elections, and they were, for the first time in all Arab history, to include Arab women among the voters. Arab representatives enjoyed the same status as any of their Jewish colleagues in the Knesset. For Arab Knesset members who did not speak Hebrew, there were head phones available to provide simultaneous translations of speeches, much like the system employed at the United Nations.

On the Statute Books

Among the laws passed by the Knesset was the Law of Return. It set forth the right of every Jew everywhere to settle in Israel. Another, the compulsory education law, required every child to attend school. There was a military draft law, which applied also to women.

In the Family of Nations

When on May 11, 1949 the Star of David was hoisted to the top of a flagpole, one of many standing in front of the United Nations building at Flushing Meadows, New York, Israel was admitted to membership.

Not even a year had elapsed between the declaration of Israel's independence and its acceptance into the UN. What greater compliment could be paid by the world to the political maturity of the new state!

The UN gave Israel a new forum for trying to settle its differences with the Arab nations. But the results often were discouraging. Israel pressed for a fair solution to its problems and often won UN support, but the Arabs remained hostile. In violation of the Rhodes agreement and in violation of international obligations, Egypt prohibited ships bound for Israel from passing through the Suez Canal. Upon Israel's complaint that Egyptian action was endangering the peace, the Security Council passed a resolution to stop the blockade. But the Egyptians ignored it.

When the question of Jerusalem's internationalization came up before the United Nations, and when the decision was made to internationalize the entire area including the all-Jewish New City, Israel saw its vital interests endangered. A Jewish state without Jerusalem seemed unthinkable. The Knesset therefore continued to meet in Jerusalem and it proclaimed Jerusalem as the capital of the state. This was followed by the Israeli government's moving its offices to Jerusalem.

The Second Knesset

In July, 1951, the citizens of Israel went to the polls again to elect the second Knesset. After another hectic election campaign, a coalition gov-

*Israel's
Second President
Itzḥak Ben-Zvi
is sworn in*

ernment, once more headed by Ben-Gurion, emerged. And Chaim Weizmann was named president. Weizmann did not serve out his second term. He died in November, 1952, at the age of seventy-six. On a site chosen by himself, Weizmann was buried in the garden of his residence in Reḥovot. Weizmann's passing plunged the Jewish people everywhere into deep mourning. World-wide tribute bore eloquent testimony to the greatness of the man and his achievements.

After the traditional thirty days of mourning, the Knesset elected the scholarly Yitzhak Ben-Zvi, a veteran of the *Second Aliyah*, to be the new president.

Retreat to the Negev

In 1953, Ben-Gurion decided to step down from his post as Prime Minister and retire to the Negev. It was a dramatic move. Ben-Gurion announced that he wanted to spend two years in the seclusion of a tiny pioneer settlement, S'de Boker, to work as a farmer. He was determined to demonstrate to the youth of Israel that the Negev needed them, that this wild, arid, unsettled desert demanded cultivation and redemption. Thousands of new settlers had crowded the cities; others had gone into rural settlements in the north; but they had shied away from the Negev. Ben-Gurion believed the key to Israel's future was in the vast desert. As he wrote in 1935: "The numerous ruins prove that a large community inhabited this area. Cities with paved streets, buildings, wells, gardens, and fenced fields were uncovered, pointing to the existence of an ancient workable system of economy. Today, there isn't a living soul there. This territory is no man's land."

Only a loose ring of sparse settlements dotted the long, lonely stretches from Beersheba to Eilat. But Ben-Gurion's decision to go to the Negev, to seek out the desert and to conquer it by steady work, had a moving effect upon the *Yishuv*. Suddenly, S'de Boker became a national shrine.

Every day busloads of Israeli citizens, school children, visitors from abroad, came to see him at work. He fired the country's determination to conquer the desert.

Ben-Gurion continued the tradition of the Labor Zionists who came

Working for "his" Kibbutz: Ben-Gurion at Sdeh Boker ➤➤

before him. Like A. D. Gordon, whose love for the soil and belief in the redemption of the Jews were more than empty words, David Ben-Gurion fulfilled his ideals in his day-to-day existence. The words he uttered in 1944 were put into practice, and men were stirred by his selfless dedication to the future of Israel:

The desert area of our land is calling us, and the destruction of our people is crying out to us. . . . The tasks that lie ahead will require pioneering efforts the likes of which we have never known, for we must conquer both the sea and the desert—by creating Jewish sailors and even Jewish Bedouin tribes. Our desert is not a Sahara or a hopelessly arid wilderness. The deserts of Israel were once inhabited in ancient times. The conquest of the desert requires bold and adventurous pioneers who will not shrink back in the face of any obstacle or hardship.

The reins of government passed into the hands of Moshe Sharett who became Prime Minister in 1953. His name was originally Shertok. He changed his Russian name to the Hebrew Sharett, which means Servant. A servant of his people from his early days in the Zionist movement, he had steadily moved up the ladder of leadership by virtue of his brilliant personal gifts and his long record of achievements. Now he became Prime Minister, leading the country through crises, both within and without, until Ben-Gurion was ready to return and again assume the responsibilities of leadership as Prime Minister and Minister of Defense.

DEFENDING Israel's borders had been one of the most crucial problems with which the young state had to cope. It strained the country's nerves, manpower, and financial resources. Though the armistice agreements had formally put an end to warfare, violations of the truce had been committed almost from the very beginning of the armistice.

Protecting Israel was extremely difficult. Its frontiers stretched for hundreds of miles. It could not be guarded inch by inch. Stretching through hills, plains, and desert, the border invited attack. For years the frontier was ablaze with gunfire and mine explosions. There were times when the jagged nerves of Israel's frontier guardsmen gave way under unbearable tension and triggered unfortunate acts of retaliation.

Border crossings from Jordan developed over the years into a regular pattern of surprise assaults by armed gangs, sabotage, and thefts. There were thousands of such incidents and numerous dead and wounded. A lone settler in a village in the Jerusalem hills would be murdered in his bed. Homes would be blown up in raids on frontier settlements. Buses would be waylaid and their passengers massacred. The Haifa-Tel Aviv passenger train would be attacked in the coastal plain from across the Jordanian border. Hand grenades would be thrown into schools and hospitals. It is not surprising that at times tension and rage reached the breaking point and retaliation followed.

A United Nations Mixed Armistice Commission investigated these incidents, censured one side or the other, but rarely could prevent them from happening.

Serious border incidents also occurred along the frontier with Syria. When Israel undertook a major drainage project in the swamps of the Lake Huleh region in the north, Syria opposed the work by force. The Syrian-Israeli frontier shook during the spring of 1951 with such violence that the United Nations Security Council had to step in and arrange

CHAPTER 3 *Defending the Borders*

for another cease-fire. Another conflict arose over an Israeli hydro-electric project involving the Jordan and Yarmuk Rivers.

After a long series of attacks by Syria, Israeli army units raided a Syrian gun position on the northeastern shore of Lake Kinneret in November, 1955. There were many casualties on both sides.

While all of Lake Kinneret and a strip of land on its western shore lay within Israel, according to the armistice with Syria, fishing in the lake became very hazardous for Israeli fishermen. From hill positions overlooking the lake, Syrian guns fired on Israeli fishermen. Armed Israeli police launches gave some protection, but the Israeli fishing fleet came under Syrian shelling time and again. The toll of dead and wounded kept mounting, until the Israeli army retaliated with a raid and destroyed the Syrian base.

The uneasy truce was broken again and again by new violations and violence. Repeatedly, the Mixed Armistice Commission met, and the complaints of Israel and its hostile neighbors were laid before the Security Council of the United Nations. From 1948 through 1956 the Palestine situation came up for review and discussion no fewer than two hundred times. To a great extent, this was because of the many armistice violations by Egypt.

The Egyptian Blockade

Those violations began very early with Egypt's blockade of Israel-bound shipping through the Suez Canal. Though the Security Council had adopted a resolution requiring Egypt to open the Canal to all shipping, it was ignored. Egypt also hindered the passage of ships to the Israeli port of Eilat through the Gulf of Aqaba. It seized an Israeli freighter en route from Eritrea, impounded its cargo, and imprisoned its crew. After the wheels of the United Nations machinery were set into motion and the Security Council's majority condemned Egypt's action, the crew was released. But the blockade remained effective.

The Gaza Strip

Before the State of Israel was proclaimed, the Haganah distributed leaflets in all the Arab villages urging the inhabitants to remain calm.

The Histadrut sent out similar messages and Jewish leaders toured Arab areas in an effort to reassure the Arab residents. However, all these attempts failed, and when the State of Israel was created, a mass exodus of the Arabs began. Three major factors caused this flight from Israel:

1) Arab anticipation of a Jewish defeat.
2) Arab fear of Jewish revenge.
3) The desire of Arab leaders to create a chaotic situation in Israel.

The wealthy Arabs who left Israel assumed that the Jews would easily be defeated. They expected to participate in a triumphal return to Palestine where they would bask in the glory of their victory. Their confidence in the future was encouraged by the Arab press. In an article published by *Al-Hoda*, the leading Lebanese newspaper, the following was found:

. . . The Secretary-General of the Arab League, Abdul Rahman Azzam Pasha, published numerous declarations assuring the Arab peoples that the occupation of Palestine and of Tel Aviv would be as simple as a military promenade for the Arab armies. He pointed out that they were already on the frontiers and that all the millions the Jews had spent on land and economic development would be easy booty for the Arabs, for it would be a simple matter to throw the Jews into the Mediterranean.

Brotherly advice was given to the Arabs of Palestine to leave their land, homes, and property and to stay temporarily in neighboring, brotherly states, lest the guns of the invading Arab armies mow them down (June, 1951).

The fear of Jewish revenge motivated the flight of many Arabs. It should be remembered that the Western style of warfare differs greatly from that of the Arabs. In the Western world, an organized military force wages battle while the civilian population remains comparatively safe. In contrast to this, Arab methods were marked by indiscriminate killings, mutilations, and lootings. They regarded every member of the opposing group, whether soldier or civilian, as an enemy to be ruthlessly destroyed.

On the eve of the Arab invasion, the Secretary-General of the Arab League described the future fate of the Jews. "This will be a war of extermination and a momentous massacre which will be spoken of like the Mongolian massacre and the Crusades." It was natural for the Arab population to expect similar treatment at the hands of the Jews.

Both the confident belief in a swift Jewish defeat and the fe[a]r harsh retaliation in the event of a Jewish victory were feelings w[hich] were fostered by the Arab governments. The basic purpose of the attack was to prevent the establishment of Israel and, in case such a government were created, to destroy it. One method of destroying Israel would be to completely uproot its Arab population. If thousands of refugees were forced to leave their homes, they could only bear an intense hatred toward the Jews. Throughout the Arab world, the existence of the refugees would be an endless source of hostility toward Israel. This is why the Arab leaders constantly roused the fears of the Arab population, urging them to leave their villages, farms, and cities.

Haifa provided a striking example of the results of this policy. When this city was captured by the Haganah in April, 1948, the Jewish authorities asked the Arabs to remain. They assured them full protection but, in spite of this, almost all of Haifa's Arab population fled. They fled because they were told to do so by their leaders. Conclusive evidence of Jewish efforts to reassure the Haifa Arabs has been obtained from both British and Arab sources. In a secret report sent by British police in Haifa to British headquarters is the following:

The situation in Haifa remains unchanged. Every effort is being made by the Jews to persuade the Arab populace to stay and carry on with their normal lives, to get their shops and businesses open and to be assured that their lives and interests will be safe . . . (April 26, 1948).

And two days later, the Haifa British police reported:

There is no change in the situation in Haifa. The Jews are still making every effort to persuade the Arab populace to remain and settle back into their normal lives in the Town. The quays and harbour are still crowded with refugees and their household effects, all waiting an opportunity to get a place on one of the boats leaving Haifa.

The Arabs themselves have admitted the great part they played in this exodus from Haifa. On August 19, 1951, the Moslem weekly *Kul-Shay* of Beirut published the following:

Who brought the Palestinians to Lebanon as refugees, suffering now from the malign attitude of newspapers and communal leaders, who have neither honor nor conscience? Who brought them over in dire straits and penniless, after they lost their honor? The Arab States, and Lebanon amongst them, did it!

At present, the Arab refugees wait in the Gaza Strip wretched, impoverished, and full of hatred for Israel. Having lost their homes, their land, their livelihood, all that remains is a nagging discontent with their present condition coupled with memories of an earlier, pleasant existence.

Gaza is bounded on one side by the Mediterranean and on three sides by the state of Israel. Israel is easily visible from Gaza. Every day, Arab refugees view their former country and contrast their poverty with Israel's prosperity. Inevitably, they feel resentful and vengeful. In an effort to create a force which will eventually destroy Israel, the Arab leaders nourish this hatred. A superficial glance at the Arab demand for complete repatriation suggests tender concern with the plight of the Arab refugees. However, on closer examination, a second and deeper purpose is discovered:

Our first urgent request must be the return of the refugees. We are unable to return them honorably. Let us therefore try to make them our fifth column in the struggle yet before us. Up to now the Jews argued that there was a state of war between us and one could not ask them to accept soldiers, enemies, into their midst. But at present, if we shall appear in the guise of peace-seekers, they will have no argument.

At the present time, the important question is not where to place the blame for this problem but how to find a solution to it. Regardless of the reasons for a man's homelessness, the misery of his daily life demands attention. Israel has made repeated offers in the UN to compensate the Arabs for their lost property. In order to reunite families separated by the war, Israel has permitted many refugees to return. The Arabs, on the other hand, have done nothing to ease the plight of the Gaza Strip refugees. In spite of their avowed plans for the annihilation of Israel, the Arabs insist that all refugees be admitted. Israel, of course, cannot invite the enemy to destroy her. In addition, the Arabs fail to realize that an exodus is not reversible. When people leave, newcomers occupy the land; the latter would have to be shifted elsewhere, and a new refugee group would be created.

The Arabs do not recognize the existence of the State of Israel. All

Arab-Israeli negotiations in the UN are carried out through a third party. Direct discussion would imply an acknowledgment of Israel as a nation. Until the Arab countries are willing to make peace with Israel, the refugee problem will remain unsolved. It is to the Arab governments' advantage to keep this problem alive, for they know that the refugees are a real threat to the State of Israel. They have become helpless pawns in the hands of a few vengeful Arab leaders who hope to use them as a weapon in the fight against Israel.

The Gaza Strip has become a vast slum of refugee misery and the breeding ground of discontent and hatred. Violence has erupted time and again on the border with Israel. At first, there were exchanges of gunfire across the border. Later, there were more serious incidents. Arab marauders infiltrated into Israeli territory to steal and to kill. There were bombings, mining of roads, and the blowing up of pipelines. Sometimes, Arab civilians staged the raids. But often aggressive actions were carried out by units of the regular Egyptian army.

After each episode of robbery, sabotage, and military attack, the Mixed Armistice Commission, under a United Nations chairman, went through the motions of investigation and condemnation. In one single period, from August 1954 through March 7, 1955, Egypt was found guilty of violating the armistice agreement no less than forty times. But UN declarations, calling on Egypt to put an end to these repeated attacks, were of no avail. The regular Egyptian army continued to infiltrate deep into Israeli territory, spreading terror in towns and on the countryside. When the Israeli army struck back, and in a sharp encounter drove the Egyptians across the border, the complaints of both sides reached the Security Council again. Impartial UN investigators blamed Egypt, and the Security Council called for a halt to the violence, but it continued. The tension sharply increased, leading to new incidents and finally to a radical showdown.

The Dictator on the Nile

Egyptian acts of aggression had taken a sharp turn ever since 1952 when Colonel Gamal Abdel Nasser gained power through a revolutionary uprising against King Farouk and installed himself as a dictator on the Nile.

Possessed by dreams of uniting the entire Arab world under his leadership, Nasser embarked upon a series of undertakings designed to inflame Arab passions against the West. He obtained arms, tanks, and planes from Soviet Russia and its satellite, Czechoslovakia. In violation of all international agreement, he seized the Suez Canal, vital to all of Europe. The complete annihilation of the Jewish state was Nasser's avowed aim. "Prepare yourselves, oh Israel," he exclaimed, "for the day of your destruction is near. . . . We want revenge and our revenge is Israel's death."

The Fedayeen

To carry out his aim, proclaimed daily to the Arabs and to the world over the Cairo radio, the Egyptians unleashed a campaign of terror in 1956 through the Fedayeen, specially trained commandos, largely drawn from the restive Arab refugees in the Gaza Strip. They penetrated deep into Israel's territory, into the Negev, into the coastal plain, and almost into the outskirts of Tel Aviv. Theirs was the mission of spreading terror and fear, of striking suddenly and of killing in surprise moves, of mining roads, blowing up vehicles, sabotaging railway traffic, destroying

After a Fedayeen Raid

wells, attacking farmers in the field, raiding settlements, and of shooting up Israeli army patrols. Murder in one form or another was their objective. Fedayeen incursions sometimes were intercepted by Israel's army; often they were not, and their violence spread. It became increasingly clear to Israel's leaders that the root causes of this disease had to be stamped out. The time had come for drastic action.

The Sinai Campaign

On October 29, 1956, the bearded chief chaplain of Israel's armed forces stood with a Torah in his arms before a jeep at the head of an armored column ready to cross the border into Egypt. Placing the Torah scroll into the jeep, he said, "You are about to enter holy soil, for on this land Moses, our teacher, received the Torah."

That was the signal for the start of the Sinai Campaign that brought Israel's army within 10 miles of the Suez Canal in only four days. It was a brilliantly executed military operation, sealing off the Gaza Strip with lightning speed, and penetrating deeply into the Sinai Peninsula. Soon the blue-and-white flag with the Star of David was raised on the hallowed peak of Mount Sinai, and Egypt's army was in tatters.

At the start of the campaign, Egypt's forces consisted of approximately 45,000 soldiers who were in a strong, well-planned defensive position. The Egyptian army was concentrated in the northeastern part of the Sinai peninsula, near Israel's western border. Three villages bounding the area formed a triangle, and it was these villages which Israel first attacked.

Though the Egyptian and Israeli forces were almost equal in size, Egypt had superior military equipment. Nevertheless, one hundred hours after the attack had begun, Israel was within ten miles of the Suez Canal. She had lost 174 men and only four had been captured. Egypt's dead numbered over one hundred, and six thousand of her soldiers were captured. In addition, Israel seized a great quantity of tanks and guns.

World-Wide Repercussions

The repercussions of Israel's move were world-wide. Great Britain and France invaded the Suez Canal area on the pretext of trying to keep the armies of Israel and Egypt apart. Their real purpose was to liberate the Suez Canal. The United Nations Assembly, called into emergency session at the insistence of the U.S.A., condemned England, France, and Israel for their actions. Russia, trying to enlarge its foothold in the Middle East, and posing as the champion of the Arabs, threatened to send volunteers into the area to fight on Egypt's side. So did Communist China. The spectre of a new world war loomed large. Under such pressures, England, France, and Israel complied with the UN order to withdraw their forces from Egypt.

Back from Sinai

Thus Israel moved its troops back from the Sinai Peninsula, then later from the Gaza Strip, and finally from the Straits of Tiran, on Israel's southern coast at the entrance to the Red Sea. There, a small barren island

Under fire during Sinai campaign

dominating the Straits had long been used by the Egyptians to block Israel's sea lane to Asia. When the Sinai Campaign started, Tiran Island was quickly overrun by the Israelis and its gun positions destroyed. On withdrawing, the Israelis handed over control to the United Nations Emergency Force, formed to serve as a buffer between the armies of Israel and Egypt. United Nations troops also manned the border separating the Gaza Strip from Israel. The right of free passage through the Gulf of Aqaba, powerfully endorsed by the United States, was a result of the United Nations' intervention. Israel's free access to the sea was solemnly proclaimed. This brought new life to the port of Eilat, vital to the development of Negev and Israel's traffic with the world.

Israel's drive to Sinai, undertaken in defense, resulted in the destruction of the myth of Egypt's military superiority and gained the respect of military leaders everywhere.

Israel's main objectives in the Sinai campaign were:

1) To eliminate the Fedayeen bases of attack,
2) To forestall an imminent Egyptian attack,
3) To open the Suez Canal and the Gulf of Aqaba to Israeli ships, and
4) To convince Egypt and the other Arab states that she had a permanent place in the Mideast.

The Sinai campaign was an ambiguous victory for Israel. From a military point of view, she had certainly succeeded. The Egyptian army suffered a humiliating defeat, and their Fedayeen raids stopped. The most important result of this victory was the opening of the Gulf of Aqaba to Israeli ships, but Israel did not gain access to the Suez Canal. Today, Israel is the only nation in the world not permitted to pass through the Canal.

Israel's military successes did not blind her leaders to the fact that the future of Israel was bound up with the necessity of establishing permanent peace with her Arab neighbors. Israel has been anxious for peace, but the Arab states remain adamant in their attitude of hatred and revenge.

THE INFLUX of new immigrants continued without letup, and Israel's population approached two million in 1958. More than one-tenth of the population was composed of non-Jews, mostly Moslem and Christian Arabs, and Druse. Almost a million Jewish immigrants entered the country between 1948 and 1957. Political and economic insecurity in some countries, outright persecution in others accounted for this new tidal wave of immigration. After the first surge of immigration from refugee camps in Europe, Jews came primarily from North Africa, later on from Egypt and Hungary, and still later, from Poland and Rumania. The gates of Israel stayed open.

Ship to Village

After the first years of immigration, with its tent cities and shanty towns, Israel was in a position to give its newcomers something better. In 1954 a dramatic experiment in human engineering went into effect. It was called the "ship to village" plan. Immigrants who agreed to participate in the program could board trucks almost immediately after landing at Haifa and be taken directly to villages and settlements that had been prepared for them. Land was already parcelled out, houses often were waiting for occupancy, the village school was already set up, and there were facilities for health and recreation. And adults could find employment immediately. Days after entering Israel, immigrants could be productive Israelis.

Very few immigrants had been farmers. Yet during the first eight years of independence about four hundred and fifty agricultural villages came into existence. In contrast, the total of farming settlements established during the preceding seventy years amounted to only two hundred and seventy-seven. These two figures alone show what growth and change had taken place in Palestine. The tractor became the symbol of a new way of life, of living on the land.

CHAPTER 4 *The Open Gates*

From Ship to Village:
Immigrants from Hungary

The Negev is almost half the territory of Israel. Before 1948, it was known that the Negev contained mineral resources, but no actual mining had been undertaken. The area was judged unfit for human habitation, destined to remain an arid wasteland. The only testimony to the contrary was the words of scholars who knew that once large sections of the Negev had been fertile and productive.

Many facts about the Negev were discovered through the Bible. It was known that patriarchs had wandered through the Negev with their cattle. Beersheba had been an oasis where Abraham lived. King Solomon had copper mines at Timna, and his merchant fleet sailed for Africa and the Orient from the Red Sea port of Eilat. King Uzziah built a network of military roads and had pastured flocks of cattle in the Negev.

Centuries after the biblical era, the Negev again became an international thoroughfare. Ruins of the great Nabatean cities testify to the existence of a highly developed civilization. The Romans and the Byzantines were in the area for 900 years, and the region flourished until the Arabs invaded in the seventh century.

The area declined, and the desert slowly took over. For 1,200 years the Negev was a desolate and uninhabitable desert where nothing grew, where the khamsin (hot desert wind) blew across vast stretches of sand, encountering no living obstacle in its path.

In 1943, observation posts were set up by the Jewish Agency and the first modern study of the Negev began. The settlers' task was to find out whether it was really impossible to live there. After much observation, they announced that the Negev could be cultivated with water. "Operation Negev" established eleven settlements in one night. By May, 1948, there were twenty-seven Negev villages. Cut off from the rest of the country by invading Egyptian troops, they became isolated strongholds. But their precious water system was destroyed and a new pipeline was not completed until 1955.

The search for mineral resources began in 1948, while fighting was still going on in the Negev. Biblical geography proved accurate time and time again. It was written in the Bible that this was "a land whose

"Somewhere in the Negev":
An Arab child leads
the family's camels

Road through the Negev:
From Beersheba to Sodom

stones are iron and out of whose hills thou mayest dig copper." And copper was recently discovered at Timna, near Eilat. After 2000 years, King Solomon's mines are in use again. The oil strike at Heletz became the best publicized of the Negev finds. However, Israel's greatest single source of mineral wealth is the Dead Sea, whose salty waters contain almost unlimited quantities of valuable minerals. It is no exaggeration to say that with the effective use of these rich minerals, Israel's life can be made to flourish.

The most dramatic event in the revival of the Negev is the growth of Eilat. The significance of this harbor town is that it is the entrance to the Gulf of Aqaba, through which Israel can reach the Indian Ocean without dependence on the Suez Canal. Six thousand Israelis have gone to Eilat to live. Life there demands toughness; conditions are hard; bus and plane transportation to other parts of Israel is limited. In many respects, Eilat has become the Israeli counterpart of the American boom town where sudden success has not yet provided an easy life for its inhabitants.

The history of the Negev is just beginning. Communications must be improved, industries expanded, and the water supply increased. There is much work to be done here. The American West represented the last frontier of the United States; it was the last place where dedication to hard physical labor, a willingness to accept a life without luxury, was rewarded with the satisfying knowledge of achievement. To the Israeli, the Negev offers the greatest challenge and presents the greatest opportunity. This new frontier gives him the opportunity to transform a barren desert into green and fertile fields.

Archaeology

In Israel, like in many other countries today, archaeology enjoys a popularity among all sections of the population. It has become a national hobby pursued by teen-agers and statesmen, generals and kibbutzniks. General Yigal Yadin and President Yitzhak Ben-Zvi are two of Israel's most famous people who have long devoted themselves to the study of their country's past.

The discovery of the Dead Sea scrolls in the Judaean Desert (1947) was one of the most important archaeological events. These scrolls were the religious literature of a Jewish community that lived in the Desert of Judah during the early years of the Common Era. The recovery of these documents provides additional background for the understanding of early Christianity.

Thousands of Israelis dabble in archaeology, hoping to turn up remains of the country's rich and varied past. Hikers, farmers, surveyors, and geologists follow the achievements of archaeologists in the press and take part in archaeological conventions. Over a hundred amateur archaeologists, scattered throughout the country, are actively associated with the work of the Israel Department of Antiquities.

Over the Seven Seas

Spectacular advances were also scored by Israel's marine. Israel had once, in the days of King Solomon, ranked among the seafaring nations. But in 1948, as modern Israel was to enter the sea lanes again, it had only a few old vessels. The gross tonnage of boats available or in service did not even reach fourteen thousand. But the years that followed saw a rebirth of Israel's merchant marine. Thirty-five ships with a total displacement of one hundred and thirty-five thousand tons were afloat on January 1, 1957. Freighters and passenger boats, manned by Israeli crews, gave proof of the young state's ambition to sail the oceans of the world. Nineteen-knot passenger liners went into regular service from Haifa to New York. Most of Israel's merchant ships were built through German reparations.

Fragment from the Dead Sea Scrolls

El Al

In the air, Israel's airline, El Al, linked the new country with Asia, Europe, Africa, and North America. The J. F. Kennedy Airport (then known as the New York International Airport) was the terminal for regular jet flights that carried passengers from Lydda to the United States in less than sixteen hours. In 1956 about eighty-seven thousand passengers reached or left Israel by air. They came from all parts of the world.

Tourism

Tourists came to Israel in ever-increasing numbers through the years, resulting in the growth of the tourist industry as an important source of revenue.

Tourism today is the second largest source of foreign currency, exceeded only by income from citrus exports. Aside from its economic contribution, the tourist industry serves to create closer ties with people the world over. Israel's attractions are widely known in many countries. The pleasant climate and scenic landscapes, the many diverse communities being molded into a nation, the biblical and historical past combine to make Israel a country of great interest to the tourist. Added to this is the fact that Israel is still new, still growing. In the eyes of the American or European visitor, Israel represents a last frontier. In many ways, she is similar to the old West of America. This is a country which still cherishes the pioneer's hard work, which eagerly embraces new ideas, and fully utilizes the talents of its people. Tourists who have visited almost always comment on the exhilarating atmosphere evident from the moment they disembark from ship or plane.

From Kindergarten to University

The school system in Israel had undergone a major change. Prior to the establishment of the state, most schools were run on a private basis by political or religious parties and groups, each with its own curriculum. In 1953, the Knesset decreed a system of universal, compulsory, and free state education for all children from the ages of five to fourteen. Parents had a choice of two types of schools—general public schools and religious

*Municipal
High School
in Tel Aviv*

*The New Hebrew University:
Administration Building*

schools. The school population jumped from ninety-eight thousand in 1948 to over four hundred and twenty-five thousand in 1956, in state-governed schools, ranging from kindergarten through a variety of high schools, to universities.

In 1958, there were three major universities. The leader was the Hebrew University, originally on Mount Scopus, but scattered over the city of Jerusalem after 1948, when its campus, lying within Jordan-occupied territory, became inaccessible to students. At first, the Hebrew University operated in temporary premises in various parts of the new city of Jerusalem. New departments of medicine, agriculture, law, economics, and social sciences were added and, later, a new university campus was opened.

Named after Rabbi Meir Bar Ilan, a leader of Mizrachi, the Bar Ilan University at Bnei Brak, near Tel Aviv, began a regular academic program in 1955. This school of higher learning is sponsored by the Mizrachi organization in the United States and in Canada.

The University of Tel Aviv came into existence in 1956 to provide the youth of that city with a local school of higher learning.

Haifa had been for many years the site of the Technion, or Israel Institute of Technology. It ranks as one of the foremost schools of higher technical learning in the world. Its academic scope has expanded rapidly since the establishment of the state and now includes departments of agricultural engineering, aeronautics, architecture, industrial chemistry, industrial management, and science.

Not only do these formal institutions of higher learning contribute to the education of the people, but education receives special emphasis in the Israel Defense forces. The armed forces absorb many young immigrants with inadequate schooling, who must be aided to adjust to their new environment, culture, and language.

Compulsory courses in Hebrew, Bible, Israeli and general history, geography, mathematics, and civics enable every recruit to meet minimum standards of education.

In addition, soldiers in the regular army receive a 50% reduction in tuition fees at institutes of higher studies. Among many who recently studied at the Technion and the Hebrew University is a former Chief

The Mann Auditorium in Tel Aviv's Cultural Center ➤➤

of Staff. Thus, the army plays a significant role in blending the diverse elements of the population into a unified nation.

Books

According to recent UNESCO figures, Israel takes second place in the world for the number of books published in proportion to the population. The great demand for books indicates that the traditional respect for learning among Jews has survived and flourished. This is a country of culture-hungry people. Plays and concerts are enthusiastically welcomed by a people whose keen interest in the arts has created a lively cultural atmosphere. Evidence of the vitality of Israel's cultural life can be observed at all levels, from the encouragement given by the government, which offers literary prizes, to the *Kibbutznik's* pride in his personal library. In Israel, it is not unusual to find a farmer who is also an avid reader of the classics. The stereotyped view that physical activities and intellectual interests are mutually exclusive has no validity here.

Music

Whether they live in the rustic simplicity of a *Kibbutz*, or whether they make their homes in the cities, the interest of Israelis in music is extraordinarily high. Musical life in Israel is not an urban monopoly. In villages, *Kibbutzim*, and towns there are thousands of men and women with a deep love for good music. Visiting conductors such as Leonard Bernstein,

Serge Koussevitsky, and Eugene Ormandy made a special point of playing with the Israel Philharmonic Orchestra in the most remote settlements. The eager response and discriminating appreciation of these audiences left a strong impression. The great maestro, Arturo Toscanini, gave the Israel Philharmonic a unique start in its career. In a series of memorable concerts, he transformed a group of individually fine musicians into a superb orchestra.

As the national character of Israel reflects the strikingly different contributions of East and West, so does its music. The Yemenite music is characterized by the lonely sound of the *Ḥalil* (flute) played by a shepherd as he watches his flock and by the syncopated beat of a clay drum filling the air with its urgency. To this is added the heritage of the West, the more restrained Russian and French melodies expressing a plaintive nostalgia for the lost civilization of the waltz and the mazurka.

The quality of Israeli music has not yet crystallized. For the moment, the influences of Russian and French music and the new "Mediterranean" style persist. The great variety of cultural backgrounds has contributed to the diversity of Israeli folk music. It is difficult to predict the future, but one can be certain that the Western musical heritage of Europe and the flavor of the Orient will combine to form a new and more distinctly Israeli folk music.

Inbal Performance

Dance

Ballet, too, fills the theatres and arouses the public's interest. Companies from London and New York, Paris and Bombay, Africa and Yugoslavia are all generously applauded.

Israel has her own dance company, "Inbal," a group of Yemenite folk dancers who interpret the ancient ways of an exotic people to enthusiastic audiences throughout the world. The themes, often taken from the Bible, are presented through the medium of modern folk dance. The Yemenites' colorful contribution to Israeli culture is nowhere seen as vividly as in their dance performances.

The Theatre

The theatre in Israel has been a national institution since 1928, when a drama group, Habimah (The Stage) arrived from Russia, where it had begun as the first Hebrew-speaking troupe ten years earlier.

Serious drama in Israel today is represented by four major repertory companies: Habimah, Ohel, the Chamber Theatre, and Zira. Their permanent home is in Tel Aviv, but they often go on tour to various towns and *Kibbutzim.* The plays presented cover a wide range including classics of many different countries, recent successes from New York, London and Paris, and original Hebrew works.

Original Hebrew plays are also coming into their own. In recent years, small theatrical groups have been formed which tour the country and bring original plays and better known works from the world repertoire to distant settlements and *Kibbutzim.*

On stage:
An actor's thanks for the
Government's proclaiming
Habimah as Israel's National
Theatre

During the Siege of Jerusalem:
Newspapers are posted on public bulletin board

Newspapers

The newspapers in Israel are as varied as its people. More than a score of newspapers appear daily, most of them in Hebrew, but also in other languages—in Arabic, French, German, Hungarian, Bulgarian, Yiddish, and English. *The Jerusalem Post*, formerly *The Palestine Post* in the days of the British Mandate, has retained its prestige as the leading English-language newspaper of the Middle East.

Most papers in Israel have definite affiliations with political parties and reflect the views of the parties which they support. There are eighteen morning and two evening papers. In addition, three hundred and twenty periodicals are published in twelve different languages. They include literary, political, illustrated, and art magazines. The press is free from all censorship, though control is exercised over matters affecting military security.

Newspapers have an added importance in Israel in that they help new immigrants learn Hebrew. *Omer*, for example, is published in vowelled Hebrew, so that beginning students may understand the news more easily.

The Voice of Israel

Israel's radio network, Kol Yisrael (The Voice of Israel), maintains a full schedule in Hebrew. It also broadcasts evening programs on a special wavelength in Yiddish, French, Ladino, Roumanian, Hungarian, Turkish, and Persian for immigrants who have still not mastered Hebrew. Regular broadcasts in Arabic are provided for the Arab population of the state, and Moslem prayers and readings from the Koran reach them over the airwaves of Israel's State Radio.

Arabs in Israel

From the beginning of the State of Israel, its Arab citizens experienced major changes in their lives. Mostly farmers, Israeli Arabs had been accustomed to hard toil with meager returns. The new government of Israel began a program of providing modern agricultural equipment, irrigation, and other modern methods of cultivation. Their agricultural output rose considerably. Mobile units of agricultural equipment were made available to the Arab farmers for a nominal rental; government loans were extended to them. Soon farms, once worked only by donkeys and oxen, hummed with the sound of tractors.

Modernization revolutionized health conditions among Israel's Arabs. Permanent clinics in Arab population centers and mobile clinics touring the Negev and Galilee did much to stamp out disease. Two plagues of the region, malaria and tuberculosis, were all but eliminated.

A fierce battle was waged against illiteracy, and special efforts were made to educate all Arab boys and girls. During the days of the British Mandate, less than half of the Arab children of elementary school age attended school, and the number of girls was minute. Woman's status among Israel's Arabs is changing completely. Equal rights for Arab women, previously unheard of, are enjoyed.

The majority of Israel's Arabs practice the Moslem religion, but there is also a sizable minority of Christians. They are divided among various denominations, including Greek Catholic, Greek Orthodox, Roman Catholic, Armenian, Maronite, Anglican, Coptic, Syrian Jacobites, Ethiopian, Assyrian, and a number of Protestant sects. The many holy places of Christianity, which dot Israel's countryside, receive special care from the government.

Chief Rabbinate Building and seat of
High Rabbinical Court in Jerusalem

Another religious group, the Druses, also makes its home in Israel. Jewish, Christian, and Moslem traditions are welded together in the religion of the Druses, who speak Arabic but live apart from the rest of the Arabic community. Their main shrine is the tomb of Jethro, father-in-law of Moses, at Hittin, near the Sea of Galilee.

Haifa is the center of another sect, the Bahai faith, founded in the nineteenth century by a Persian, Mirza Ali Mohammed of Shiraz, who proclaimed himself as successor to Moses, Jesus, and Mohammed. Bahai, which has adherents throughout the world, looks to Haifa as its head-quarters. On the slopes of Mount Carmel, a splendid Bahai temple was erected in 1953. Its golden dome has become one of the landmarks of the city. The number of Bahai adherents in Israel is rather small.

Judaism

Jewish religious observances are bound up with public life in Israel. The Sabbath brings all business and public activity to a halt. Holidays have both religious and national forms. Passover, Shavuot, and Sukkot are commemorated by traditional observances ·as well as by new public celebrations. Hanukah is marked also by torchlight ceremonies in Modiin, the town where the revolt of the Maccabees began. Tel Aviv provides a setting for an internationally famous Purim carnival. And Tu Bishvat is a national occasion for tree planting.

From time to time difficulties have arisen between those who insist on strict adherence to the traditional Sabbath laws and those who are less observant. Ultra-religious groups have lined the roads near Jerusalem, stoning buses and cars which travel on the Sabbath. The *Kibbutznik*, among others, whose day off is Saturday, objects to this infringement of his right to travel when and where he pleases. The people who stone buses, however, are not really representative of Israel's religious population, most of whom leave the matter of religion up to the individual.

The question, however, of separation of church and state in Israel is a vexing one. Religious authority in Israel is vested in the Chief Rabbinate, headed by the Ashkenazi and Sephardic Chief Rabbis. The country has been described—perhaps in a spirit of overstatement—as a theocracy. It is true that civil marriage does not exist in Israel; one can be married only by a rabbi. However, many observers feel that the tenor of the state is largely secular.

Zionism After Statehood

The realization of Zionist aspirations through the establishment of the Jewish state did not mean the end of Zionism, as some were inclined to believe. But it is true that the Zionist movement had to pass through some phases of uncertainty, aimlessness, and confusion. The reality of Israel posed the question of whether Zionism was necessary at all, since its original aims had been accomplished. Finding new direction and setting new goals occupied two Zionist Congresses, convened after Israel's independence.

The Twenty-Third Congress, the first to meet on Israeli soil, opened with a solemn ceremony at Herzl's Grave in Jerusalem. The flag of the State of Israel and the Herzl flag with seven golden stars were raised at the summit of Mount Herzl. Twenty-two children of twenty-two youth organizations took their place around a raised platform with the banners of the past twenty-two Zionist Congresses.

Two and a half hours later, the Twenty-Third Congress was called to order in Jerusalem's convention hall. Dr. Isidor Schalit, one of Herzl's ardent co-workers, a man of over eighty, called the Congress into session with three taps of his gavel. He had used the same gavel to open the First Zionist Congress in Basle. He and two others were the only veterans of the Basle conference to witness the homecoming of the Zionist movement to Zion. There were four hundred and forty-five delegates, representing over two million organized Zionists from all parts of the world except the Soviet Union and its satellites.

For sixteen days the Congress deliberated, taking stock of the relationship of the new state and the Zionist movement, reviewing immigration to Israel and its financial requirements, discussing the role of American Zionists in fund raising and settlement, and formulating the future tasks of the movement. It defined the new tasks of Zionism as these:

The strengthening of the state of Israel
The Ingathering of the Exiles in Eretz Yisrael
The fostering of the unity of the Jewish people

Naḥum Goldmann had emerged over the course of the years as a leading personality in world Zionism. When the Twenty-Fourth Congress took place in Jerusalem in 1956, he was elected president of the World Zionist Organization.

The intense flare-up of Arab hostility towards Israel, the flow of Russian-sponsored arms to Egypt while Israel could not obtain arms from the Western powers for its defense, the danger of a new world war—these alarming conditions occupied the attention of the Twenty-Fourth Congress. In a manifesto to world Jewry, it proclaimed the indissoluble and historical bond between the Jewish people and the land of Israel, and called upon Jews throughout the world to rally to Israel's support. Then the Congress found itself deeply embroiled in a debate on basic questions of what forms Zionism should take in the future. That problem, overwhelmingly important to the destinies of the Zionist movement, remained unresolved. The question promised to reappear at Congresses to follow.

Israel's Future

As Israel entered her second decade of statehood, Jews throughout the world rejoiced with her, marvelling at her success. Two thousand years of homeless wandering had ended, and every Jew who desired it could freely enter his homeland. Israel's doors were opened wide, and the newcomers were welcomed. Men who had fled from country to country, who had been hunted by beasts of prey and routed from every hiding place, found a place to rest, a land where they could again taste freedom. As dignity was restored to human beings, they recaptured faith in the future. The wonder of the present helped soften the suffering of the past.

The emergence of a Jewish national identity also affected those outside the state of Israel. Jews throughout the world were proudly conscious of the fact that there was a Jewish nation, and Israel became the vital center of Jewish life.

On the occasion of her tenth anniversary, both idealists and objective observers expressed their hopes for Israel's future. Some hoped that the voice of the Orient would soon disappear, leaving the Western influence in complete control. Others dreamed of a nation whose diverse peoples would create a dynamic union of East and West, where the best qualities of both cultures would combine to form a unique Mediterranean nation.

Israel today has come a long way. Since 1948, her population has almost tripled in size. Export of goods has steadily increased, and she is gradually becoming self-sufficient. During the ten years from 1948 to 1958, the land under cultivation increased 2½ times. Her mineral resources are being exploited, and industry has greatly expanded. Thus the nation of Israel has shown phenomenal growth.

Economy

Israel's economy is one in which both capitalist and socialist enterprises exist side by side. Cooperatives have been highly developed. Most of the agriculture, almost all passenger transportation, and a significant part of industry, are run by cooperative associations.

The *Kibbutz* movement, which played such an important role during the early years of the state, has shown some signs of decline. Temporarily, at least, the *Kibbutz* has lost some of its attraction. The reasons for this are varied. One of the major goals of labor Zionist idealists was the creation of the State of Israel. It was this struggle, this call to idealistic self-sacrifice, which drew many people into its ranks. Now that Israel

*Hora in Haifa:
A street scene during
Israel's Tenth
Anniversary
Celebration*

is an accomplished fact, the pioneer's life of dedicated labor has lost some of its appeal.

The role of the *Kibbutz* continues to change. There has been a trend towards allowing individual members to own more personal property. People want to spend more time with their families and less with the group. They want their children to live at home with them rather than in separate children's houses. Nevertheless, the great majority of *kibbutzniks* are convinced of the validity of their way of life and, whether new people join them or not, their communities will continue to exist.

The conquest of the desert has yet to be completed. Until that time, the importance of the *Kibbutz* will not diminish. The *Kibbutz* is particularly suited to this purpose, and groups of youngsters are forming new collective settlements in dangerous and deserted areas of the Negev. They are determined to transform this land into a fertile farming area.

The major problems facing the *Kibbutz* movement today are how to arrange its life so that individual members will feel freer; how to increase production and absorb new immigrants; how to utilize its strength in the service of the Zionist ideal. It is likely that this movement, which has accomplished so much in the past, will continue to exist alongside Israel's capitalistic enterprises.

Social Factors

What will the character of the State of Israel be in the years to come? Will she be just another country on the Mediterranean, with a Mideastern personality, or will she be able to draw from both East and West those elements which will combine to form a culture uniquely Israeli? Israel is a small country containing a wide range of conflicting customs and attitudes. Some of her people must be inducted into the world of the twentieth century while others must patiently wait for them. Questions of which cultural standards will become the norm are really irrelevant. Those who pose these questions assume an inevitable choice between one culture and another. They fail to see an obvious alternative: the co-existence of differing cultures bound together by an allegiance to the State of Israel.

The mass immigration to Israel has created social problems. Some

Israelis of European origin find it difficult to accept the Oriental Jew. In addition to linguistic barriers there are vastly divergent social and cultural backgrounds. It is sometimes hard for a Jew of the Western world to realize that an illiterate and dark-skinned man is his brother. However, until the European can rid himself of his prejudice and help these immigrants accustom themselves to a new life, Israel will not have an integrated community.

Political Life

Israel has gained prestige in the UN and has won friends throughout the world. Her foreign policy has been particularly successful in Asia and Africa. Both Burma and Ghana are receiving aid through Israel's program of technical assistance. Israeli aid has special significance for these emerging nations which can look to Israel, also a young state, for guidance. One of the most important ventures in the Black Star Line, a shipping company in which Israel and Ghana were partners, but which is now ready to be independently controlled by Ghana.

The Arab refugee problem remains a major political vexation. Though Israel has repeatedly tried to solve this problem, the Arab leaders have refused to discuss the matter. They continue to hold these refugees as a

future threat to Israel's security. Until the Arab nations decide to recognize the existence of the State of Israel and are willing to negotiate with her, this problem will remain unsolved.

Related to the question of the Gaza Strip refugees is the Arab refusal to allow Israel the use of the Suez Canal. Today, Israel is the only nation in the world not allowed passage through these waters. Passage to Asia and East Africa is thereby made very difficult, necessitating roundabout routes and high costs.

Israel's position in the Middle East is unique. She is the only democratic state in an area still controlled by feudal regimes. From the Arab point of view, Israel constitutes a threat to the continuance of the feudal system. As news of Israel's prosperity spreads across her borders, as the higher living standards of her workers become known to the Arab world, discontent with the present Arab regimes will undoubtedly follow. This is what the wealthy Arab landowners fear: the eventual destruction of a system which allows them great profits. While the Arab worker lives in ignorance of a better way of life, feudalism has a chance to survive. As soon as he realizes that poverty can be eliminated, that better conditions can be attained, the economic structure of the Arab countries will come into question. Added to this is the awakening nationalism of the Arabs, a nationalism which is chauvinistic and uncompromising. In time this nationalism may become less aggressive and peace may yet become a reality.

Science

The Research Council of Israel is now at work on two major projects: the utilization of solar energy and the desalination of water. Both are critically important to Israel which has unlimited quantities of sunlight but lacks fresh water.

Four countries are working on the problem of harnessing the sun's energy—the United States, Soviet Union, France, and Israel. The ultimate object is the direct conversion of solar radiation into electricity. Israel has a more immediate need: to use solar energy to cool houses, generate steam for industry, and to run small power units for farmers. The chemical factory at Beersheba is the world's first sun-operated industrial plant.

←◄ Study mission from Ghana receives instruction in poultry farming at a Kibbutz

There are many ways in which small quantities of sea water can be converted into drinking water. The problem, however, is how to desalinate large quantities of water cheaply enough to make it usable for agricultural purposes.

Israel is also working on the peaceful uses of atomic energy in the hope that it will provide a cheaper and more efficient source of power.

Israel and American Jewry

The relationship between Israel and world Jewry is a complicated one. Israel derives much of her financial support from the contributions of Jews in the United States. Nevertheless, there are Israelis who have argued that a vital Jewish life outside of Israel is impossible. This is heatedly denied by many Jews in this country. While recognizing the inspiration provided by Israel, they insist that an authentically Jewish life can be created in the peaceful and democratic atmosphere of the United States. Others see the relationship between Israel and the United States Jewry as one of rich cultural and spiritual interchange. They talk meaningfully of the "bridge" that must be built between these two major centers of Jewish life.

But one thing is clear: the emergence of the State of Israel has infused Jews everywhere with new pride and security. Traditionally the man without a country, the Jew now has the self-confidence that comes with the knowledge that he need never again be homeless. In Israel a new type of Jew is developing—self-reliant, free, and fearless. Jews everywhere in the world draw strength and courage from his achievements.

A. D. Gordon's words, expressing the hopes of thousands who came after him, have finally been realized: "We seek the rebirth of our national self, the manifestation of our loftiest spirit, and for that we must give our all. It is life we want, no more and no less than that, our own life feeding on our own vital sources, in the fields and under the skies of our Homeland."

A

Abdul Hamid. See Sultan of Turkey.
Abdullah, Emir of Transjordan, 129
Abraham, 4, 24, 216
Abu Isa, 18
Abyssinia, 163. See also Ethiopia.
Aden, 195
Adler, Dr. Herman, 59
Adrianople, 28 .
Africa, 57, 63, 83, 216, 220, 225, 234, 235
Africa, North, 191, 214
Africa, South, 116
Agnon, Samuel Joseph, 100
Agudat Yisrael, 199
Ahad Ha'am, 45, 46, 87, 100, 113, 130. See also Ginsberg, Asher.
Akiba, Rabbi, 12, 17
Albania, 29
Alexander II, Czar of Russia, 37–39, 81
Alexandria, Egypt, 114, 163
Al-Hoda, newspaper, 206
Aliyah (immigration), 43, 94, 96, 98, 137, 138, 140, 151, 152, 164, 202
Aliyah Bet (illegal immigration), 161
Allenby, General Edmund, 115, 118, 119, 121
Alliance Israelite Universelle, 34, 37, 102
Allied Powers, 127
Allies' Supreme Council of Ten, 123
America, United States of, 38, 41, 63, 85, 105–10, 112, 115, 116, 133, 139, 173, 220
America, South, 172
American Army, 115, 187
American Jews, 105–10, 112, 113, 115, 173, 196
Americans, 120, 169
Amman, capital of Jordan, 119
American Zionist Federation, 112
Amsterdam, 27
Anglo-American Committee of Inquiry, 169
Anglo-Palestine Bank, 70
Anglo-Palestine Company, 151
Aqaba, Gulf of, 205, 213, 218
Arab Army of Liberation, 180
Arab Governments, 207, 209
Arab High Committee, 175–77, 177, 181
Arab League, 206
Arab Legion, 177, 185, 187
Arab National Committee, 125, 126
Arab States, 119, 174, 176, 177, 201, 208, 213, 235
Arabia, 20. See also Saudi Arabia.
Arabian Peninsula, 19
Arabs, 6, 18, 42, 43, 118–20, 124, 126–30, 145–48, 152–60, 162, 167, 168, 172, 173, 175, 177, 178, 180, 181, 184, 186, 190, 191, 200, 205–10, 212–14, 216, 217, 227, 228, 231, 234, 235

Argentina, 56, 116
Arlosoroff, Dr. Chaim, 149
Armenia, 126
Aryans, 51
Asia, 213, 220, 234, 235
Asia Minor, 111
Assarah B'Tevet, 11
Atlit, prison camp, 161
Attlee, Clement, 169
Auschwitz, concentration camp, 160
Australia, 174
Austria, 60, 169, 191
Austrian Jews, 53
Austro-Hungarian Empire, 111
Austro-Hungarian Monarchy, 46
Avignon, France, 27
Azzam Pasha, Abdul Rahman, 206

B

Babylon, Babylonia, 3, 4, 12
Babylonians, 6, 11
Baden, Grand Duke Friedrich of, 73, 87
Bahai Faith, 229
Balaam, 17
Balfour, Lord Alfred James, 93, 114, 117, 118, 121, 129
Balfour Declaration, 116, 118, 124, 127, 131, 135, 147
Balkans, 191
Baltimore, Maryland, 105, 109
Bar Ilan, Rabbi Meir, 222
Bar Ilan University, 222
Bar Kokhba, 3, 6, 17, 18
Basle, Switzerland, 63, 65, 67–9, 76, 79, 83, 85, 93, 105, 143, 198, 230
Basle Program, 67, 79, 85
Bat Tzion (Daughter of Zion), 8
Bedouins, 119, 125, 153
Beersheba, Israel, 202, 216, 217, 235
Beirut, capital of Lebanon, 207
Ben-Gurion, David, 114, 139, 148, 173, 183, 189, 198, 200, 202, 203
Ben Yehuda, Mrs. Deborah, 48
Ben Yehuda, Eliezer (Eliezer Perlman), 47–49, 100, 102
Ben-Zvi, Yitzhak, 114, 139, 148, 201, 202, 218
Berlin, Germany, 39, 62, 80, 152
Bernstein, Leonard, 223
Betar, Fortress of, 18
Bevin, Ernest, 164, 169, 172
Bezalel School of Arts & Crafts, 102
Bet Hamikdash (the Holy Temple), 3
Bialik, Hayim Nahman, 100, 101, 130
Biluim, 41–43
Bismark. See von Bismark, Otto.
Black Sea, 165
Black Star Line, 234

Blum, Leon, 144
Bnei Brak, 222
Bombay, India, 59, 225
Borochov, Ber, 98
Bosphorus, 27
Boston, Massachusetts, 105
Boston Jewish Advocate, newspaper, 109
Brandeis Group, 134
Brandeis, Justice Louis D., 108–10, 113, 118, 132, 134
Brenner, Hayim Joseph, 99, 100
Britain, 18, 60, 79, 113. See also Great Britain, England
British (people), 113, 114, 124, 155, 156, 161–65, 167, 168, 169, 170, 171, 175, 177, 181, 183, 207
British Alien Commission, 79
British Army, 59, 124, 127, 162, 163, 168, 170, 177, 178, 184
British Empire, 164
British Government, 80, 83, 114, 116, 118, 120, 124, 127, 129, 130, 142, 146, 158, 159, 160, 169, 171, 184
British Isles, 59, 78
British Jews, 116
British Mandate, 175, 183, 185
British Naval Intelligence, 165
British Navy, 165, 167
British Parliament, 79, 131, 157, 158, 169
Buchenwald, concentration camp, 160
Budapest, Hungary, 50
Budapest, University of, 77
Bulgaria, 62
Bunche, Dr. Ralph, 190
Burma, 234
Byzantines, 216

C

Cairo, Egypt, 25, 26, 80, 210
Cairo Jews, 26
Canaan, Land of, 6
Canada, 222
Cardiff, Wales, 59
Carmel, Mount, 229
Caucasus, 126
Chaibar, region of Arabia, 20
Chamber Theater Repertory Company, 225
Chamberlain, Joseph, 83
Charkov, Russia, 41
Charles V, Emperor of Germany, 21–23
Chicago, Illinois, 105–6
Chief Rabbinate, 228, 229
China, 56, 118, 212
Christianity, 17, 21, 23, 33, 53, 175, 219, 228, 229
Christians, 19, 25, 27, 51, 52, 59, 62, 121, 186, 214, 228
Churchill, Sir Winston, 131
City of David Fortress, 7
Clemenceau, Georges, 88

Cleveland, Ohio, 110, 134, 135
Cochin, India, 196
Columbia University, 106
Constantinople, Turkey, 27, 41, 74, 86
Crete, Island of, 18, 163
Cyprus, Island of, 78, 165, 177, 191
Czarist Empire, 126. See also Russia.
Czarist Russian Army, 125
Czechoslovakia, 137, 190, 210

D

Dachau, concentration camp, 150, 160, 163
Damascus, capital of Syria, 34, 125
Daniel, 12
Danzig, 139
Dardenelles, 114
David, House of, 6
David, King, 6, 7, 15, 28, 30
Dead Sea, 218
Dead Sea Scrolls, 218, 219
Deborah, 137
Deganya, Galilee, 95, 96, 98, 125, 188
de Haas, Jacob, 106, 109, 110, 113
de Hirsch, Baron Moritz, 56, 63
Democratic Fraction, 94
Denmark, 112
Devil's Island, 54
Displaced Persons, 164
Dizengoff, Meir, 140
Dome of the Rock, Jerusalem, 126, 145
Dreyfus, Captain Alfred, 54, 55
Druse, 214, 229

E

East European Jews, 69, 92, 100, 105, 107, 111, 172. See also European, West European Jews.
Ecole Militaire, Paris, 55
Edom, 17
Egypt, 14, 19, 25, 114, 146, 163, 180, 190, 196, 201, 205, 209, 211, 212, 213, 214, 231
Egyptian Army, 187, 190, 209, 211, 213, 216
Egyptian Government, 80
Egyptian Palestine, 78, 79
Egyptians (people), 210, 213
Eilat, Israel, 190, 202, 205, 213, 216, 218
Ein Harod, 138
Einstein, Dr. Albert, 133–5, 144
Einstein, Mrs. Albert, 134, 135
El Al, 220
El Arish, 78, 79, 80
Elijah, 2, 15, 26
Emek Valley, 137, 138, 158, 175, 177, 180, 188. See also Jezreel Valley.
Empress of Russia, 125
Engels, Frederick, 33
England, 34, 56, 78, 79, 85, 93, 111–13, 116, 147, 157, 162, 172, 212. See also Britain, Great Britain, British Isles.

English (people), 51, 116, 120
English Government, 118. See also British Government, British Parliament.
Eritrea, 163
Ethiopia, 154, 191. See also Abyssinia.
Europe, 6, 19, 20, 23, 25, 33, 34, 36, 46, 51, 56, 62, 63, 79, 92, 100, 105, 107, 111, 112, 137, 149, 151, 214, 220, 224
European Jews, 33, 34, 66, 172, 173, 184, 234. See also West and East European Jews.
Exodus, ship, 166–167.
Ezekiel, 15

F

Farouk, King, 209
Fascist Black Shirts, 154
Fedayeen, 210, 211, 213
Federation of American Zionists, 106, 110
Feisal, Emir; later, King of Iraq, 119, 120, 129
Felsenthal, Rabbi Bernard, 106
Ferdinand I, King of Bulgaria, 87
Foundation Fund (Keren Hayesod), 133, 135, 142
France, 19, 27, 34, 55, 60, 111, 116, 118, 123, 163, 165, 167, 176, 191, 211, 212, 235
Frankfurt, Germany, 36
French (people), 54, 125, 167
French Army, 54
French Guiana, 54
French Jews, 27
French Labor Party, 144
French Parliament, 56
Friedenwald, Dr. Harry, 109
Frischmann, David, 100

G

Galicia, 46, 62
Galilee, 17, 95, 125, 153, 155, 158, 175, 228
Gallipoli, Turkey, 114
Gaza, 26
Gaza Strip, 190, 208, 210, 211, 212, 213, 235
G'dud Ha-Avodah (Labor Legion), 138
General Federation of Labor. See Histadrut.
General Zionists, 148, 200
Geneva, Switzerland, 159, 160, 172
German Ambassador in Vienna, 74
German Army, 54
German Chancellor, 74
German Emperor, 57, 73
German Jews, 33, 35, 64, 151, 152, 160, 172
German Kaiser, 73, 74, 75, 77. See also Wilhelm II.
German Parliament, 53
German Reich, 74
Germans, 33, 35, 51, 54, 75, 121, 151

Germany, 22, 35, 53, 54, 64, 71, 73, 77, 113, 151, 166, 167, 169, 177, 191
Ghana, 234, 235
Gilboa, Mount, 138, 139
Gilead, 15
Ginsberg, Asher, 44. See Ahad Ha'am.
Givat Brenner, 163
Goldmann, Nahum, 231
Goldsmith, Colonel Albert Edward, 59
Goldsmith, Carmel, 59
Goldsmith, Rachel, 59
Goliath, 184
Gordon, Aaron David, 96–98, 203, 236
Gottheil, Prof. Richard, 106, 109
Great Britain, 116, 123, 127, 130, 142, 157, 158, 172, 176, 177, 198, 211. See also England, Britain, British Isles.
Greece, 19, 25, 29, 118, 163
Gruner, Dov, 170
Guatemala, 174
Gymnasium (Hebrew High School, Jaffa), 102. See also Herzliah.

H

Haas, Jacob de. See de Haas.
Habimah Drama Group, 224, 225
Hadassah, 108, 142, 152, 173
Hadassah Hospital, 178
Hadrian, Emperor, 3, 17
Haganah, 146, 156, 161, 167–70, 174, 178–180, 184, 188, 205, 207
Haggai, 15
Haifa, 145, 148, 149, 153, 167, 175, 177, 180, 181, 204, 207, 214, 219, 222, 229, 232
Ha-Kibutz Ha-M'uhad, 138
Haluka, 101
Halutz, halutzim (pioneer), 98, 139, 140, 142, 163
Hamburg, Germany, 167
Ha-M'orer, magazine, 99
Hanita, 156
Hanukah, 229
Hapoel Hamizrachi, 148
Ha-Shahar, 46
Ha-Shomer (The Guard), 189
Haskalah movement, 46
Hebrew University, 48, 107, 120, 129, 131, 133, 165, 178, 221, 222
Hebron, 43, 101, 146
He-Halutz, 139
Heidelberg, University of, 71
Heine, Heinrich, 33
Heletz, 218
Herut (Freedom Party), 200
Herzl, Mount, 88, 230
Herzl, Theodor, 32, 50, 52, 53, 55–66, 68–70, 72, 73, 75, 77–81, 83, 84–86, 90–94, 99, 101, 105–107, 109, 110, 143, 183, 198, 230

Herzliah Gymnasium, Tel Aviv, 102, 103, 141
Hess, Moritz (Moses), 32, 33, 34
Hilfsverein, 102
Hirsch, Baron Moritz de. See de Hirsch.
Histadrut (General Federation of Labor), 148, 149, 199, 206
Hitler, Adolf, 149, 160, 161, 167
Holland, 118
Hov'vei Tzion (The Lovers of Zion movement), 36, 41, 47, 64, 71, 105. See also Lovers of Zion.
Huleh, Lake, 204; — Swamp, 153
Hungarian Jews, 215
Hungarians, 36
Hungary, 50, 62, 163, 214, 215
Hussein, King of Hedjaz, 119

I

Inbal, folk dancers, 225
India, 59, 174, 191, 196
Indian Ocean, 218
Ingathering of the Exiles, 197. See also Kibbutz Galuyot.
Inquisition, 23
Iraq, 180, 183, 188, 191, 196, 197
Irgun Zvai Leumi (National Military Organization), 164, 165, 170, 174, 178, 200
Isaac, 4
Isaiah, 11, 15, 128
Islam, 19, 28, 175. See also Moslems.
Israel Department of Antiquities, 219
Israel Army, 184, 186, 190, 197, 209, 211, 213, 222, 223. See also Jewish Army.
Israel Philharmonic Orchestra, 224
Israel National Theater, 225
Israel State Radio, 227
Italians, 120
Italy, 20, 22, 26, 82, 116, 118, 127, 154, 163, 191; king of, 82, 86, 88, 163. See also Victor Emanuel III

J ✓ ✓ ✓ ✓

Jabotinsky, Vladimir, 114, 126, 127, 143, 147, 149, 200
Jacob, 2, 3, 4, 14, 17, 41
Jaffa, 36, 41, 75, 90, 91, 104, 129, 140, 145, 154, 155, 175, 181
Japan, 118
Jebusites, 7
Jellinek, Dr. Adolf, Chief Rabbi of Vienna, 39
Jeremiah, 15
Jerusalem, 2–12, 23–26, 43, 53, 54, 75, 85, 88, 93, 101, 102, 114, 118, 121, 126, 128, 129, 145, 147, 153, 155, 158, 167, 170, 171, 175, 177–179, 183, 184, 187, 188, 190, 191, 201, 204, 222, 226, 228–231
Jerusalem Post, daily paper, 227

Jesus of Nazareth, 17, 229
Jethro, 229
Jewish Agency, 142–145, 147, 149, 152, 162, 168, 170, 173, 175, 216
Jewish Army, 20, 115, 126. See also Israel Army.
Jewish Brigade, 162, 163
Jewish Chronicle, 79
Jewish Colonial Trust, 70, 91, 104
Jewish Colonization Association, 56
Jewish Legion, 114–116, 118, 126, 143
Jewish National Council, 174
Jewish National Fund (Keren Kayemet), 70, 71, 95–97, 104, 111, 133, 140, 142
Jewish National Home, 132, 133, 142, 147, 153, 159
Jewish Territorialist Organization, 100
Jewish Theological Seminary of America, 107
Jezreel, Valley, 137–139. See also Emek.
Joao III, King of Portugal, 20, 21
Jordan, Kingdom of, 119, 129, 204, 222
Jordan, River, 20, 105, 129, 143, 157, 205
Jordan Valley, 95
Joseph, 14
Joshua, 4
Judah Halevi, 100
Judaism, vii, 21, 23, 29, 30, 33, 34, 37, 53, 59, 64, 93, 105, 107, 110, 175
Judea, 17, 43
Judean Desert, 218, 219
Julius Severus, 18

K

Kalischer, Rabbi Zebi Hirsch, 35–37
Karlsbad, Czechoslovakia, 137
Kattowitz, Silesia, 41, 71
Katznelson, Berl, 43
Kentucky, 109
Keren Hayesod. See Foundation Fund.
Keren Kayemet. See Jewish National Fund.
K'far Gileadi, 125, 126
Khedive, Turkish ruler of British Egypt, 79
Kibbutz, kibbutzim, 138, 143, 156, 197, 202, 223, 225, 232, 233. See also K'vutzah.
Kibbutz galuyot (ingathering of exiles), 191
Kinneret, Lake, 205
Kishinev, Russia, 80, 83, 84, 106
Knesset, 198–202, 220
Kol Yisrael, 227
Koussevitsky, Serge, 224
Kovno, Lithuania, 62
Kul-Shay, Moslem weekly, 207
K'vutzah, k'vutzot, 96–98. See also Kibbutz.

L

Lag Ba-Omer, 12
Lansdowne, Lord, 79

Lassalle, Ferdinand, 33
Lawrence, Colonel T. E., 119
Lazarus, Emma, 41
League of Nations, 123, 130, 142, 152, 157, 160
Lebanese (people), 183
Lebanon, 155, 162, 180, 191, 206–208
Lemberg, Poland, 62
Levin, Dr. Shmaryahu, 87, 112
Lida (Russia) Conference, 99
Lilienblum, Moshe Loeb, 38
Lipsky, Louis, 109, 112, 113, 135
Lisbon, Portugal, 22
Lithuania, 48
Lloyd George, David, 114
Lombroso, Cesare, 69
London, 39, 56, 59, 60, 62, 78, 80, 93, 132, 133, 158, 169, 173, 225
Lovers of Zion, 59, 105. See also Hov'vei Tzion
Lydda, Israel, 220

M

Ma'abarah, ma'abarot, 195
MacArthur, General Douglas, 187
Maccabean, The, magazine, 109
Maccabeans, 59
Maccabees, 229
MacDonald, James G., 152
MacDonald, Ramsey, 147
Mack, Justice Julian W., 113, 134
Magnes, Judah L., 107
Maimonides, 19, 20
Mainz, Germany, 53, 55
Malta, Island of, 163
Manchester, England, 93
Manchester, University of, 93
Mantua, 22
Mapai, 148, 199
Mapam, 199
Marcus, Colonel Mickey, 186, 187
Marranos, 21, 23, 66 ("new Marranos")
Marseilles, France, 167
Marshall, Louis, 144
Masliansky, Zvi Hirsch, 107
Marx, Karl, 33
Mauritius, Island of, 161, 165
Mediterranean Sea, 73, 140, 183, 206, 233
Melchett, Lord, 144
Mesopotamia, 126
Messiah, 6, 14–16, 18, 19, 21–28, 30, 36, 37, 64, 99, 194
Metulla, Israel, 125
Mexico, 23, 116
Middle East, 19, 20, 119, 154, 212, 213, 227, 235
Migdal Oz, 28
Mikveh Israel, 37, 75
Mixed Armistice Commission, 209
Mizrachi party, 99, 148, 173, 199, 222

Moab, 17
Modiin, Palestine, 229
Mohammed, Mirza Ali, 229
Mohammedan, 52. See also Moslem.
Mohilever, Rabbi Samuel, 38
Molkho, Solomon (Pires, Diego), 21, 23
Montague, Sir Samuel, 59
Montefiore, Sir Moses, 34–36
Mordecai Zevi (Sabbatai Zevi), 24
Moriah, Mount, 12, 126
Morocco, 191
Mosensohn, Dr. Ben Zion, 134, 135
Moses, 14, 17, 126, 211, 229
Moslem, Moslems, 6, 19, 29, 77, 121, 145, 194, 207, 214, 227–229. See also Islam.
Motele, Russia, 92
Motza, Israel, 37
Munich, Germany, 64
Mussolini, Benito, 154

N

Naples, 86
Nasser, Col. Gamal Abdel, 209, 210
Nathan Gazati, 26–28
Nazis, 151, 162–164
Near East. See Middle East.
Nebuchadnezzar, 3, 11
Negev, 169, 175, 177, 188–190, 202, 210, 213, 216–218, 228, 233
Nehemiah Ha-Kohen, 28
Neue Freie Presse, Viennese daily, 54, 62
Neumann, Emanuel, 135, 173
"New Palestine," 83
New York, 80, 105, 109, 112, 134, 135, 177, 200, 219, 225
New Zionist Organization, 149
Nile River, 80, 209
Nitzanim, Israel, 188, 189
Nordau, Max, 58, 59, 65–67, 84, 85, 132
Normandy, 187

O

Odessa, Russia, 38, 44, 47
Ohel, repertory company, 225
Ohio, 173
Omer, newspaper, 227
Oriental Jews, 234
Ormandy, Eugene, 224
Ottolenghi, Giuseppe, 86
Ottoman Empire, 73, 111. See also Turkey.

P

Pacific Ocean, 187
Pakistan, 191
Palestine Cooperative Co., 135
Palestine Development League, 135
Palestine Economic Council, 135
Palestine Endowment Funds, 135

Palestine Labor Party, 148. See Mapai.
Palestine Post, daily, 227
Paris, 39, 44, 48, 54, 55, 78, 80, 93, 121, 123, 131, 225
Passover, 2, 34, 229
Patria, ship, 161
Patterson, Colonel Henry, 115
Peel, Earl, 157
Perlman, Eliezer. See Ben Yehuda, Eliezer.
Persia, 18, 19, 77
Petah Tikvah, Israel, 44
Philadelphia, Pennsylvania, 105
Pinsker, Leon, 38, 39, 41
Pires, Diego, 21 (See also Molkho)
Plehve, Count Von. See Von Plehve, Count.
Poale Zion, Zionist Labor Party, 94, 98, 99, 148, 173
Poland, 28, 46, 69, 139, 140, 142, 214
Polish Jews, 139, 140, 172
Pope Benedict XV, 118
Pope Clement VII, 20, 22
Pope Pius X, 86
Port Arthur, 125
Port Said, 90
Portugal, 21
Prussia, 35, 60
Purim, 141, 229

R

Rabbinical Court, Jerusalem, 228
Radical Zionists, 143
Ratisbon, Germany, 22
Red Sea, 190, 212
Reform Temple, Budapest, 50
Rehovot, 75, 173, 202
Reines, Rabbi Isaac Jacob, 99
Research Council of Israel, 235
Reubeni, David, 20–23
Revisionist Party, Revisionists, 143, 147–49, 164, 200
Rhine River, 53
Rhodes, Island of, 189, 190, 201
Rishon L'Tzion, 42, 44, 75
Rochester, New York, 109
Romans, 6, 10, 11, 17, 18, 216
Rome, 17, 20, 21, 22, 131
Rome and Jerusalem, 34
Rosh Hashanah, 11, 26
Rothschild, Baron Albert, 57
Rothschild, Baron Edmund, 42, 44, 63
Rothschild Family, 57
Rothschild, Lord Nathaniel Mayer, 79
Rothschild, Lord Walter, 117, 118
Round Table Conference, London, 158
Rumania, 46, 62, 69, 214
Ruppin, Dr. Arthur, 137
Russia, 36–39, 41, 42, 44, 46, 60, 62, 69, 70, 80, 81, 84, 92–95, 98, 104–107, 111, 116, 123, 125, 126, 137, 174, 176, 199, 210, 212, 225, 231. See also Soviet Union.
Russian Army, 125
Russian Government, 80, 81
Russian Jews, 37–39, 41, 69, 80–84, 92, 94, 99, 105, 114, 123, 137
Russian Parliament, 112
Russians, 37

S

Sabbatai Zevi, 23–29
Sabbath, 8, 11, 99, 128, 141, 183, 229
Safed, Israel, 21, 43, 101, 145, 146, 180
Sahara Desert, 203
Salonika, 24, 25
Samarkand, 77
Samuel, Sir Herbert, 127–129
San Remo, Italy, 127, 132
Sarah, wife of Sabbatai Zevi, 26, 28
Saudi Arabia, 184, 191, 194. See also Arabia.
Schalit, Dr. Isidor, 230
Schapiro, Prof. Herman, 71
Schatz, Prof. Boris, 102
Schechter, Dr. Solomon, 107
Schneur, Zalman, 100
Scopus, Mount, 121, 129, 131, 178, 222
Scotland, 27
S'de Boker, 202
Sdot Yam, 163
Sea of Galilee, 229
Seder, 2
Semlin, Yugoslavia, 62
Senesch, Hannah, 163
Serbian Jews, 62
Sereni, Enzio, 163
Seth, 17
Sharett, Moshe, 148, 162, 203
Shavei Tzion, 105
Shavuot, 229
Shiraz, Persia, 229
Shivah Asar B'Tammuz, 11
Siam, 118
Silesia, 41
Silver, Rabbi Abba Hillel, 107, 173, 175
Simon, "Son of the Star," 17. See Bar Kokhba.
Sinai, Mount, 211
Sinai Peninsula, 78, 79, 211, 212
Singer, Reverend Simeon, 59
Smyrna, Turkey, 23, 25–28
Society for the Colonization of Palestine, 37
Society for the Spreading of Culture Among the Russian Jews, 38
Sodom, Israel, 217
Sofia, capital of Bulgaria, 62
Sokolow, Nahum, 113, 118, 122, 123, 133
Solomon, King, 8, 24, 216, 218, 219
Sons of Moses, 46
Smolenskin, Peretz, 46, 47

Smuts, General Jan Christian, 116
Soviet Union, 176, 230, 235. See also Russia.
Spain, 6, 19
Spinoza, 27
Stern, Abraham, 165
Sternists (Fighters for the Freedom of Israel), 165, 178
Stoeker, Frederick, 53, 55
St. Petersburg, Russia, 36, 80, 81
Struma, ship, 161
Suez Canal, 80, 201, 205, 210–13, 218, 235
Sukkot, 9, 229
Sultan of Turkey, 28, 38, 74, 76–78, 91
Supreme Moslem Council, 155
Switzerland, 34, 63, 172
Syria, 34, 125, 155, 162, 188, 191, 204, 205
Syrian Jews, 34
Syrians, 183, 205
Szold, Henrietta, 108, 113, 152

T

Tardieu, Andre, 123
Technion, Haifa, 48, 102, 222
Teheran, capital of Persia, 152
Tel Aviv, Israel, 73, 140, 141, 149, 153, 154, 170, 176–78, 181, 187, 190, 198, 204, 206, 210, 221, 222, 225, 229
Tel Aviv Art Museum, 183
Tel Aviv Cultural Center, 223
Tel Aviv Municipal High School, 221
Tel Aviv University, 222
Tel Hai, Israel, 125, 126
Tel Yosef, Israel, 138
Temple (Holy Temple in Jerusalem), 2, 3, 6, 8, 11, 13, 23, 36, 85, 145
Temple Emanu-El, New York, 107
Territorialists, 99, 100
Thorn, Prussia, 35
Tiber River, 22
Tiberius, Israel, 43, 180
Timna, Israel, 216, 218
Tiran Island, 213
Tiran, Straits of, 212, 213
Tishah B'Av, 6, 11, 24, 85, 111, 128
Toscanini, Arturo, 224
Transjordan, 129, 158, 183, 191. See also Jordan.
Transjordanian Arab Legion, 183
Transjordanians, 187
Tripoli, North Africa, 163
Truman, President Harry, 169
Trumpeldor, Joseph, 125, 126, 138
Tu Bishvat, 11, 229
Tunisia, 191
Turkestan, 77
Turkey, 21, 23, 29, 41, 73, 74, 76, 86, 111–14, 127. See also Ottoman Empire.
Turkish Empire, 78
Turkish Government, 81, 92, 104

Turks, 20, 22, 25, 28, 29, 75, 111, 112, 114, 115, 118
Tzioney Tzion (Zionists of Zion), 100

U

Uganda, 83–85, 88, 92, 93, 100, 113
Ukraine, 123
Ulpan, ulpanim, 197
UNESCO, 223
United Jewish Appeal, 173, 196
United Nations, 107, 171, 174, 175, 177, 181, 183, 186, 190, 200, 201, 205, 208, 209, 212, 213, 234
United Nations Emergency Force, 213
United Nations Mixed Armistice Commission, 204, 205
United Nations Security Council, 205, 209
United Nations Special Committee, 171
United Nations Special Committee on Palestine (UNSCOP), 174, 175
United States, 56, 69, 105–107, 112, 114, 116, 139, 140, 144, 169, 174, 176, 199, 200, 212, 213, 218, 220, 222, 235, 236. See also America.
United States Congress, 135, 196
United States Export-Import Bank, 196
United States Jews, 236. See also American Jews.
United States Supreme Court, 113
Ussishkin, Menahem Mendel, 122, 123, 134, 135, 137
Uzziah, King, 216

V

Vaad Leumi, 183
Vambery, Herman, 77, 78
Vatican, 131. See also Pope.
Venice, Italy, 20
Versailles, France, 123
Vichy Government, 162
Victor Emanuel III, King of Italy, 85. See also King of Italy.
Vienna, Austria, 39, 46, 53, 54, 56, 62, 74, 80, 86, 88, 131
Vienna, University of, 53, 62
Vilna, Russia, 81
Von Bismark, Otto, 57
Von Plehve, Count, 80

W

Wailing Wall, 5, 145, 175
Wales, 59
Warburg, Prof. Otto, 92
Warsaw, capital of Poland, 62
Washington, D.C., 169
Wasserman, Oscar, 144
Weizmann, Dr. Chaim, 70, 87, 92–94, 114,

119, 120, 122–24, 127, 130, 133–35, 142, 143, 147, 159, 160, 172, 173, 174, 198, 199, 202
Weizmann, Mrs. Chaim, 134, 135
Weizmann Institute, Rehovot, 48
West European Jews, 85. See also European and East European Jews.
Wolffsohn, David, 90–92
Wilhelm II, German Kaiser, 75, 90. See also German Kaiser.
Wise, Rabbi Stephen S., 106, 107, 113, 118
Wilson, President Woodrow, 113, 123
Wingate, Orde, 184, 186
Witte, Count, 81
Women's Zionist Organization of America, 142. See also Hadassah.
World, The, Zionist Weekly, 73
World Zionist Movement, 131, 172
World Zionist Organization, 85, 92, 99, 112, 122, 133, 143, 147, 149, 174, 231

Y

Yadin, General Yigal, 189, 218
Yarmuk River, 205
Yemen, 19, 20, 191, 192, 194
Yemenite Jews, 19, 20, 191–96, 225
Yishuv, 44, 102, 104, 111, 112, 126, 128, 129, 133, 135, 140, 141, 146, 148, 149, 156, 161–

65, 168, 170, 171, 173, 178, 180, 183, 187, 202
Yom Kippur, 2
Young Judea, 107, 135
Young Turks, 92
Yugoslavia, 62, 163, 225

Z

Zangwill, Israel, 59, 99
Zechariah, 15
Zion, 1, 4, 7–9, 11, 14, 30, 32, 35–37, 41–43, 45, 47, 84, 90, 91, 108, 125, 135, 186, 230
Zion, Mount, 8
Zion Mule Corps, 114–16, 125, 126
Zionist Commission, 120, 124
Zionist Conference, 124, 133
Zionist Congress, 63–67, 69, 71, 76, 83–85, 90–94, 100, 105, 131, 137, 143, 147, 158–60, 172, 173, 198, 200, 230, 231
Zionist Congress House, 65, 70
Zionist Federation, 118
Zionist Organization of America, 134, 135, 173
Zionist World Organization, 67, 90, 91
Zira Repertory Company, 225
Zola, Emile, 54
Zurich, Switzerland, 144, 145, 158